UNLIKELY HEROES

A Chronicle of the Men of Company H, 2nd Battalion,

291st Regiment, 75th Infantry Division in World War II

James Slagle McClintock

2014

Cover: Oil Painting by James Slagle McClintock, based on a series of photos provided by S. Phillip Lawson.

Printed in the United States of America

First Printing, 2015

ISBN-10: 1517688345

ISBN-13: 978-1517688349

This book is dedicated to my Grandfather,

Robert O. Slagle,

who encouraged me to pursue my interests in history

To the men of H Company

and 2nd Battalion, 291st Infantry

And to all those young men of the 75th Infantry Division

with their bravery and sacrifices that helped to liberate

Europe from Nazi tyranny

Contents:

III.   <u>Overseas Duty: The ETO</u>

VII. The End of the Battle of the Bulge

1. Into Vielsalm
2. Handling German Prisoners
3. A POW Incident
4. Coffee and Doughnuts
5. Clear Skies
6. Threats from Above
7. Trench Fever
8. Hygiene
9. Into St. Vith
10. The "Bulge Busters"
11. Unlikely Heroes
12. Replacements and Promotions
13. A New General

VIII. The Colmar Pocket

1. No Rest for the 75th
2. Preparing for Combat
3. Actions of the 291st Infantry in the Colmar Pocket
4. Losing an Officer
5. H Company's New Commander
6. Long Awaited Equipment
7. Scouting Ahead
8. Wells' Departure from H Company
9. The Andolsheim Canal Crossing
10. Casualties on the Canal
11. Snipers in Fortschwihr
12. Worse than the Bulge!
13. The Colmar Forest

XII.   **The Ruhr Pocket**

XIII. <u>Clearing the Ruhr Pocket</u>

XVII. <u>The Men of H Company After the War</u>

Introduction:

There has been a library of books written about WWII. There seems to be a law of inverse distance: The farther you get from the war the more books that get written.   These books are mainly concerned with the "big picture" matters of geopolitics and grand strategy or they are a presentation of personal experiences. This work is different. It is a history constructed by James Slagle McClintock of his grandfather supplemented by interviewing men who served with him and reviewing primary source documents such as after action reports. This material is seldom consulted and it will not soon be around because it hasn't been preserved and is deteriorating. In addition while writing this book McClintock was taking a master's degree at a National Defense Institute in Washington DC and used some of this material for term papers. Along the way he received help and encouragement from professors.

The division first formed in April 1943. This was late in the war to be forming new divisions. The manpower resources of the country were low. About 2/3 of its initial complement were young soldiers who had been in ASTP programs. This meant that from 1-2 years they had been in college studying. They had no regular military training. The other third had many young men from rural areas who did not have a lot of education. The division early acquired the nickname of the "diaper division". They embarked for the ETO in November 1944.

Around the 19th of December they and the 106th division, another late formed unit, were assigned to what was a quiet sector of the line. This was one of the great miscalculations for the war. For within a day the German attack which became known as the Battle of the Bulge was launched through this sector. The division was ill-prepared for this. Not all their weapons had arrived. Some men were still in summer uniforms and ammunition was short. Most historians are right in characterizing this as a division that was a lot less than elite. They, however, leave out a critical fact. Despite taking substantial casualties they and the 106th held their ground and delayed the German forces long enough for a counterattack to form. The 106th was hit even harder than the 75th in that two of their regiments were surrounded and had to surrender. This book will provide an important corrective to the estimation of the 75th division's role in WWII.

The other important axis of the work is Robert O. Slagle's career as a soldier. He was a most unusual soldier. Early in his service he received training in intelligence and had this as a military occupation specialty (MOS) number. He also completed basic training in heavy weapons and was a gunner in the first platoon of Company H. 291 Inf. In addition to this he was a member of the division band and would go from the unit to play at Division military and social events. Whether any of this was related to intelligence activities is not known but he certainly had much more freedom of movement than the average GI.

The one concrete example of intelligence activity was at the end of the war when in the middle of the night Slagle received a call from division headquarters requesting him, a man named Cohen who also had intelligence training, and Siegfried the company translator. When a messenger arrived to pick them up a man named Lawson who was awake was added to the group and a small convoy headed by General Mickle the Deputy Division Commander went to a holding camp near Czechoslovakia that had been used to distribute people to concentration camps. There they were asked to search through dead bodies for dog tags. One of the untold stories of the war which has only come out in recent years is that almost 300 American GI Jewish POWs were sent to concentration camps.

There is a personal observation I have concerning my participation in the later events described in this book. While seeing this work come together I became aware of how exclusively my attention was focused only on what was directly in front of me. Several events where heavy fighting occurred are described in what follows. They were within a few hundred yards of me. Until I read about them here I had no idea that these had happened. As I think about it in combat the only thing that matters is what is directly in front of you.

This is a well written and interesting tale. It not only provides a picture of a beloved grandfather but it also is a corrective for some misimpressions of the role of the 75th Division. At a personal level it had a profound impact. I was in the last group of replacements to the division. Whatever information I had about the month preceding my arrival was of a bragging nature designed to show that I had missed the real war. As I read through this history I came to understand that my first day in combat was as real as war gets and that such things as duration of being engaged and weather added complicating factors. I had started out early that morning at division headquarters in formation on a parade ground with a few hundred other replacements. We arrived there the night before after having moved through several replacements depots in Belgium in the last few days trying to catch the division which was on the move to the extreme northern flank of the 9th Army. Along the way we didn't get much to eat and someone shot himself in the toe to avoid combat. They then took away the pistol and ammunition I was carrying and gave me an empty M1 rifle. They did the same with the whole group except that those with rifles only gave up their ammunition.

Early the next morning all the division replacements were in parade formation at Division headquarters. A two star general gave us a pep talk. All I remember is that his last words were something like I expect you to come back with your chest covered with medals. We then got into trucks and convoys headed toward regimental headquarters. Midway between division and regiment we got strafed. Everyone jumped out of the trucks and moved away from them taking cover and starting to dig in in drainage ditches alongside the road. One man panicked and started to run across a farm field. On its second pass the plane got him. He was the heavyweight champion of my basic training camp. What I got from this incident was the confidence that I could handle combat. Later when I thought about it the plane left after two passes and never hit a truck. If probably was not a fully armed fighter plane but a reconnaissance plane with limited armament and ammunition.

Arriving at company headquarters we were quickly split into groups. I was sent to the first platoon, second squad of H. Co. I arrived at the platoon just as they were coming back from firing a mission on the Maas River. They came under pretty heavy artillery fire. It was then I met one of the two people significant to me in my military experience in the 75th Division. It was my squad leader. He was much different than the other GI's since he was 38 and had two kids. He volunteered to come into the army. With shells coming in he said to me, "Junior get out of the way and don't try to be a hero." The platoon was staying in an old tavern and I ended up under a pool table.

When it was quiet a couple of minutes I came out. In a minute or so a jeep came roaring up accompanied by more shellfire. It was the platoon Lieutenant, Bergheimer. His driver slammed on the brakes and rushed inside yelling something like, it was the Goddam Jews that started this war and a few other choice remarks. I had no ammunition but moved my finger toward the M1 trigger guard.   Bert saw this and told me he would take care of it. I don't know what he said but the guy quieted down. Bergheimer began shouting orders, none of which I understood, and soon got to me. "Who are you?" I said I was a replacement and then asked, "when do we eat?" He exploded, "Here I am fighting a goddam war and this son of a bitch asks when do we eat?" Since I hadn't eaten in about 3 days it was a natural question to me. For a long time I thought he was only on my case. Reading this book made me realize that he was universally despised as a coward, drunk, and a thief. I later also found out that the British water cooled gun had a greater range than ours. Their emplacements that we had only taken over a day or two before were in the back of the tavern. The Jerries were still zeroed in on these guns so when the platoon returned from the Maas they ran into artillery directed at the British emplacements. I suspect it was Bergheimer who placed the guns there.

When things had quieted down the other guys in the platoon began going over the duffel bag full of clothes I had hauled over from the states. I objected saying I was signed out for all of that stuff. Bert politely told me I could keep anything I could carry. Thus ended my first day in combat.

Sometime during the day I heard mention that Lt. Goodnight was coming back to the company. Toward the end of the Battle of the Bulge Captain Haddock the company commander lost both legs. The executive officer Lt. Goodnight had just been operated on for appendicitis. The only other thing I heard was that he was an All American football player and had played pro ball. We stayed in this area about a week covering patrols or guarding against them on the Maas River at night. We then went by truck to the Rhine River where we did the same thing until the crossing. It took only a few days to get a Bailey Bridge across the river and then we were assembled as a company to relieve the troops who had crossed.

It was there I saw for the first time what was now Captain Goodnight. He was a solidly built man with a brown skin. Later I found out he was an Indian. The things I remember most about him was that his neck was so big I did not think he could button his shirt if he had to and that he was deliberate and soft spoken in his language. There were no 4 letter words in his vocabulary. Until the end of the war I saw him a couple more times like this in company assemblies, when Roosevelt died and the war ended.

There was one time when he interviewed me. Bert had shot his nephew by accident. He was an ambulance driver and he was visiting. We were sitting in a circle when it happened. Naturally there was an investigation and since I was in that circle I was to be interviewed by the regimental commander. He saw me before to reassure me. As I found out he also remembered me.

Within a month we were in camp New York in Suippes France. Toward the end of June a call went out that volunteers were needed to cook in the kitchen because the cooks had high points and were going home. We had gotten a new Lieutenant from the states that was angry he had missed the war and quick promotion. When we guarded POWs he insisted we carry a live round in the chamber. That is an invitation to an accident. As it was we couldn't drive a POW away. If the French caught them they worked them 15-16 hours a day. And besides I was hungry. So I volunteered. Captain Goodnight interviewed me. He remembered our prior meeting. I had no previous kitchen experience but he put me in the kitchen anyway. He used to come in every morning at about 10:00 am for a cup of coffee. After a while he began to talk with me. I was awed. It was just that he was not just an officer but he was a pro football player. Once he asked me about college. I told him I had thought about it but the papers said colleges were full. I told him I didn't know if I could make it on the GI Bill and he told me about how he had worked in an ice house summers moving big blocks of ice.

It was just the kind of encouragement I needed. Later when I got out of the army I went back to work for my uncle in butter and eggs. The papers once again said colleges were full. I went to the VA to find out how to sign on a ship as a cook. There I met another helpful person, Dave Brown. He gave me an intelligence test. After it he asked me about college. I went into my money and full routine. He told me to apply to UConn and he would write a letter. I was accepted and in turn accepted buoyed up by the thoughts of the encouragement Goodnight had given me. I haven't looked back since.

Of the two I did keep in touch with Bert by mail. Never could afford to go to a Division reunion. I visited him once on the way to teach a summer quarter on the West coast. Until the advent of the internet I could not find out about Goodnight. He became a high school football coach and teacher in San Marcos Texas. He died too young at 50 but not before he had become known as a coaching legend and inducted into the Hall of fame. They named the San Marcos Middle School after him. That does not happen too often to football coaches.

One other thing. On reading this whole book I got the feeling that Goodnight should have gotten a higher award than the Silver Star he did get. Owen L. Goodnight was a hero in any way you think of him.

Dr. Harris Chaiklin,

Columbia, Maryland

Author's Note

     The following account details a history of the men that served in Company H, 2nd Battalion, 291st Regiment, 75th Infantry Division during World War II. My grandfather, Robert O. Slagle is one of the men depicted. Though he passed away in 1996, his stories, written accounts, and old hand-written notes (including names of men from H Company) were used to track down the last surviving veterans of the unit. Interviews with each of these men, many of who had not been in contact with each other since the end of the war, validated my grandfather's stories. I not only learned more about my grandfather, but also a wealth of information about H Company; the men, what they went through, and the result of their actions. Thus, combined with the official Army records, a daily combat diary, and the First Sergeant's Morning Reports, I was able to write a nearly complete, chronological narrative of H Company's involvement in the war. The story is told at times, through the eyes of many of the men of H Company.

     This book was written with the direct assistance of all known, surviving veterans of H Company and in addition, veterans of G Company as well. This is written from the GI's perspective and includes much more than stories of combat. It includes stories of both the mundane, daily activities of the GI, but also the strong bonds of friendship made between many of these men after going through combat together. There are many stories of heroism in H Company and also stories of hardship and great tragedy. The 75th Division was the youngest US Army Division to serve in World War II. The average age of these men was only 18 or 19, which earned them the nickname of "Diaper Division." They would prove themselves during the Battle of the Bulge and earn their place in history as the "Bulgebusters." After nearly 70 years, an important tale of unlikely heroism emerges from the "Fog of War".

James Slagle McClintock

December 2014

UNLIKELY HEROES

Owen L. Goodnight Jr

Robert O. Slagle   S. Phillip Lawson   Saul Cohen

"Hay Seed"   "Kirk"   Stan Slawson

Mike Murza   **Luther Siegfried**   **Harris Chaiklin**

Billy G. Wells   Wallace Kravitz   Henry H. Smith

Bill G. Prater   John Malarich   Floyd R. Ross

Leslie Hicks   **Jim Strong**   **Ira Posnak**

"In battle, all we had was each other. We depended on one another and fought together. We were very close. Being in a war like that and seeing that kind of devastation is hard on a person. You develop a camaraderie in wartime that is the type of relationship that is similar to that of family. It is that common bond of working together to stay alive that helped us to save one another and fight to save the lives of others."

Floyd R. Ross, Third Platoon (Mortars), H Company

The ASTP Program

From ASTP to the 75th Division

On a night in mid-March 1944, Robert O. Slagle found himself in an Officer's Club with several classmates, having a fine meal and listening to Big Band music. Life was good for Slagle; he was a student at Xavier University in Ohio studying engineering and he would soon be commissioned as a navigator to a bomber crew. The next morning he woke up to find that the Army Specialized Training Program (ASTP) had terminated and that he was reassigned from the Army Air Force to the US Army 75th Infantry Division. When he asked what happened, Slagle was told that the Air Force had more than enough pilots, but the Army needed more infantrymen. Slagle boarded a train that afternoon bound for Camp Polk, Louisiana where the 75th Division was then on 3rd Army Maneuvers.

Robert O. Slagle

Slagle became a union musician in 1940 during his junior year in high school. He began to work as a replacement sax player in many of the Big Bands in New Jersey. He played in Camden, New Jersey and made many trips to play in Philadelphia. He was quite grown up for his age and no one questioned him even when he bought a drink for the female vocalist in the band. When the United States entered World War II in late 1941, Slagle noticed how so many young men in the bands he played with were lost to the draft. One by one, all the best musicians disappeared until the bands were left with young boys and old men. In January 1942, during his senior year in high school, Slagle got the opportunity to play with some of the big name bands at the Steel Pier in Atlantic City, some forty miles from his home town of Hadden Heights, New Jersey. Slagle played six nights a week and wondered if he would make it through high school. He also became the only white member of an all black band called "Harlem on the Bay," that was a big attraction. When he graduated from high school in June 1942, Slagle decided to become a full-time musician in Atlantic City; he was making much more money than his father. Slagle wanted nothing to do with the military; he loved his music, but continued to watch as all the men of age were drafted. Finally, in May 1943, 11 months after his high school graduation, Slagle received his draft notice.

Slagle reported to Fort Dix, New Jersey in June 1943 to take his physical and receive his shots. As he stood in line, each man walked through a doorway and were unsuspectingly given two shots; one in each arm. The man in front of Slagle screamed and almost fainted, causing a big stir. Due to the disturbance, Slagle turned abruptly and found that the two shot needles broke off into his arms. He could not use his arms for a day or more and was given time to recover. He was given a written IQ test when he recovered and he scored very high. He went through Basic Training at Camp Croft, South Carolina. On Slagle's first day at the camp, an over-weight draftee was driven to the front gates by his mother. During their first march, this "Tiger" complained that he was tired, his feet hurt, and he did not want to walk anymore; he also was a bed wetter. The "Tiger of Camp Croft" was discharged the next day. After completing his training, Slagle was given the opportunity to join the ASTP program and was sent to Rhode Island State University. He remained there until late December 1943 when he joined the Army Air Corps. The ASTP program was something of a sped up equivalent of Officer's Candidate

31

School and was developed in an effort to get more educated young men into all branches of service. Slagle then went to Tex Arkana for additional training and to Biloxi, Mississippi for jump training, a requirement for all pilots and aircrew. At Biloxi, Slagle was on top of a bell tower, pushing off GIs for their first parachute drop, when a sergeant got behind him and pushed him off too. Slagle found that he despised the soggy okra that was served daily and was glad to leave Mississippi when his training was completed. The ASTP program then transferred Slagle to Xavier University in Ohio to continue his studies.

Wallace Kravitz

Wallace Kravitz from Springfield, Massachusetts had completed high school in 1941. He worked part time as a clerk in a men's clothing store and attended American International College in his hometown, where he studied accounting. He was granted a temporary deferment from military service, but ended up being inducted in March 1943. Kravitz was assigned to Fort Devens, Massachusetts, but as a capable typist, Kravitz was offered an assignment with an Airborne Engineer Company at Westover Field, an Army Air Force Base in Massachusetts. After battling pneumonia for many weeks and then returning to complete Basic Training, Kravitz was given the opportunity to take the IQ test to get into the ASTP program. A week later, Kravitz was assigned to the College of the City of New York (CCNY). He completed one semester from October to December 1943 and was in his second semester when the ASTP program terminated abruptly in March 1944. About a week later, Kravitz was on a troop train bound for Camp Polk, Louisiana and the 75th Division.

Bill G. Prater

Bill G. Prater from Springfield, Missouri also joined the ASTP program. He was playing sandlot football on 7 December 1941, when he heard the news that the Japanese had attacked Pearl Harbor. At that time, Prater was a senior in high school. The following September, he and several high school friends decided to join the Armed Forces. Prater enrolled in Drury College, and signed up for the Army School Program. By the Spring of 1943, the students in Prater's military school program as well as those across the United States were called into active military service. Prater's group reported to Jefferson

Barracks in St. Louis for induction into the Army and then went to Camp Roberts in California for Basic Training. At the end of Basic, Prater was offered to join ASTP and he was eager to go back to college studies. Prater was assigned to the City College of New York, just as Kravitz was.

Floyd R. Ross

Floyd R. Ross of Santa Paula, California joined ASTP as well. He was drafted in February 1943 at 19 years of age. Ross was put on a Greyhound bus and was taken to the Fresno, California Medical Examination Center, where he waited in long lines with other draftees to take his medical exam. When he passed his exam, Ross was enlisted in the Army and put into the Enlisted Reserve Corps. On 16 February, Ross was sent to the induction station at Fort Ord in Monterey, California to get his shots, his uniform, and a G.I. haircut. Ross was then sent to Camp Shelby, Mississippi for Basic Training and boarded a troop train to make the trip. The Pullman Car coaches were converted into bunks for sleeping at night and back to regular coach seats during the day. The raw recruits on the train were the lowest priority and they frequently were left waiting at stations as freight trains carrying war supplies, other troop trains, and passenger trains moved along the tracks. Ross' train did not have a dining car and they had to stop at stations with a restaurant for their meals. Once, at a station that lacked a restaurant, the recruits fell into formation and marched into town to a local restaurant. The whole trip to Mississippi took about a week. When he arrived to Camp Shelby, Ross was assigned to a field artillery battalion. Ross asked for non-combat duty and was assigned to a medical detachment, but they were not equipped to provide Basic Training and he went back to artillery training.

In late June 1943, Ross' Battalion was sent to Louisiana for maneuvers, which lasted until August. When the maneuvers concluded, the trucks and equipment were loaded onto railroad flat cars and the GIs were put aboard troop trains bound for California and desert training. After a week's furlough, Ross returned to his unit and received news that he had been selected to attend Surgical Technician School at O'Reilly Army General Hospital in Springfield, Missouri. Ross completed his thirteen week long course on 31 December 1943 and he was qualified to serve in a battalion aid station or as a medic in the field artillery battery. Ross then learned about the ASTP program, took and passed the IQ test, and was sent to Grinnel College in Iowa. After more tests, Ross was sent to study at CCNY, where Kravitz and Prater were also studying.

An ASTP Student's Routine

A basic engineering course was the first task of the ASTP student. It was very similar to a freshman's first year in college. The ASTP men received a wakeup call at 0600 hours, cleaned up, had breakfast, and were off to class by 0800 until about 1600. An hour of physical activity would follow which included close order drill or a march around the campus. After dinner at 1800, they would attend a three-hour study session to complete their homework. On weekends, the students were free to do what they pleased from noon Saturday until bed check on Sunday night. At CCNY, those who lived in the area went home for the weekend. Kravitz was only a three-hour train ride from his hometown and occasionally spent the weekend at home with his girlfriend. The others would venture out and explore New York City. Advertising agencies would often give away free tickets to radio broadcast shows and Ross went several times to see Frank Sinatra on the Lucky Strike Hit Parade. Restaurants also offered free meals to GIs many of whom were a long way from home. The Pepsi Cola Corporation had a recreation room at Times Square that provided all the Pepsi you wanted for a nickel. The ASTP men could also sightsee all over New York City as subway rides cost only a nickel too.

Termination of ASTP

When the ASTP program terminated in mid-March 1944, everyone who was in the program was assigned to an infantry division. The program had come to a very abrupt halt with little explanation as to why. For the men who had been in the program, they were left to assume that more men were needed for the upcoming invasion of Europe. Those at CCNY were put aboard a troop train with triple deck bunk beds. The baggage car was converted into an Army kitchen to feed the one thousand or so men on board the train. Their destination was Camp Polk, Louisiana, where the 75th Division was participating in 3rd Army Maneuvers. Slagle woke up one morning at Xavier University, ready to go to class and within hours was on a troop train. Slagle, Kravitz, Prater and Ross, upon termination of the ASTP program were pushed into the 75th Division; Company H, 2nd Battalion, 291st Regiment.

Joining the 75th Division

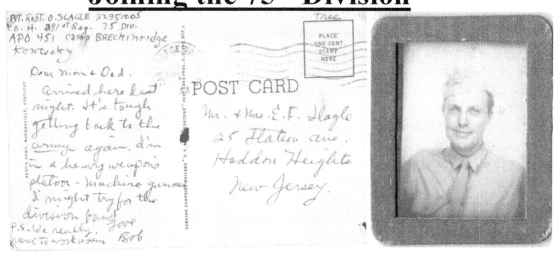

PVT. RobT. O. SLAGLE 3295/005
CO. H. 291st Reg. 75 DIV.
APO 451 Camp BRECKINridge
Kentucky

Dear Mom + Dad,
Arrived here last
night. It's tough
getting back to the
army again. I'm
in a heavy weapons
platoon - machine gunner
I might try for the
division band. Love
P.S. We really
have to work again   Bob

POST CARD

Mr. + Mrs. E.F. Slagle
25 Station ave.
Haddon Heights
New Jersey

Slagle's Letter Home	Robert O. Slagle

291 Inf. Kentucky Colonels Band	291 Inf. Drum and Bugle Corps

35

Camp Polk

The men from ASTP were taken aboard troop trains and sent on route to Camp Polk, Louisiana. A bus then transported them from the train station to the camp. They arrived at Camp Polk with uniform and full pack and were trucked out to the field to join the rest of the 75th Division, which was in the midst of 3rd Army Maneuvers. The men from ASTP found themselves in an awkward position, some having been in a cozy university classroom less than a day earlier. Instead of "the good life," the men from ASTP were out on maneuvers in the field. The days were hot, humid, and the terrain was formidable. The men would march five miles each morning through marsh and swamps, full of snakes and mosquitoes. Maneuvers continued through rain and mud. Slagle watched as many men dropped during marches that were not accustomed to the climate. Slagle tolerated the heat and humidity well, from having spent several summers of his youth in Norfolk, Virginia where the climate was similar. The night after Slagle left the comforts of the nightlife around Xavier University, he found himself in a kitchen at Camp Polk, peeling potatoes.

A Confusing Time

Being on maneuvers meant that the men slept in the field as they would in a combat situation. That first night at Camp Polk was quite an event, with the newly arrived ASTP men tasked with setting up their tent in the field for the first time. Prater and Slagle both were experienced outdoorsmen and had little difficulty: others had much more difficulty. Each man carried half a tent in their pack and they could find a buddy and setup a pup tent for two. That first day, Prater met his tent-mate, Private Harry Osborn, a man who had already been through Basic Training like himself and was fresh out of Army Air Force studies with ASTP. For the ASTP men, that first day out in the hot sun in the field was quite a shock after spending many months in the classroom. The ASTP men had grown soft from the comforts of university life and this was their wake up call; they had to work hard again.

Billy Wells

While H Company was still on maneuvers at Camp Polk, men who were to join the 75th Division began to arrive at Camp Breckinridge, Kentucky. One of these men was Private Billy Wells of Lyons, Indiana. Wells had little to do but polish shoes and scrub floors as he awaited the 75th Division's arrival. Three-day weekend passes were frequently granted, leaving Wells to believe that he had died and gone to Heaven. He hitchhiked or when he had the money, took a bus home: it was only a three-hour ride. Wells formally joined the 75th Division on 6 June 1944. He was glad to have joined a fresh division rather than serving as a replacement to a division already in combat where pecking orders had already been established. Wells was one of many men too young to serve as a replacement overseas, who instead were to join the 75th Division. Thus, with the average age of a GI in the Division being just 18 or 19, the 75th Division received the nickname of "Diaper Division."

Wells finished high school early and went to work for a US Navy ammunition depot. When he turned 18 in September 1943, Wells registered for the draft. He was inducted on 15 November 1943. Wells was sent from Indiana to Texas, where he took Basic Training. At the end of his training he was assigned a mosquito net and assumed he was going to a place he did not want to go: the Pacific. One day, Wells' name was called and his duffel bag was put aboard ship, yet he was not told of his destination. Later that day, Wells found out that a law had been passed that required all men going to war to be at least eighteen years and six months old; Wells was too young to make the cut. Wells' bag was returned and he would not be shipping off to the Pacific after all. Wells was sent to the 45th Division at Camp Butner, North Carolina. There, he was trained on the .30 caliber machine gun. Wells was taught to disassemble the machine gun blindfolded, in preparation for doing so under cover of darkness in combat. When classes were complete, leave passes were granted to the town of Durham: it was here that Wells quickly learned the differences between his hometown of Lyons, Indiana and the "Old South." Wells was walking through town when a black man stepped off the sidewalk and into the gutter. Wells' first action was to try to help the man up, he thought he had slipped. Someone quickly told Wells to mind his own business; such behavior was normal there. Wells did not think it was normal, but such was the difference in customs between the North and South even in 1944.

Henry H. Smith

Henry H. Smith from Covington, Virginia had been going to vocational school in Manassas, Virginia to lean to be a welder, when Pearl Harbor happened. Smith took a job in Potsdam, New York working for the Alcoa Aluminum Corporation, until he enlisted on 23 March 1943. He went from Fort Niagara, New York to Fort Custer near Battle Creek, Michigan to become a Military Police Escort Guard. After completing Basic Training, Smith was sent to Boston, Massachusetts to pick up a load of German prisoners and take them to Mehacia, Texas. Smith then went on to Spence Field, Georgia where he guarded German POWs and took them out on farms to work. Smith then was sent to Anniston, Alabama for more POW guard duty. In the spring of 1944, Smith was then sent to join the 75th Division at Camp Breckinridge, where he took a second round of Basic Training.

Elton T. Page

Elton T. Page from Burlington, North Carolina was drafted into the Army after turning 18. He was inducted at Camp Croft, South Carolina and went through Basic Training at Camp Shelby, Mississippi. Page kept getting extra duty in the kitchen during Basic Training, either for having a dirty rifle or being late for roll call. Page found he liked KP duty and told his mess sergeant that he would like to go to school to become a cook. After two months, Page completed Cook and Baker's School and became a Cook First Class. Shortly after becoming a cook, he was sent back to his platoon and then was sent to Camp Breckinridge where he joined the 75th Division. Page was one of the last replacements to fill the 75th Division's ranks, having arrived just a short time before the Division was prepared to depart to the ETO.

S. Phillip Lawson

Phillip Lawson from Savannah, Georgia grew up on his large family farm. He had only a 6th grade education. He worked long, hard hours on the farm since he was 11 years old. He was the youngest child of fifteen siblings, living in a four-room shack with no electricity or running water. He learned to fire a rifle as a young boy and was an excellent shot. His family was so poor that when he went hunting with his father, he was given only a bullet or two and he was punished if he did not shoot something. Lawson was drafted in August 1943 and took Basic Training at Camp Croft, South Carolina. He did not want to be in the military, but decided that since he was drafted and could do nothing about it, he was determined to be the best soldier he could be. After battling an illness that persisted for almost six months, Lawson returned back to duty and was sent to Camp Breckinridge where he joined the 75th Division in June 1944.

"Kirk"

"Kirk," from Philadelphia, Pennsylvania was born into an immigrant family from Greece. They were very poor and he just barely passed high school. With a heavy Greek accent, "Kirk" had a hard time finding a job, so he tried his hand with many different odd jobs, but he did not like any of them. He and his younger brother both found part-time work in a diner and they both learned how to cook. He got married in 1943 and found out that he had a child on the way. "Kirk" could not find regular work and decided to enlist in the Army to get a steady paycheck. He arrived to Camp Breckinridge with a trainload of replacements and joined the 75th Division in July 1944. "Kirk" received a leave pass in late September and got to see his baby girl just weeks before he was sent to the war.

"Willard"

"Willard" grew up in the suburbs of Philadelphia. He was a very tall and gangly man with red hair. When he finished high school, he found a job as a server in a diner in town. "Willard" enjoyed working in the diner, but could not decide what he wanted to do with his life; he knew he had no interest in joining the military and hoped he would not get drafted. Just as he was about to propose to his high school girlfriend, he received his draft notice. He was sent to Camp Croft, South Carolina for Basic Training. He had a leave pass home in June 1944 and told his girlfriend that he wanted to marry her as soon as he got out of the Army. His mother was terribly worried about sending off her only child to war, she had a bad feeling that something was going to happen to him. "Willard" joined the 75th Division at Camp Breckinridge in July 1944.

Camp Breckinridge- Enlisted Barracks

S/SGT William Wilson   **SGT Leslie Hicks**   **SGT Colin Chisholm**   **SGT Johnny Stewart**

40

Top Left: Billy Wells and buddies from 2nd Platoon

2nd from left S/SGT Clarence Carroll- right S/SGT Bob Galway- holding flag SGT Colin Chisholm

Holding Flag- SGT Chisholm, Front 2nd from left- Bruce Reynolds,
 Back row, 2nd from right- 1st SGT Mike Whalen

On Leave in Evansville, Indiana: 2nd from left- Henry H. Smith

From Polk to Breckinridge

The 75th Division had been at Camp Polk from 9 February to 3 April 1944. No one was sorry to leave "Camp Swampy" when the time came. The 75th Division then moved on to Camp Breckinridge, Kentucky and spent much of the month of April organizing its outfits and providing advanced training to those who qualified. Slagle found himself in an intelligence-training program with daily classroom instruction, following his regular duties. The men were back in the grind of daily marches and training while at Breckinridge. The 75th Division formally organized itself at Camp Breckinridge; final personnel decisions were made and empty positions were quickly filled. A three month Basic Training program began soon after arriving to Breckinridge, intended for all the new draftees entering the 75th Division's ranks, but it also included the men from ASTP who had completed Basic Training a year or more earlier. For

Slagle, his second round of Basic was almost routine; it was hard work, but he had been through a lot more in the 11 months since he entered the service.

Assignments

The 75th Division had already been activated a year earlier in April 1943 at Fort Leonard Wood, Missouri. Men from the 75th Division were repeatedly being drawn away to serve as replacements with the divisions already serving in Europe. Thus, the ASTP men served as replacements in the 75th Division. After that first day, the newly arrived ASTP men went to an office in camp where a second lieutenant gave them their unit assignments. Slagle was put into First Platoon, H Company of the 291st Regiment as a machine gunner. Lawson also joined First Platoon as an ammunition bearer. Kravitz told his First Sergeant that he was a typist, which made no impression on him. Kravitz became a replacement ammunition bearer in Second Platoon, carrying two containers of machine gun bullets and a rifle over his shoulder. Wells and Smith also joined Second Platoon. Prater was asked what he wanted to do; he wanted to be with mortars and he was put into Third Platoon as a mortar man. Ross mentioned that he was a medic and was told that the Division had all the medics it needed. Due to his artillery training, Ross was assigned to the Mortar Platoon. Page also joined Third Platoon. H Company was the heavy weapons company of Second Battalion and was composed of two machine gun platoons and one mortar platoon. The Company's complement was 138 men.

Marksmanship

At Camp Breckinridge, the men of H Company had their daily routine like any other company, which included time at the firing range. As an infantryman, each member of a company, despite their MOS, had to be familiar with firing a rifle. The M-1 Garand was the basic weapon. Many GIs preferred the M-1 to smaller and lighter weapons. Training also included use of the M-1 Carbine and Colt .45 pistol. The men got to try every weapon in the American arsenal, including flame-throwers. As H Company was a heavy weapons company, its men primarily trained on machine guns and mortars. The basic machine gun used was the water-cooled .30 caliber. The machine guns required a 51-pound tri-pod that the assistant gunner in a squad would carry. H Company also had a

.50 caliber heavy machine gun mounted onto a jeep. The mortar used was an 81-mm and it also required a heavy bi-pod and base plate.

Company Headquarters Structure

H Company was commanded by Captain Richard Haddock with First Lieutenant Owen L. Goodnight Jr serving as his Executive Officer. Mike Whalen was the First Sergeant. Staff Sergeant Lyons was the Mess Sergeant and Richard Jones was the Supply Sergeant. Hoffman Wong was the Map Sergeant, John Bessner was the Communications Sergeant and Richard Thorpe was the Company Clerk. There were three cooks: Ray Casper, Ross Simms, and Raymond Ott. There were also two cooks helpers. H Company also had 25 privates that made up other duties in Headquarters Platoon. Slagle was the Company Bugler and Arnie Spade was the Motor Pool Sergeant. There were three messengers, two of whom were also jeep drivers.

The Platoon Structure

H Company's two machine gun platoons were each broken up into two sections, which were arranged into two squads, each possessing one gun: with a gunner, assistant gunner and four ammo bearers. There were fifteen men in each machine gun section and seven men in each squad. The machine gun squads were lead by a buck sergeant and a staff sergeant commanded each section. A tech sergeant or "platoon sergeant" commanded the two sections in each platoon. The mortar platoon was broken up into three sections, which were arranged into two squads, each possessing an 81-mm mortar. There were seventeen men in each mortar section and eight men in each squad. A corporal led the mortar squads with a gunner, assistant gunner, four ammo bearers, and a driver. A second lieutenant commanded each mortar section and a staff sergeant served as section chief. Third Platoon also had a "platoon sergeant."

Equipment

As Second Battalion's heavy weapons company, H Company carried a quantity of munitions. Privates in Headquarters Platoon carried M-1 Garands. Privates in the machine gun and mortar platoons carried either the M-1 Garand or M-1 Carbine. The

Carbine was a lighter weapon and was preferred by the ammo bearers who already had a heavy load to carry. However, the M-1 Garand was the preferred weapon of an experienced rifleman. Headquarters Platoon had two jeeps, a three-quarter ton truck, and a .50 caliber machine gun. The machine gun and mortar squads each had a jeep with trailer. There were sixteen jeeps in H Company. Each machine gun platoon had two bazookas, while each mortar section had two bazookas. Pistols were carried by the officers and were a secondary weapon carried by sergeants and gunners.

Life in the Barracks

Privates lived in their own quarters building and slept in bunk beds arranged against the wall, in a rectangular room. They had a footlocker containing their possessions at the foot of their bed and a small space on the wall between their beds to hang their shirts and coats. The sergeants and staff sergeants slept at the end of the rows on a single bed. H Company had two barracks. The first building housed First Platoon on the bottom level and Second Platoon on the upper level. Third Platoon was in the second building; two sections lived on the bottom level, the third section lived on the upper level along with H Company's cooks and headquarters staff. First Sergeant Whalen had an office in this building. About forty men lived on each level. The platoon sergeants lived in a closed room at the end of the room that housed the privates. The cramped space brought about plenty of socializing among the privates and whether they liked each other or not, they learned all there was to know about each other. Many stories could be recounted about life among one's platoon buddies. In many ways, the men of a platoon were very much like a group of close friends, almost like brothers. Some might call them a "clique." They would not always agree on everything and many would love to argue with each other. Yet, there was no one else that a member of a platoon would rather argue with or haze than his buddies. When a letter from home arrived for a member of the platoon, either he would read it aloud or one of his buddies would swipe it and read it to the others. Such was the lack of privacy among one's platoon mates.

When someone ventured into town on leave, they bought a magazine or a newspaper and it made the rounds through the platoon. Some men in H Company could not read and Wells once read an issue of Stars and Stripes to one such man. If a member of the platoon had a date while on leave or was invited to a home-cooked meal or picnic off base, the poor man would be poked and prodded for every last detail of the event. Many were homesick and such outings were as close to "home" as one could get. There was a Cajun in H Company; a large and rowdy man. He was loud and wanted to roughhouse all the time. If a GI left his bunk, the Cajun liked to rip it up; he was too big to take down for it.

The Men of First Platoon

Perhaps the most notable character in First Platoon was the soft-spoken Bert Larson from Minnesota. He was 38 years old, married and a father of two. He did not have to be there, but he volunteered for military service. Larson was very much a father figure to the men in the Platoon that were nearly 20 years his junior. In fact, Larson had a habit of calling many men in the platoon "Junior," his choice term of endearment. His friendly, outgoing personality kept many of his platoon mates both entertained and away from thoughts of being homesick. Others in First Platoon included Mike Murza, a musician from Philadelphia. Phillip Lawson was a farmer from Georgia and a crack shot with a rifle. Then there was Stan Slawson, a Staff Sergeant and member of the Division Band. Their superiors often confused Slawson and Lawson even though they looked nothing alike as Slawson was tall and thin with dark hair and Lawson was a blonde and built like a football player. Slawson was from Wisconsin and a college graduate. He was studying to be a pastor, when he decided to volunteer for the Army. Slawson and Larson were the oldest men in the Platoon and the younger men looked up to both. There was also a big, husky young man from Mississippi that was nicknamed "Hay Seed;" he had such a heavy accent that no one could understand anything he said. Everyone liked to tease "Hay Seed," because he was very satisfied with his life in the Army; he liked the food! "Kirk" was a Greek from Philadelphia and "Willard" was from the suburbs of Philadelphia. Saul Cohen was from the Bronx, where he grew up working in his father's pawnshop. Cohen consistently used foul language to describe his superiors and even his Platoon mates. He was a very hard man to get along with. Then there was Slagle, a union musician, who had played in the Big Bands in New Jersey.

The Men of Second Platoon

Second Platoon had several stand out characters. Staff Sergeant Don Stewart was a sad faced man who often talked of his wife and family. He was older than the others in the Platoon and was called "Pop." Staff Sergeant William Wilson was a very likable fellow who was nicknamed "Stretch" for his 6-foot-6 stature; he was a college basketball player before being drafted. Colin Chisholm, nicknamed "Chissey" was a Sergeant and he came from Massachusetts. He and "Stretch" were among the few remaining members of H Company that had been there since the formation of the 75th Division at Fort Leonard Wood, a year earlier. Galen Hummel was nicknamed "Happy" because he was always unhappy. Bob Cage had a habit of grinding his teeth, especially in his sleep. He was nicknamed "Itchy" for his constant habit of scratching. John Welch from Maine was the comedian of the Platoon and had quite an accent. John Henry was from Pennsylvania and he and John Welch became great friends: as close as brothers. Bruce Reynolds was a strange, but funny fellow from Chicago. Billy Wells was the youngest in the Platoon and was nicknamed "Willie." James Siggelakis or "Greek" as he was called was a rough looking, stocky man, yet always jovial. He would receive letters from his girlfriend and pass them along to his buddy, Wells who responded with "It looks Greek to me," which it was. Howard Schaefer was called "Red Dog," being the only redhead in the platoon. Henry Smith was from Covington, Virginia. Then there was Wallace Kravitz from Springfield, Massachusetts.

The Men of Third Platoon

Third Platoon was H Company's mortar complement and it too had some notable characters. Jim Strong from Long Island was athletic and exceptionally intelligent. He too came from ASTP. Larry Silverstein was also from New York and came from a family involved in the diamond business; he was a very talented artist. Ira Posnak was a friendly and talkative fellow, who was also from New York. John Malarich's family was from Yugoslavia and he was perhaps ten years older than most in Third Platoon. Malarich was short, stout, and bald. He was a factory worker before enlisting and he was very strong: he was also a boxer. Richard Modrzejewski was a Staff Sergeant. He was part of the 75th Division since it was formed at Fort Leonard Wood a year earlier. Modrzejewski was from a coal mining family in Pennsylvania and was crude and not particularly bright; it is doubtful if he even finished high school. Many of the men in the Platoon made jokes about him. Despite his overall lack of intelligence, Modrzejewski was a very capable soldier. Floyd Ross was from California and Bill Prater was from Missouri. Leslie "Joe" Hicks was from Massachusetts and was a Sergeant; he too had been with H Company since Fort Leonard Wood and was buddies with Chisholm and Wilson. Then there was Elton Page who was from Burlington, North Carolina.

A German in H Company

Slagle had an interesting first day at Breckinridge. The man who slept in the bunk above him was a German who had escaped his homeland just prior to the outbreak of World War II. He had seen Hitler up close in 1938 during a military parade and saw what was happening to Germany. After being drafted into the German Army while still in high school, Luther Siegfried managed to escape from Germany and make his way through Europe. Siegfried arrived to the United States in 1939 and spoke very little English. Living in the United States and enjoying the freedom it offered even to a foreigner came as a shock to Siegfried, who volunteered for military service the day that he became an American citizen. Siegfried recognized that Slagle was a German name and they struck up a friendship. Siegfried taught Slagle some basic German and Slagle helped him make sense of the many slang terms used by Americans. Siegfried also went through the intelligence-training program and had a secondary duty as translator for H Company.

Music

The morning after arriving to Camp Breckinridge, Slagle was awakened to a familiar sight: a parade of musicians marching past him. In high school, Slagle had a music instructor that was a former military man and he made all members of the high school band march around in military procession. Slagle soon volunteered for Colonel Robertson's 291st Infantry Drum and Bugle Corps and became one of its 23 members. As the Company Bugler, every morning Slagle would get up and make the Company Bugle Call and rouse everyone out of their sleep. Then, he would join in the Drum and Bugle Corps that would march down the street and around all the barracks buildings before breakfast. Slagle discovered that many of the men in the Drum and Bugle Corps were also in the 291st Infantry "Kentucky Colonels" Band. At Breckinridge there were dance bands and jazz bands that entertained the troops on weekends, in addition to the actual Division Band. The "Kentucky Colonels" Band had already formed some time before Slagle was transferred to the 75th Division, but Slagle managed to join up and he played the alto sax and clarinet. The 75th Division Band was a different story: there were few open slots and it was very competitive. Many of the band members had been front men in the Big Bands prior to joining the Army. Slagle had to wait some time for an appointment to the Band. The 75th Division Army Band was composed of men from the three Regimental Bands of the 289th, 290th, and 291st. Band members had an MOS of "Bandsman" in addition to their MOS of infantry.

Weekend Leave Passes

At Camp Breckinridge, each soldier would be granted leave passes for two or three days away from their duties. Leave passes were granted in rotation, so that after the full cycle of men had received leave, the cycle would begin again. There was little to do in the immediate area around Breckinridge, so men would frequently take a trip on an Ohio River paddle boat and cross into Indiana where there was the small town of Evansville and nightlife. Evansville was a very enjoyable spot for an evening or for a full weekend. The GI could get treats, coffee, doughnuts, and more. Evansville had a movie house and even dance halls for meeting girls. Some soldiers got friendly with nurses working on base who went home to Indiana. GIs on leave were frequently invited to dinner at the nurses' homes. Many locals in Indiana would invite GIs to spend the weekend at their homes; many a homesick GI gladly accepted the offer to sleep in a bed and eat home-cooked meals. There were many old couples in the small town in Indiana that enjoyed the company of a GI and asked them to return for dinner whenever they had leave. Local girls would often invite GIs to a picnic or an outing with the family. Smith enjoyed venturing into the small town of Owensboro, Kentucky on leave with some of his platoon buddies. While in Owensboro, Smith met a girl and had three dates with her during his time at Breckinridge.

An Honorable Duty

Every day, one man from each regiment would be chosen to be the commanding general's guard. The man chosen would have to be the neatest soldier in his company.

Each company within each regiment had their chance to be represented; the companies were rotated daily. The company first sergeant would select the man to be chosen as the general's guard. Prater once earned himself a weekend leave pass by becoming the general's guard. He went home to Springfield, Missouri and surprised his family. In October, Prater had a weekend leave pass and decided to go to the World Series in his home state of Missouri. After leaving the gates of Breckinridge, he was picked up by a truck of factory workers going into Evansville, Indiana. Prater hitchhiked the rest of the way to St. Louis and saw a World Series game between the St. Louis Cardinals and St. Louis Browns. He watched from "box seats," standing in the very back row, high up in the stadium. Ross had met a girl while in medical training in Springfield, Missouri and asked First Sergeant Whalen for a three-day pass so he could give her an engagement ring. Whalen would not give Ross a pass, but told him to volunteer for guard duty and he would see that Ross was selected as the general's guard when H Company's next turn came.

Furloughs

When the 75th Division arrived to Camp Breckinridge, one of the first orders of business was to issue furloughs to those who had not yet had one. For the GI returning home, it was a big event and his family and friends would want to visit and take pictures of him in uniform. In early May, Kravitz got his furlough home to Springfield, Massachusetts to visit his family and his girlfriend. In July, Slagle got his furlough and he returned home to Hadden Heights, New Jersey and a visit to the Steel Pier in Atlantic City, where he had been a musician in the Big Bands a year earlier. After two weeks of visiting family and friends and a few days at the beach, Slagle was on his way back to H Company.

A Pleasant Divergence from the Daily Routine

Kravitz was a capable typist, this being a trait that few other privates in H Company possessed. As a result, Kravitz would on occasion have the opportunity to work as First Sergeant Whalen's office clerk. Thorpe was the Company clerk, but Bessner also worked in the office as a typist. Sometimes they were both away on leave. This gave Kravitz a day or two out of the field and away from the routine of daily training. Typists were needed not only in H Company, but also throughout the Division. When a clerk was away on a leave pass or furlough a backup would be needed and Kravitz would sometimes find himself in the Battalion Headquarters Office. The monotonous daily training went on from May through to September and until October when rumors began to surface about deployment to the war. The opportunity to leave the rigors of daily training, if only for a short time, was not passed up by anyone who received an offer of temporary duty away from the field. One night, when Kravitz was working as Whalen's assistant, he was ordered to setup the First Sergeant's pup tent on a week when H Company was in the field on maneuvers. It was dark and Kravitz could not see where he was setting up the tent, but he set it up anyway. The next morning, Whalen emerged from his tent with a bright red face and yelled for Kravitz. Whalen was scratching all over. Kravitz had setup Whalen's tent atop of a chigger's nest!

Meals at Breckinridge

The men of H Company would eat together by platoon in the dining areas. There would be three or four sittings for each meal to accommodate the whole Company. The men received class-A food; hot meals. Army food has never been known to be the best food in the world, but it was filling. Some who had grown up in poverty during the Great Depression were glad to have a full belly. Other than the usual grumbling, there were few serious complaints about the grub. "Hay Seed" absolutely loved the food. He lived a very simple life in Mississippi and grew up without indoor plumbing. He was raised on "meat and potatoes" and when he had spaghetti for the first time at Breckinridge it was a big event for him and something he enjoyed very much. Others who were accustomed to specific delicacies from their time as college students in ASTP grumbled over some of the food. Slagle enjoyed many Southern specialties such as succotash that was served often, but he despised the soggy okra that resembled slugs in texture. Over the many months spent at Breckinridge, many of the skinny boys became filled out men from having balanced meals.

H Company's First Sergeant

First Sergeant Mike Whalen was a soldier's soldier. He was tall and a bit overweight and had a loud, forceful voice. Whalen was a draftee like most of the other enlisted men and they identified with him in that way. He was a capable taskmaster with the enlisted men and very congenial with the officers. Whalen had been with H Company since Fort Leonard Wood and had weaseled himself into the position of First Sergeant by cozying up with his superiors. He was Captain Haddock's right hand man. He was a tough and rugged man who was not necessarily the most friendly or likable man, but he was well respected by H Company: he was fair to the enlisted men. Whalen was a red faced Irishman and enjoyed his weekend leave passes as much as the next guy, perhaps more. As enlisted men did not qualify for a liquor ration, Whalen would buddy up with the lieutenants that did not drink and get their ration. He would go into Evansville, Indiana and have quite a weekend of drinks and parties; he was a borderline alcoholic. On Monday morning he somehow managed to stagger back to his duties. His condition was quite evident when he frequently referred to Kravitz as "Kra Vitz," emphasizing the second syllable. Slagle was on somewhat good terms with Whalen, as the First Sergeant would frequent the Saturday night jazz band performances where Slagle played. Whalen enjoyed the music and especially the steady supply of drinks, offered to all those who attended.

Punishments

Captain Haddock was very strict with his men and depended on First Sergeant Whalen to discipline the men of H Company. "Hay Seed" was somewhat of a challenge in this respect; he was a hard man to discipline. On his first day at Breckinridge, the Company was lined up for inspection after dinner. Each man wore a collared shirt and tie. "Hay Seed" rolled up his sleeves, let his shirttail out, and used his tie to wipe his face; he did not know what it was for. Whalen exploded when he saw "Hay Seed's" appearance and gave him punishment detail of doing KP duty for a week. "Hay Seed" thanked him for the duty; he did not understand that it was a punishment. When Whalen got fed up with his behavior and started yelling at him on a daily basis, "Hay Seed" became very confused. He noticed that Whalen was always drinking. After a furlough home, "Hay Seed" came back with a bottle of "White Lightning" moonshine that his family bottled and gave it to his First Sergeant. "Hay Seed" quickly became Whalen's favorite in the Company! Kentucky was dry; you could not buy alcohol. The day after "Hay Seed" returned from his furlough, Whalen issued him another one and told him to go home, spend time with his family and say "hello" to his parents for him. Whalen also told "Hay

Seed" how much he loved the moonshine. In the summer of 1944, "Hay Seed" spent more time at home than any other man in the Company and Whalen really enjoyed his weekends.

On Base Entertainment

There were several outlets for entertainment at Breckinridge, including movies, dances, and bands. On weekends, a movie would be shown on base and due to the frequent over-crowding of GIs it would have several different screenings. Dances were arranged with nurses and also local girls were invited; many being girls that the GIs knew from their visits to Indiana. Then, there were live band performances by the dance and jazz band ensembles. Slagle spent most of his weekends at the band performances, playing and then fraternizing with the musicians in the Division Band. Ray Brejcha was one such musician. Brejcha had a different path than Slagle did in the 75th Division, as he was a member of the Division Band and was not attached to an infantry company as well. The band performances would often end very late and with alcohol available, it led to lots of GIs with hangovers the next morning. One of the other less advertised venues of entertainment were the card games, played during off hours and out of eye shot of any officer. Card sharks were quite prevalent and a wise GI would do little more than be a spectator during such games. Some were so desperate for a game of poker that they crowded under bed sheets with a flashlight for a late night game. Of course, there were also the games of craps that were played in the barracks. Ross often played craps with the man in the bunk above him. One had to be sure that the dice landed flat to avoid a dispute. In his first game, Ross won about one hundred dollars and did not realize that the so-called "winner" of a game of craps, really was not much of a winner after all. When all his Platoon buddies realized Ross had some money, many of them wanted loans.

Games

While at Breckinridge, hard work and intensive physical training was not the only activity that men from H Company did as a group: there was also softball. Slagle was a pitcher on his high school baseball team and he pitched on his team in H Company too. First Lieutenant Goodnight, H Company's Executive Officer was a professional athlete. He was a Native-American from Texas who, before the war, was an All-American college football player. He spent a year in the Pros with the old St. Louis Rams before being drafted. Goodnight was a great athlete in all sports and was the envy of many of the young privates in the Company who enjoyed playing ball with a Pro football player. Lawson and "Hay Seed" enjoyed watching the baseball games. One hot summer day, one of the team members asked "Hay Seed" if he wanted to hit a few balls. Lawson encouraged him to give it a try. "Hay Seed" had never played baseball before and they told him to swing the bat and hit the ball. He missed the first few pitches, but then hit the ball so hard it split the seams! "Hay Seed" decided that he preferred to be a spectator.

A Role Model

Many of the young GIs looked up to the older men in their platoons. Many of the men were naïve and impressionable, while others were more grown up and street smart. Yet, all of them whether they wanted to admit it or not, were looking for some measure of guidance and acceptance from the older guys. The afternoon baseball games drew a crowd of onlookers. Most of the men playing were privates and only a few officers would play. Slagle prided himself on striking out almost anyone who came up to bat. In the early summer, a lot of the privates were still unfamiliar with their superiors. A stocky, broad shouldered man came up to bat. Slagle threw a pitch and the man knocked the ball clean out of the area for a home run. Slagle must have had a look of shock on his face as the batter, Lieutenant Goodnight patted him on the shoulder and said, "Think nothing of it, I played pro football." Slagle immediately found a friend among Goodnight. In the weeks to follow, Slagle made it a point to get Goodnight a cup of coffee in the morning. Goodnight was a friend to many, he was very humble and approachable, unlike most other officers. One morning Slagle made the Company Bugle Call and the Company Commander was unsatisfied with it and he told Slagle that right after breakfast, he was to go out behind the barracks and get some practice in. Slagle did as ordered, but he was yelled at by the First Sergeant. Whalen was recovering from a hangover and was very angry at the noise. He assigned Slagle latrine duty. Goodnight intervened and it was Whalen that got stuck with cleaning out his own latrine for drinking while on duty.

Shooting Competitions

During H Company's training at Breckinridge, time was spent at the rifle range. For some it was an opportunity to learn to fire a rifle well; some for the first time. For others, it was a time to show off their skills. The farm boys were without question the best shots. "Hay Seed" was often teased by his Platoon buddies for coming from a humble background and not being familiar with a lot of things that many others took for granted. "Hay Seed's" handling of the M-1 Garand at the rifle range was quite a sight. Soon his Platoon buddies came to him asking for advice on handling the Garand. Third Platoon also had some competitions and sometimes betting a little money on the side to keep one's mind off the boredom of training. The mortar men even had some competitions involving the speed of setting up their mortars into position to fire. Some of the men were very poor shots even with frequent training. The men had to achieve some measure of accuracy to remain in the platoon.

Captain Haddock

H Company's Commanding Officer, Captain Richard Haddock from Long Island, New York, was not the most pleasant officer. He was in his late 30s or early 40s and was a career soldier; he was not a draftee. Haddock was a strict disciplinarian. He had been with H Company since the 75th Division was first activated in April 1943. On one occasion, a man from the Company was very disorderly and Haddock issued him a violent beating with a belt. Haddock did not associate with enlisted men in the Company at all. He wanted everything done by the book. He hated having a company of men with dirty weapons; everything had to be spotless. If someone needed to meet with him, they made an appointment. Captain Haddock was not popular with his men: in fact, many were afraid of him. It was impossible for enlisted men to get acquainted with their commander.

An Infamous Officer

H Company's First Platoon had one less than adequate First Lieutenant as its commanding officer, by name of Bergheimer. Lieutenant Bergheimer was from New Jersey and possessed a personality that could be easily compared to that of a mobster. He was rough with his men, taken quick to anger, and possessed a desire for alcohol unrivaled by any other man in H Company, with the exception of First Sergeant Whalen. He acted self-important and perhaps his most noticeable trait: he did not listen. In short, to the average private under his command, Bergheimer was the officer from Hell. On one very hot afternoon, Bergheimer lined up his Platoon with full pack and gear in a trench and made them stand at attention. They stood for possibly two hours, as the hot sun beat down and the men began to drop in the heat. Bergheimer stood there, berating each man for the most miniscule of issues, offering personal insults to any man who dropped or twitched in the heat. After his disordered inspection, he revoked all privileges and leave passes and angrily sent the men back to their duties. Many men in First Platoon held a grudge with Bergheimer.

A Little Prank

Officers in the military lived in separate quarters from enlisted men. They had privileges not allocated to the numerous enlisted men that make up an infantry company. Officers did not spend their free time getting involved with interpersonal issues surrounding those under their command that is with the exception of Bergheimer. At night, men from First Platoon would play a game of poker in their quarters, out of sight from officers. One evening, Bergheimer came upon the game and sat in on it; he wanted to play. The privates in First Platoon were very nervous and the atmosphere of the game quickly changed. When Bergheimer lost his hand, he told the privates that their game was against the rules and he would turn them in; that is unless they would hand their Lieutenant the pot, which they did. The privates were very intimidated by Bergheimer, who began to haze many of his men over the next few days. The card games ended and Bergheimer continued to visit the privates in their quarters and try to involve himself in their business. Eventually it led to privates doing errands for their Lieutenant and if they did not fetch him a beer or deliver a newspaper or magazine to him when he asked for it, he would see that their leave passes were revoked. When he had a bad day, or was recovering from a hangover, Bergheimer would just report them for nothing. This led to First Sergeant Whalen paying frequent visits to First Platoon's Barracks and wondering why they were getting a reputation for being so misbehaved. Whalen knew many of the men in First Platoon well and realized that something was wrong.

Several of the privates in First Platoon tired of this poor treatment by Bergheimer and they decided to do something about it. Bergheimer would frequently get drunk after dinner and turn in for the night. On a dare, a few privates walked out of their quarters late one night and intentionally got themselves caught. Their answer for what they were doing out at that time of night was "Getting beer for our Lieutenant, he ordered us to." The privates got a verbal scolding by an MP and were sent back to their quarters, but what happened to Bergheimer was not such a light scolding. Lieutenant Bergheimer was roused out of bed in a drunken stupor and berated by Captain Haddock. The next morning Bergheimer emerged and was strangely quiet and almost polite to his platoon. He said little. The privates in First Platoon also said little as they tried to contain their laughter as they watched their Lieutenant serve them breakfast and proceed to do KP duty. It was well worth losing their weekend leave passes just for the sight of watching Bergheimer clean the grease pit below the grill. Bergheimer was also demoted that day to Second Lieutenant, but he still was the platoon leader.

The Incident

On Saturday nights, the men of H Company would enjoy themselves in some way, with either the on base entertainment or by taking a leave pass and venturing to one of the nearby towns. On one particular Saturday night, a lot of the men had too much to drink and staggered back into their barracks. Some had returned to the barracks earlier and were reading a magazine or getting ready for bed. Kravitz was in his bed on the second floor of the barracks building when some of the guys staggered in. Kravitz was an average guy, like any other in the Company. The fact that he was Jewish was the only thing that made him any different and no one really paid much attention to it. After all, there were other Jews in H Company too. That night, one of the medics could not hold his liquor and threw up on the top of the stairs. Kravitz told him to clean up his mess. The looped medic walked over to Kravitz and called him a "Dirty Jew." The chatter in the room suddenly became silent. Kravitz punched the man in the face and down he went. One of the men in the barracks yelled "Good for you!" to Kravitz. The medic got up and left the room. In the morning, Kravitz discovered that the mess was cleaned.

Slagle's Weekend Pass

Slagle received a weekend leave pass and along with a few platoon buddies, decided to venture across the Ohio River and into Indiana. Slagle had a date with a 23 year old nurse who worked on base. Even though Slagle was 19, he handled himself like a man much older. The nurse's parents invited Slagle to their home for the weekend and they also invited two of his friends. Slagle left Breckinridge for his leave; many others were also on leave and heading for the same destination: a popular weekend outing. When Slagle arrived to board the paddleboat that would take him across the Ohio River, they spotted Lieutenant Bergheimer, also out on a weekend pass. Slagle did his best to stay out of Bergheimer's sight. Slagle and the nurse got to their seats with his friends sitting close by. They were enjoying their trip when Bergheimer finally spotted them and made his way over. He ordered Slagle to get out of the seat and Bergeimer proceeded to sit with the nurse. It was mid-afternoon, but Bergheimer reeked of alcohol. Somehow he lost his balance and fell down, before he could get to the seat next to the nurse. Laughter ensued. Bergheimer got up, mumbled something to himself and walked back to his original seat. He continued to mumble unintelligibly to himself until he fell asleep. Slagle managed to avoid his Lieutenant for the rest of his trip.

A Shortcut

The 106th Division was also training at Camp Breckinridge and men from the 75th and 106th would meet while on leave in the surrounding areas. Some friendships were made. Also at Breckinridge, there was an all black company that was training. Slagle had no issues with race, he had played in an all black band before he was drafted. Slagle often took a shortcut back to his barracks through the area where this black unit was training. The company had a Southern white officer commanding it and Slagle overheard his harsh words to the men in his company. One day, Slagle walked through and the black soldiers gave him dirty looks. Slagle said, "How is that old slave master treating you?" Some of the men laughed. In the days to follow, Slagle was always saluted as he walked through; he was friendly to the men of the company. One day Slagle and Lawson took the shortcut to the barracks and the white officer in command chewed them out. He shouted, "You don't belong here, get out!" Slagle pulled up his sleeve and looked at his skin and said,

"Yes Sir! I do not belong here!" A round of laughter ensued among the black soldiers. Slagle continued to take his shortcut every afternoon.

Intelligence Training

During the summer of 1944 at Camp Breckinridge, some men were hand picked for classroom training. By that time American soldiers had arrived onto the European mainland by the thousands; they had invaded Fortress Europe. The average GI knew nothing more than that they had a job to do; to defeat Hitler. However, there was a lot more happening. Lieutenant Bergheimer was a platoon commander, but he also was a classroom instructor in intelligence. Bergheimer was not a draftee, he was a career soldier and had been in the service for some time. One day an officer arrived to First Platoon's barracks with a message. Three names appeared on a list and they were to report for a special assignment every afternoon. The men selected were Slagle, Cohen, and Siegfried. There were many other men from Second Battalion also in the same class. They were taught methods of gathering intelligence in the field under combat conditions. These men were also instructed to assume command if their superiors were killed or wounded. They were briefed on the many situations that could play out under combat conditions and what was expected of them. Most of all, these men were expected to hold themselves together psychologically, no matter what horrors they might find should they make it into Germany.

Rumors of Assignment

In September 1944 another round of furloughs began. Kravitz was one of the first to receive a furlough when the 75th Division arrived at Camp Breckinridge in May, now he had a second one. Kravitz returned home once again, but he was not the same skinny fellow from months before, he gained weight and was in great shape from all the training he had went through. Others awaiting their second furlough were not so lucky: furloughs were abruptly cancelled. Rumors spread through camp that the 75th Division would soon be sent overseas. Men argued where they would be sent; to the war in Europe or to the Pacific. On 1 September, Slagle was promoted to Private First Class. At dinner one evening, Slagle overheard some officers discussing the war effort in Europe and figured that was their destination. His assumption was quite correct. Training intensified in

September; long marches with full pack were issued every morning. It was evident to everyone that a major move was in the planning. Slagle was not to make the journey across the Atlantic with H Company; he was very abruptly admitted to the 75th Division Band when an opening was made available due to a transfer. The 75th Division Band was setup at the train station near Breckinridge and they played as each unit of the 75th Division boarded the trains and departed. Slagle watched as H Company and his buddies in First Platoon boarded the train on route to Fort Dix, New Jersey.

Overseas Duty: The ETO

North Sands- Tenby, Wales   75th Division's Barracks, Wales

Preparations for Deployment

By early October, the 75th Division prepared to ship out. Most of the Division was sent by train to Fort Dix, New Jersey for a week long period of inspection. Men received their shots, had physical examinations, and were issued their uniforms and duffel bags. On 15 October 1944, the first wave of the 75th Division, including a portion of Division Headquarters, was sent to Camp Shanks, New York. Camp Shanks was the staging area for the Port of Embarkation. The daily routine was intensive, with training revolving around what the GI would need to know while aboard ship. The training included escape, evasion, and the abandon ship drill. The men were warned about the dangerous U-boat infested waters that would be crossed during their voyage. There were a few Italian

POWs in camp and they made good spaghetti suppers that were enjoyed very much by the GIs.

First Glimpse of the Big City

On Friday morning, leave passes were issued to many men from the 75th Division. Larson, Lawson, and "Hay Seed" received their leave passes and they decided to venture into Manhattan. Lawson and "Hay Seed" both grew up in the country and had never been to a big city before; they were very excited. They walked along the street in the late morning and women smiled and waved at them. Old men tipped their hats and shouted greetings. As they walked by many stores, shop owners came out and shook their hands and invited the GIs inside. Lawson could not believe how friendly everyone was to a man in uniform. Larson took them to a YMCA building and it was an amazing sight for the two country boys. They saw teenagers playing pool, indoor tennis, and they saw the snack bar. "Hay Seed" saw the huge swimming pool and stared at it in disbelief. Lawson and "Hay Seed" took a very welcomed hot shower, got a towel and bathing suit and jumped in the pool. When they got out of the YMCA, they smelled something good. A little cart with a sign that read "Kosher Sandwiches" was sitting right out front. Lawson had no idea what it was but he wanted to try it. Larson, Lawson, and "Hay Seed" each had a sandwich with pastrami, sauerkraut, and mustard on rye bread. Lawson and "Hay Seed" just loved it.

They walked through town for the rest of the day took a bus ride into Times Square and as nightfall approached, they saw the city light up with activity. Big Band music blared out of clubs and bars and the smell of food cooking was very tempting. On the side of a building was a sign that read "Pizza," which the country boys did not understand. Larson took them to a soda shop and treated them. A pretty young girl worked at the counter and was surrounded by GIs impatiently waiting for their chance to talk to her as they put in their order. "Hay Seed" had his first taste of ice cream and wanted more. The shop owner was so pleased to have GIs in his establishment that he gave out seconds for free. By 2000 hours, the men fell into formation and marched to the bus stop for transportation back to Camp Shanks. Lawson and "Hay Seed" had a wonderful experience during their first visit to a big city.

Deployment Overseas

On Friday night, 20 October, leave was issued, and the men had one last Coca-Cola, ice cream soda, or beer before they departed the United States for war. The next morning embarkation began and was completed late on Saturday night. Each man was given a printed card with the exact deck and bunk number he was assigned. The 291st Regiment boarded the US Army transport Edmund B. Alexander that was part of a large convoy of about dozen troop ships, escorted by destroyers on their perimeter. The 106th Division that trained at Camp Breckinridge at the same time as the 75th, was also a part of this convoy. The GI's last sight as they left New York was the Statue of Liberty out on the horizon.

Crossing the Atlantic

During the voyage, the time on deck was spent with drills and inspections. Many weary soldiers took a look over the side of the ship, hoping to see just water and no U-boats. Guard duty on deck was continuous day and night. In the ship's recreation hall, there were movies shown nightly. Prater manned the projector that ran the movies for the troops. As a result of running the projector, Prater did not have to do KP or guard duty, which was a pleasant change in pace from what the other privates were doing. Boxing bouts on the aft deck were another entertainment venue. Then, there were the poker games in the hold with the usual card sharks. Some men in H Company wagered a month's salary in a game of poker; the stakes were high! Wells among others spent much of his time reading in his bunk. For those that smoked, a cigarette did much to settle one's nerves and seasickness. Wells did not smoke and he traded his cigarettes for Tootsie Rolls, a valuable commodity in their own right. Wells ate so many Tootsie Rolls during the voyage that it made him ill. The bunks were six high, which made moving about something of a challenge. A conversation with the man in the next bunk or the bunk above or below was the routine. Many of the men talked of home, already missing it and their families. Some talked of the medals they were going to come home with. Others talked about leaving their personal footprint on Hitler. By the end of the twelve-day voyage, the men were glad to make landfall.

Disembarking in Wales

The 75th Division arrived at the Port of Swansea, Wales on 2 November. The first night was spent aboard ship, with disembarking beginning the next morning. Troops disembarked by unit with the whole of H Company arriving on the shore together. They were then transported by truck to the town of Havorfordwest in South Wales. H Company lived in an empty clothing store downtown; it was big enough to house all three platoons. There was no furniture so the men slept on the cold floor. Eventually, bunks were setup, three high with straw mattresses; some had fleas. Havorfordwest was in the county of Pembrokeshire, where other elements of Second Battalion, 291st Infantry were camped. As soon as the housing situation was taken care of, the men of H Company began training once again, as they knew that their call to the front could come at any time. This time, they were in a new land, with a vastly different climate than that of Kentucky where they had trained for seven months.

Training in Wales

On their first morning in Havorfordwest, H Company began its new training program that would prepare the men for the tough days to come. A five-mile march each morning with full field pack and gear was the first duty of the day. The men would march in the gray mist along the coastline in the cool, damp climate of Wales. A chilly rain was frequent. In the town's courtyard, the men would train on their equipment with an emphasis spent on setting up their machine gun or mortar as swiftly as possible. As they were in the middle of a town, no munitions were expended in training. Other activities including calisthenics and sometimes basketball games were played in the gym of a school in town. Staff Sergeant "Stretch" Wilson, due to his thin, gangly appearance at 6 foot 6, was at first not taken seriously, but he quickly showed his skill in the game. It was impossible to get the ball past him.

Life in Wales

Other than the usual daily training, the men of H Company had a relatively lax period while in Wales. When H Company first arrived in Wales, the kitchen had not yet arrived and the men were fed a steady supply of Brussels Sprouts, cabbage, and mutton. The GIs hated the food, especially the soggy, overcooked Brussels Sprouts! The inhabitants of Wales were living with a very meager food supply, but they were gracious to their American allies. Many men in H Company got friendly with Welsh girls, who invited the GI to a home cooked meal with their family. When H Company's kitchen arrived, it was stocked with canned foods and even though it was against regulations, it was common for a GI to swipe a can or two of meat or fruit to give to the family he was dining with. The GI found the local food quite different from traditional American eats. Fried fish and greasy fries wrapped in a newspaper was the local delicacy. It may not have been the best meal they ever had, but for most, it was better than what was coming out of the Company kitchen. There were fish and chips carryouts and pastry shops down the hill from town, toward the docks. Wells lived on fish and chips before the Company kitchen arrived. He got his meal from the carry out and walked along toward the pastry shop where there were many kinds of fruit tarts under glass. Two older women owned the pastry shop and they mothered Wells, telling him he looked too young to be in the war. Wells, like so many other young GIs serving in the military and far from home, missed his mother and enjoyed the attention. The GI's free time was spent taking in the sights and visiting the beaches for a walk along the coastline.

The Brawl

Passes into town were regularly granted and the men of H Company would often meet groups of men from the other companies of Second Battalion. There was little to do other than drink or fraternize with the local girls. One night Lawson entered a bar on the edge of town and thought he would try to get something to eat; he was sick of Brussels Sprouts. There were a few enlisted men in the bar and a lot of officers. Lawson thought he looked out of place and was about to leave when he noticed his platoon buddy "Hay Seed" in the bar. He motioned for Lawson to come in. "Hay Seed" did not drink, yet had a full glass in front of him so as not to look too innocent. First Sergeant Whalen was also in the bar, drinking with two girls. A second lieutenant from another company sat with "Hay Seed" and Lawson. At first he said little, until he noticed the full glass in front of "Hay Seed." The man was looped. He said, "What have we got here a big baby who doesn't drink? Maybe we should get him a diaper." The lieutenant threw the drink all over "Hay Seed." Lawson tried to hold him back, but "Hay Seed" lost his temper. Being a big man, well over 200 pounds, "Hay Seed" picked up the lieutenant and threw him across the room, knocking over a table or two. A big brawl began. Glasses flew across the room, tables and chairs were tossed around. Glasses smashed and fistfights erupted everywhere. Lawson and "Hay Seed" left the bar, got back to their barracks and said nothing of the incident. Lawson could not sleep that night; he was worried. The next morning, First Sergeant Whalen arrived for duty with quite a hangover, but bearing no signs of the brawl. Lawson was very nervous, fearing some kind of reprimand for the bar incident. Later that afternoon, Whalen stopped Lawson and with a hand on his shoulder said, "We are a Company of fighting men, aren't we?" Lawson had no reply, with his legs still quivering. No reprimand was issued and "Hay Seed" and Lawson were both promoted to Private First Class that afternoon.

Slagle's Departure

While H Company was settling into their routine in Havorfordwest, Wales, Slagle was preparing for his own departure. The 75th Division Band was one of the last elements of the Division to cross the Atlantic. Slagle was still attached to H Company, but his promotion to the Division Band left him behind at Breckinridge. During the first week of November, the remaining elements of the Division left Camp Breckinridge on a train bound for Fort Dix, New Jersey. Slagle moved through Camp Shanks, New York and to the Port of Embarkation. Unlike the large convoy that the majority of the 75th Division had left on three weeks earlier, the remainder of the Division left on a single ship, the Aquitania, sister ship to the Titanic. The Aquitania was converted into a troop ship and was manned by a British crew. The GIs including officers were fed squares of mutton fat. A revolt nearly broke out. The Americans would not tolerate such lousy food, yet to the English who had suffered greatly in the war, such food was commonplace. When the ship's captain told one of the commanding officers of the 75th Division to control his men, the officer told the captain that neither he nor his men would eat the food. Slagle survived on candy bars for most of the voyage. Slagle spent much of his time pulling guard duty on deck. One morning, he sighted a periscope near by. Slagle put his rifle over his shoulders to signify "enemy sighted" and motioned to the first officer. Alarms went off and the crew scrambled about. The ship took evasive maneuvers and easily outdistanced the U-boat. The Aquitania was a fast ship and required no escort. On 21 November after just a six day and seven-night voyage, the Aquitania arrived to the port of Glasgow, Scotland.

The Band in Wales

One night was spent in Glascow, with many of the GIs taking in the sights, fraternizing with the local girls, and spending time in bars. The next morning, the 75th Division Band members boarded trains bound for Wales. They traded their instruments for M-1 Carbines. Later that day, they arrived on the coast of Tenby, Wales and their barracks. The Band and 75th Division Headquarters had more luxurious quarters than H Company. They lived in a building that had once been a hotel and popular vacation spot. They spent time with the locals on the beach at Tenby. Slagle and Brejcha also took up horseback riding on the sandy coast. In the evenings, the Band members would get to know the locals, visit families, or go out to get fish and chips. While living near the coast in Wales, Slagle was reminded of a year earlier when he had played nightly in the Big Bands on the coast of Atlantic City.

Visits to London

Three-day leave passes were granted in rotation to all American units stationed in Wales. In mid November, Kravitz received his leave pass to London. Kravitz took the three or four-hour train ride into London with others from Second Platoon. The city was on black out and was heavily damaged by German bombs. London had been a war zone and was still littered with debris. It was eerie wondering through the streets and taking the underground subway to get around. Kravitz stayed in a group with his buddy, Reynolds and men from other companies and divisions. Members of the 106th Division were also part of the group. Members of the 75th and 106th mingled on their three day leave and were on good terms; even some friendships emerged. At the end of his leave, Kravitz returned to Havorfordwest to find that he was promoted to Private First Class.

Slagle received his first leave pass to London shortly after arriving to Wales. When he boarded the train, he saw a familiar face: Bert Larson from H Company. Slagle and Larson spent the train ride catching up on each other's movements. In London, Slagle and Larson both went their separate ways. Slagle got off the train to buy fish and chips for lunch. He walked a short distance and heard a buzz overhead. A German V-2 rocket crashed into the train station, blowing it up! Fortunately the trains were further down the track and were undamaged. The blast threw Slagle off his feet along with several civilians who were on the street. An old lady was walking down the street with groceries and she and her groceries were thrown about. Without alarm or hesitation, she dusted herself off, picked up her groceries and with a curse against the Germans, was on her way. Slagle had his introduction to war while in London and his first close call. Other than the V-2 incident, Slagle enjoyed his leave in London. He met a girl there that he might have married had he stayed there. She took him to see all the sights across London. On Slagle's second trip to London in December, he met up with his girlfriend and they were walking down a street when a politician from the Labor Party stopped and offered his greetings. The politician was quite talkative and told Slagle that Churchill was nothing but a figurehead and was good for a morale boost to the population, but as soon as the war ended, his popularity and political career would be over. At the end of his leave, Slagle returned to Tenby and learned that another move was in the works.

Deployment to the Mainland

The 75th Division received its orders to make its way onto mainland Europe on 11 December 1944. Trucks took the men of H Company to the port of Southampton; Slagle and the Division Band followed close behind. As they arrived to the port, there were three LSTs waiting to take them across the English Channel. The men boarded the LSTs and stayed aboard them overnight. The Port of Le Harve, France on the other side of the Channel was full and only a certain number of ships could disembark at once. On 12 December, the whole 75th Division crossed the English Channel. The crossing was riveted with rough seas. Many men got horribly seasick. The GIs had to eat standing up at a high table. The food served aboard the English crewed LSTs was inedible. Some sort of soup with peas in it was served and the peas were so hard you could not bite them. After the first meal, Captain Haddock gave the order to break out their ration packs. Seasickness became even worse after eating. Lawson watched as a man next to him turned various shades of green in the face. Nausea was prevalent even among the most rugged of men. It was a relief to finally see land: the Port of Le Harve. The night was spent aboard the cramped LSTs.

Le Harve

The next morning, 13 December, the LSTs arrived to the Port of Le Harve and one of them hit the remnants of a wrecked ship and caused quite a stir. For a brief few moments, some of the men thought they would have to abandon ship. The port was badly damaged and the Germans had mined it. The LSTs could not reach the port and this left the GIs with a daunting task. Each man had to descend a rope ladder with full field pack and rifle and board a landing craft that could more easily navigate the various obstacles on route to the port. Descending the rope ladder was no easy task; it swayed and shook as the LST and landing craft bumped about in the rough sea. Many GIs were quite scared, as their training had not prepared them for such an obstacle. When the landing crafts were full, they made the short trip to the shoreline. When they arrived on shore, the men were picked up by trucks and taken about thirty miles to St. Paer. While sitting in the troop truck, Slagle spotted a teenage girl and boy riding bicycles on the side of the road. They stopped to wave at the GIs and then the girl held both bicycles while the boy took a leak in clear view. All the men on Slagle's truck laughed, they knew they were no longer in America anymore; Europeans were very different people. The weather was quite cold and the ground was saturated from heavy rains that had continued on since September. The mud was thick and deep and one could easily sink up to the tops of their high top shoes while trying to walk through it. This was the terrain that the GIs were expected to live in, out in the elements.

Camping in the Mud

The men of H Company had to camp in the cold mud in a field in St. Paer. It rained almost all day for a week and the ground was beyond saturated. Pup tents were set up and the conditions were just miserable. One had to eat, sleep, and wake up in the mud. Feet got cold and wet, with saturated shoes. One excursion for the GI was to walk to the road and meet the local French people and their children that were happy to see Americans in their country. One afternoon, Lawson gave a chocolate bar to a young French boy. Over the next few days, every time he hiked up the road, he had to bring a chocolate bar or something good to eat, or the boy would chase after him. Lieutenant Bergheimer also hiked up the road and met the French people. When he returned to camp he said loudly in front of his Platoon, "I have never met so many bright young kids. How did they ever learn to speak French so well?" The men of First Platoon had no response for such a comment, but they certainly learned one thing about their commanding officer: they would have liked a new one! While in camp, Prater thought about his father, who had been in France during World War I as a sergeant in the Medical Corps.

News of the Offensive

While in camp at St. Paer, the men of H Company heard the news about the surprise German offensive that began moving through Belgium on 16 December. The news came as quite a shock and rumors circulated around camp that another move was in planning. Some thought they would end up in the middle of this battle. News came in that the 106th Division had already been deployed and would soon arrive at the Belgian front. Hitler's plan was to smash through the Allied line in Belgium, divide the American and British armies, and reach the channel ports of Antwerp, possibly changing the outcome of the war. The 75th Division was the youngest and most inexperienced division serving in the ETO. The men had barely been in Europe for a month. The men were untested in combat and their immediate future was uncertain.

The Battle of the Bulge

*"We first entered combat along the Ouerthe River, facing an
SS Panzer Division. I saw many boys become men – I was one of them."*

-Robert O. Slagle, First Platoon, H Company

1ˢᵗ Platoon, H Company- march to Ouerthe River, Rochefort, Belgium
S. Phillip Lawson- Mike Murza- "Hay Seed"- 2LT Bergheimer- Robert O. Slagle- Bert Larson

The Actions of General Collins' VII Corps

The Battle of the Bulge began with great confusion to the Allies. General Montgomery ordered General J. Lawton Collins' VII Corps, which included the 75th Division, to patrol the flank of the Allied Army and not to engage the enemy. Much of Collins' Corps was made up of men with little or no combat experience. Montgomery had little faith in Collins' "green" men. However, war rarely goes as planned and Collins' inexperienced men would become fully engaged in combat against some of the finest units in the German Army. The German westward advance was rapid and its focal point of penetration came on 24 December when German engineers built a large bridgehead across the Ouerthe River where the 2nd SS Panzer Division prepared to cross directly into the Allies flank. Elements of the US 2nd Armored Division were in the vicinity, but were not engaged. Direct orders from General Collins placed Second Battalion, 291st Regiment of the 75th Infantry Division (which was in reserve at the time) into the path of this great German advance. The men of Second Battalion, with little ammunition and very limited artillery support were ordered to hold their ground at all cost (and they did). Other units of the 75th Division took part in vicious and desperate combat against the German advance. The actions of the young and inexperienced men of the 75th Division contributed to the close of the Bulge. These men truly were "unlikely heroes."

The German Breakthrough

As news continued to pour in about Von Rundstedt's offensive in Belgium, the 75th Division awaited orders. On 19 December, their orders finally came. The 75th Division was to proceed to a reserve area in Holland, behind the British Army. The untested 75th Division was not considered for a part in the battle in Belgium. In the morning of 19 December, H Company climbed aboard troop trucks and jeeps and traveled fifteen miles to the rail station at Yvetot. The convoy passed through the French countryside and through small towns. The French civilians came out to greet the Americans, waving flags and cheering. The civilians handed the GIs postcards and apples. Prater was riding in the back of a jeep through all this friendliness. At the time, the men of the 75th Division did not know that they were about to take part in a battle that would decide the fate of these very people.

A Lack of Privacy

When they arrived to the train station in Yvetot, the men of H Company had some time on their hands waiting for their train to arrive. All men who had been assigned to duties outside of their units, were returned. Slagle rejoined H Company at the train station. The men ate from their ration packs. Slagle looked for a bathroom and found one beside the station. It was a large enclosed room with a concrete seat and a hole in the ground. Seats were arranged in a line, one next to the other. The French did not share the same concern for privacy as Americans did. Slagle watched as First Sergeant Whalen marched into the bathroom, sat down and put a newspaper in front of his face. The bathroom was the only one in the area and it was not organized into halves for men and women; it was just one room. An old lady sat down next to Whalen and did her business. Whalen put his newspaper down and turned his face to see that it was a woman sitting next to him and she smiled at him. Whalen yelled and ran out of the bathroom as fast as he could go. Slagle and his buddies in First Platoon had quite a laugh.

Train Ride to Belgium

The 75th Division boarded the infamous "40 and 8" railcars that had moved soldiers of the First World War to the front. The "40 and 8s" were designed to carry forty soldiers with equipment or eight horses. The fifth train carried the men of First and Second Battalions of the 291st Regiment. The 75th Division's gear including winter coats, gloves, boots, and rifles were packed up and were sent ahead to Holland to await the Division's arrival. At the last moment, in the late afternoon of 19 December, the 75th Division's orders changed. They were to proceed to Belgium and to the front. The Germans had broken through creating a bulge in the Allied front line that was quickly moving westward. It was a period of great confusion and all available divisions were desperately needed to close this bulge. The 106th Division was already moving toward the front. Hitler's plan appeared to be working. The men of H Company knew their part in the war was coming and soon.

On Route to War

The train proceeded on its route to the front under blackout conditions. Little was said during the two day long trip. Tension was high. Some men smoked to calm their nerves, while others made limited idle conversation. Some tried to crack a few jokes, but no one thought they were funny. Each man prepared himself for battle in his own way. The cocky guys seemed much less so, the talkative became suddenly quiet, and the religious were in prayer. The train stopped abruptly in the early morning hours of 21 December. Under cover of darkness, the men were told to quickly get out and form a line. Most of their equipment had been sent ahead to Holland. The men of First Platoon lacked their machine guns. Lieutenant Bergheimer handed each man in his Platoon an M-1 Garand, fresh from the crate. The rifles were soaked in Cosmoline, but there was no time to clean them or to sight them. Each man was handed a single clip of ammunition; there was nothing to spare. The men of Second Platoon did have their machine guns and they carried their guns, tripods, and ammunition. The men of Third Platoon also had their equipment and they carried their mortars, base plates, bi-pods, and ammunition. H Company marched toward Hosselt, Belgium where they were to stay the night in cold barns and a vacant village; the civilians offered their homes to the GI The next morning, 22 December, all excess equipment was turned into Company supply. Gas masks were dumped and anything else that could not easily be carried during a march was left with the supply clerk.

The Survivors

On the march to Tongres, H Company passed by a line of soldiers walking in the opposite direction. Their heads were down, their eyes focused only on their feet. They were wearing the lion's head patch of the 106th Division. On 20 December the 106th Division was caught by the Germans and was virtually destroyed. The battered remnants of two of its regiments were forced to surrender. As many as 8,000 men were killed, wounded, or surrendered. Lawson stopped and tried to ask one of the men what had happened to them. The man said nothing as he handed Lawson his Garand. An older soldier from the 106th defiantly told Slagle, "You kids will never hold, we couldn't." As H Company moved to the front, they passed more small bands of the 106th; the few survivors. Kravitz pondered the fate of those nice fellows from the 106th that were on leave with him in London just a month earlier.

Prater spotted a jeep covered in mud with a panic-stricken officer and two enlisted men driving as fast as they could away from the front. They were from the 106th Division. The officer got out of the jeep and asked Captain Haddock if he had any food for his company. Haddock said that he did not have anything to spare. The officer then told Captain Haddock that he, his driver and the other enlisted man in the jeep were all that remained of his company. Haddock saw that they were fed. Page from the Mortar Platoon had stood by and witnessed this confrontation. It upset him greatly and he strode off to be by himself. To the men of H Company who were in the immediate area, it was a realization of what could happen to them in the days ahead.

To the Front

On the afternoon of 22 December, H Company organized for its final movement: to the front line. Each member of the Company climbed aboard the troop trucks with what equipment he could carry. It was freezing cold and the men lacked any winter gear. Their coats, boots, and gloves did not meet them in Belgium. The men were left wearing long wool underwear, a wool shirt and pants, a wool sweater, and summer issue overcoat that was olive drab in color. Many of the men did not even have an overcoat. They had only cotton socks, high top shoes, and galoshes: they had no boots. If he was lucky, the GI had an extra pair of socks; however not everyone did. Few gloves were available: most men had to do without. Some men smoked in the truck to keep warm; others huddled together. During the night, the men of H Company began to hear artillery in the distance; sporadic at first, then more intense as they moved closer up to the front. No one slept. After a twelve and a half-hour truck ride, the men of H Company arrived to defensive positions near Marche in the town of Tohongue, Belgium in the early morning hours of 23 December. Roadblocks were quickly setup and alert defenses established. Artillery was heard coming from what seemed like every direction.

The Eve of Battle

The men of H Company spent the night in a theatre in the little town of Verlaine; no one slept. Artillery and the sound of German V-1 and V-2 rockets on their way to Antwerp and London kept them awake. On the morning of 24 December, the 291st Regiment assembled as a unit for the first time. It was a time of great confusion and fatigue. The men were tired, cold, and hungry. The constant movement over the previous few days left little time to eat or sleep. On Christmas Eve, the skies cleared and the American Air Force came out in droves. Hundreds of B-17 and B-24 bombers with their fighter escorts flew overhead in formation on route to Germany. It was one of the largest bomber formations of the war. The men of H Company stood up and waved and cheered. A sullen morale was suddenly lifted. They watched as German fighters came up to meet the American bombers, and some of the American aircraft were shot down. The afternoon was spent with commanding officers giving briefings on the situation. One of the briefings warned about Germans dressed in American uniforms moving through the American lines. Tension quickly rose. That Christmas Eve, the men of H Company spent the night in the open field and in an abandoned barn in the town of Forse, a few miles from Rochefort, Belgium. It was the coldest winter in Europe in over 100 years. The clearing skies brought the temperature down even further. Patrols were sent out and sentries made their rounds, always moving just to keep warm. Those trying to sleep in the open fields were prone to frostbite on their feet if they were not careful. Sleeping with wet socks and shoes was a constant danger. It was learned quickly that to keep your feet intact, one had to take his shoes and socks off and put them into his sleeping bag to keep warm. The GI had to tie his wet socks around his neck to dry. If they were left in the open, someone else with cold and wet feet would swipe them. Such were the terrible conditions of an army lacking adequate clothing and sleeping in sub-zero temperatures in the dead of winter.

"I Can Drive"

Early Christmas morning, Second Lieutenant Bergheimer, leader of First Platoon emerged from the barn where many men of H Company had spent the night. His driver could not be found and he needed to be driven to the Battalion Command Post immediately. He asked if anyone knew how to drive. Slagle said he could drive and

Bergheimer got into his jeep. Slagle had never driven a car before, let alone a military jeep. Lawson took over the machine gun on back of the jeep. Slagle managed to start up the jeep and throw it into reverse! He hit the brakes and screeched to a halt. Bergheimer said, "Where the Hell did you learn to drive Slagle!?" Slagle switched gears and drove straight toward the barn. Lawson jumped off just before the jeep went straight through the open barn door and out the back. GIs ran out of the barn and scattered in all directions. They had quite a wake up call! Lawson got to his feet and was nearly run over as the jeep circled around the barn and got back on the road. Lawson got back on and they all made it intact to their destination.

The First Casualty

On Christmas Day, 25 December, Second Battalion marched to an area near Marché. There they were to prepare for their first action. Artillery and heavy machine gun fire could be heard in the distance. The Germans had left the area sometime before Second Battalion arrived. H Company took over an abandoned German outpost on the outskirts of town and was weary of a German attack. The Mortar Platoon was ordered to a forward position to watch for the enemy. Lieutenant Wallis and a few of his men kicked in the front door of a farmhouse. Three German troops were inside and they tried to run. Two of the Germans were killed and the third was taken prisoner. In this forward area, the mortar men heard many sounds; artillery in the distance and what they thought were voices behind them: German voices. The rifle companies of Second Battalion also heard these German voices and with the recent rumors of Germans in American uniforms behind American lines, they fired. H Company's two machine gun platoons also heard these voices and they too opened fire. The first casualty was the Company Barber, PFC Hain who was killed by friendly fire. He had gone off into the woods for a pit stop and did not hear the soft-spoken guard ask for the password upon his return. A few casualties were taken among the rifle companies from a skirmish with German troops. Prater fired smoke rounds from his mortar, which his Squad had named "Smokey Christmas" as it was fired for the first time on Christmas Day. The Mortar Platoon was tasked with bringing up a smoke screen so the wounded men could be evacuated. That night, patrols were sent out and H Company was on full alert for Germans who might be behind their lines.

Christmas Dinner

Late on the evening of 25 December, a Christmas Dinner was served to the GIs They were served turkey, cranberry sauce, and peas. Deep snow covered the ground. Some of the men of H Company sat down in the snow to eat their Christmas dinner. The GIs lined up to have their mess kits filled from the back of the Company kitchen truck. Many of the men close to the front lines had their meal brought to them by the kitchen truck late at night. The cooks moved as close as they could up to the front to feed the freezing cold and starving GIs, some of whom had not eaten much or anything in days. A hot meal did much to lighten up what was otherwise a very sullen mood. After dinner, the GIs were issued their first cigarette ration. First Sergeant Whalen walked into a small abandoned house and came out swigging down a bottle of wine. He passed a few other bottles around, out of sight from the officers. Many in H Company wondered if their Christmas Dinner would be their last meal. Tensions were high and they knew the enemy was not far away.

The First Encounter

Late on Christmas Night and into the early hours of 26 December, Captain Haddock had sentries sent out in all directions, to scout for a potential German attack. The other company commanders in Second Battalion issued the same orders. Some scouts were sent out as far as 500 yards ahead of the front line. Wells, Second Platoon's messenger was also sent out to the front to look for locations to setup H Company's machine guns in the morning. As Wells neared the front, well-camouflaged Germans wearing snow suits, stood up and fired at him. Wells laid flat on the ground and started looking around when he felt something hit his side and felt liquid running down his leg. He thought for sure he was hit, but remembered he carried his canteen underneath his clothing to keep the water from freezing. A bullet had put a hole through his canteen! The rifle companies in the area returned fire and Wells ran back to the Company Command Post to report the situation. The Mortar Platoon's patrol that included PFC Posnak discovered two German patrols operating behind their lines. First Platoon spotted the German patrols and ambushed them with machine gun fire. One German officer and two enlisted men were captured and taken to the Company Command Post. The situation became very tense and confused.

The Opening of Battle

On the afternoon of 26 December, Second Battalion of the 291st Regiment marched up to the front to serve as infantry support to the 2nd Armored Division's tanks. Some of the men of H Company rode in jeeps or climbed aboard the tanks on their route to Rochefort, where they had been ordered to clear out what was thought to be another German outpost. The Germans in Rochefort were actually a well-equipped advance force scouting for a clear route for several Panzer Divisions to move through. This German advance group was not expecting a confrontation at Rochefort and they retreated, regrouped, and attempted a counterattack. They fired mortars and machineguns in an attempt to push back Second Battalion. The 2nd Armored Division did not bring its tanks up to the front, as they did not know the strength of the Germans opposing them. Machine guns were in short supply. Second Platoon had machine guns, but First Platoon did not as their supplies had not yet arrived prior to this attack. The men of First Platoon were forced to fight with M-1 Garands. The rifles were not calibrated and they were effective only for making a lot of noise. The Germans were much more heavily armed. Second Battalion's rifle companies managed to force the Germans to retreat to the banks of the Ouerthe River, just outside of town. The Germans had constructed a bridgehead across the Ouerthe and were planning to use it as a major crossing point for their Panzer Divisions.

Utter Confusion

Lieutenant Colonel Drain issued orders for his Battalion to pursue the enemy over the bridgehead. G Company, under the command of Captain Druillard, led the attack. As they reached the banks of the Ouerthe, the men of Second Battalion found that they had an SS Panzer Division and a Volksgrenadier Division opposing them on the other side. Heavy fire was exchanged. The Germans had plenty of ammunition and heavy artillery; Second Battalion did not. Supplies were very limited and ammunition ran out quickly. The Germans bombarded Second Battalion with heavy mortar fire. Tanks were heard in the distance, but were not visible. As darkness fell, the situation was very confused.

Second Battalion could not hold if the Germans decided to cross the Ouerthe during the night. H Company had little to fight with as most of their ammunition was spent. If Second Battalion were to withdraw, the Germans would continue their westward push. The Germans were desperate to find a clear route and the Ouerthe was just such a crossing point. Several other divisions were just a few miles behind the 2nd SS Panzer and 560th Volksgrenadier Divisions.

"Hold Your Ground at all Cost"

Lieutenant Colonel Drain sent messengers back to Regiment and Division, requesting support. His Battalion was low on ammunition and there were no reserves. Drain issued orders to his company commanders to dig in and hold their position and await further orders. Messengers returned from higher command with orders for Drain's Battalion to hold their position at all cost. They were the extreme end of the Allied line in their sector. All other units had either engaged the enemy or were otherwise held up from sending support. As one of the messengers was about to leave in a jeep, a shell came down directly on the jeep, lifting it 30 feet into the air and it crashed down on its side. The messenger and several privates were killed. Drain dispatched another messenger on foot back to Regiment, but he was also hit by a mortar shell. Drain had no more ammunition other than that which his men carried and there were no reserve forces. The young and inexperienced men of Second Battalion were all that stood in the way of the focal point of penetration by the German westward push through the Ardennes.

Assuming Command Under Fire

Just after nightfall, the German artillery quieted down. A few shells continued to come in, but they were sporadic. The First Platoon of H Company was sent up to the front as infantrymen; they did not have their machine guns. After darkness fell, Lieutenant Bergheimer told his Platoon to prepare to attack in the morning. Staff Sergeant Slawson informed Bergheimer that the men had Cosmoline soaked rifles to fight with and they were not sighted. Despite this, the men had little to shoot with, as ammunition was scarce. Bergheimer ignored Slawson altogether as if he had not even heard his concerns. Bergheimer said, "We are going to clear out those Germans in the morning." Bergheimer took a swig of whiskey from his canteen, smiled, and walked away. Larson and "Kirk" voiced their concerns to Slawson. Larson took notice of the young boys in his Squad. They did not show expressions of fear, but surely they felt it. They were as quiet as stone. Larson told them to hold onto their rifles and await their orders. Above all, Larson told each of them to be careful and not take any unnecessary risks. Lawson must have looked more tense than his squad mates, as Larson patted him on the shoulder. Lawson was scared, but more anxious than anything else. He was comforted to have a father figure like Bert Larson in his Squad.

In the morning, through very dense fog, the artillery barrage resumed. Heavy fire came in from the Germans; they were determined to push back the American force that stood in their way. Bergheimer ordered his men to return fire. Just then, a few shells came in close. Bergheimer called his driver and they left in the jeep. The privates did not know what to do and there was confusion. Someone shouted, "Our Lieutenant abandoned us!" Some of the men tried to fire their Cosmoline soaked rifles, but this did little but provide the Germans with more targets. Staff Sergeant Slawson quickly took command. He ordered everyone to take what cover they could. "Keep your heads down!" Slawson shouted. Shells began to come in very close to First Platoon's position. Shrapnel was prevalent and shells hit trees and debris clanged off of helmets. Slawson continued to shout, "Take cover!" Despite the incoming shells, Slawson checked to make sure that all of his men had some measure of cover. A thunderous barrage came in; it was deafening and to the young privates caught in the middle of it, it was terrifying. Lawson thought for sure he would be killed. Cohen tripped as he was trying to get into a foxhole and was left out in the open. Slawson saw this and without concern for his own life, sprang out from his foxhole, ran over to Cohen and helped him into a nearby foxhole. Despite the heavy incoming fire, Slawson was emotionless; he did his duty without any concern.

As the shelling concluded in the afternoon, the men of First Platoon got out of their foxholes to check for wounded. Amazingly, not one man was wounded. Slawson had held the Platoon together during an intense shelling. Bergheimer arrived just as soon as the shelling had ended. He was pleased to see that no one was wounded, but he berated Slawson for disobeying his orders. Bergheimer wanted his Platoon to return fire, not to take cover. Bergheimer strode off again and his men were glad to be rid of him, if only temporarily. The men were glad to be alive and knew it was because of Slawson's actions. Lawson asked him how he could run through the shelling without any expression of fear. Slawson replied, "I prayed. I trust that God will take care of me, so that I can do my duty."

A Close Call

Sergeant Chisholm's Second Squad of Second Platoon was moving up a road on the outskirts of Rochefort, looking to find good cover to setup their machine gun. They were walking through deep snow when suddenly a German Tiger started up and moved up the road toward them. It was covered in snow and had been well camouflaged. Chisholm's Squad quickly dove into a ditch on the side of the road. Kravitz was the assistant gunner in his squad and he dropped the machine gun tripod that he was carrying and reached out and grasped it just before the tank moved through. The Tiger's crew either did not see Kravitz or did not want to risk an engagement without infantry support, as the Tiger moved uninterrupted on its way across the Ouerthe and back to the German lines.

On Patrol across the Ouerthe

Late at night on 26 December, Second Battalion decided to send patrols across the Ouerthe River to determine the strength of the Germans. One of these patrols was First Platoon, Second Squad with Larson, Slagle, Lawson, Murza, "Kirk," and "Hay Seed." As they crossed the frozen Ouerthe River and onto the German side, their route was surprisingly clear. They heard German voices everywhere, but saw no one. As they pushed through some brush, they saw several tanks idling; awaiting their infantry support. The Germans seemed to be as confused as the Americans. The little opposition that Second Battalion offered them, in addition to American GIs wearing olive drab clothing against the snow, must have made the Germans believe they were falling for a trap. Second Squad's leader was an old Regular Army sergeant. He had been a soldier in the Peacetime Army and this was his first taste of actual combat. Slagle and Lawson wanted to take a more risky move and probe further into the German line to locate the position of their infantry support: their Sergeant was against it. Suddenly, tanks were heard close by and were closing in on them from either side. The squad moved quickly toward cover, but their Sergeant tripped and injured his leg: He could not run anymore. The Sergeant told them to leave him behind and get back to the American lines. They did not want to leave him behind, but through the wise urging of Bert Larson, they left their Sergeant behind. The squad dove into brush just as the tank moved past them. German infantry captured their Sergeant. Larson took command of the squad and they made it back to their lines safely with their intelligence report. The Germans, fearing a trap, chose to dig in on their side of the Ouerthe.

A Stalemate

By 0200 hours on 27 December, the firefight resumed. The Germans who dug in were Volksgrenadiers made up of old men and boys; they were not Wehrmacht troops. However, when dug in with good cover, even old men and boys could put up a substantial fight. Rifle fire was exchanged throughout the night. The Germans were very cautious and did not bring their tanks up to the front. The 2nd Armored Division's tanks also stood down. By this time Second Battalion had little left to fight with and German artillery fire continued throughout the pre-dawn hours. The Germans were hesitant to force an attack and this resulted in a stalemate. By around 0330 hours sounds of tanks could be heard; they were at first idling and then moving about. German voices were heard and much movement. The Germans grudgingly left their positions and the Panzer Division with its infantry support slid south along the Ouerthe River without a full engagement. Second Battalion's first combat was decided in a draw. The only casualties in H Company were Gardner and Hain from the Company's Motor Pool, both of whom had been killed by friendly fire.

A Jewish Delicacy

On the night of 26 December as the Germans were preparing to withdraw, H Company spent the night in foxholes. During an artillery barrage, Slagle had jumped into a foxhole with a man he detested, Saul Cohen from First Squad. Cohen was not well liked and was thought of by many to be the stereotypical Jew. Cohen's father owned a pawn shop in the Bronx and back in Wales, Cohen started up his own little business of supplying cigarettes, chocolate bars, candy, and even beer to members of the Company. He knew how to make a buck. He also was involved with arranging bets on the poker games back at Camp Breckinridge. Slagle and Cohen had despised each other from the start. A few days earlier, H Company received letters from home and even a few parcels. Cohen had gotten a little jar of Gefilte Fish from his parents. He and Slagle had not eaten that day and Cohen opened up the jar, ate some, then offered some to Slagle, who sarcastically proclaimed, "My life is complete and I can now die, I have tasted a Jewish delicacy!" GIs on the front line and in the face of impending danger often form strong bonds, whether the men like each other personally or not. For Slagle and Cohen, a dedicated and lasting friendship emerged that cold night in the foxhole.

The Duty of a Platoon Medic

Each of the three platoons that made up H Company had a medic that accompanied them into combat. Louis Romano was assigned to First Platoon, Eugene Dempsey was assigned to Second Platoon, and "Red" Hayes was assigned to Third Platoon. Romano was a talkative and motivational character; he kept the men's spirits up. Dempsey was a very well liked medic: he was a personal friend to many in Second Platoon. Hayes was not the best medic, he took to the bottle quite frequently. He was something of a "happy go lucky" man who liked to have a good time. He was also older than most in the Company. If a GI in one of the platoons were wounded, his platoon medic would rush to the scene to help him. If a GI were seriously wounded, the platoon medic would arrange to move him back to the Battalion Aid Station. A platoon medic always had to be alert of his surroundings. He had more to worry about than just himself, he had to worry about what would happen to the men in his platoon if he got hit. Though the medic was not a front line soldier, he saw just as much combat as the others did in his platoon and he saw the most horrible sights imaginable. The medic had to psychologically prepare himself for the casualties that were a matter of daily life in the Ardennes.

From Trench Foot to Aid Station

The GIs that lived in the field and battled the cold day and night had to be careful of their feet. The men that lacked a second pair of socks or who went to sleep with wet feet, risked getting trench foot. Each morning, the men of H Company would report for roll call. Those with illnesses reported to sick call. The platoon medic would check all such cases each morning. If a GI was diagnosed with trench foot or had any symptoms thereof, they would be taken to the Battalion Aid Station. Those that suffered from severe bouts of cold or pneumonia would also be taken to the Battalion Aid Station. The trip would be made by jeep and the aid station was very rudimentary: it was little more than a large tent in most cases with several medics there. In some locations when the battalion was near to a city, the Battalion Aid Station would be setup in a building, away from the front. Often, it would be setup in a church or a home and civilians would frequently help the sick and wounded.

That Bitter Cold

The men of H Company were on the battlefield and the sounds of artillery were continuously heard, day and night, yet combat was not foremost on their minds. The bitter cold was the greatest adversary of the GI It never left them, day or night. The men of H Company were enduring the extremes of a brutal winter: weather that no one in the Company had ever experienced before. Many of the men believed that if combat did not get them, then the cold certainly would. Yet, the men of H Company persevered, mostly. There were those men who just could not take it. Corporal Thorpe, the Company Clerk shot himself in the foot, claiming he was knocking snow off the barrel of his M-1. Another man claimed he was sitting with his back against a tree, when he "accidentally" shot himself in the leg when his pistol fired through the holster. Another man just could not emotionally handle being in combat and in such cold weather. He ran off towards the rear and was never seen again. The rest of the Company held together. In many cases, it was the hazing from one's squad buddies that kept him going, as together they braved the severity of living out in the elements during the harshest winter that anyone could remember.

Foxholes

When the men of H Company moved into a new location during the night, they would quickly get to dig foxholes to serve as cover the next day. Each GI carried an entrenching tool to dig with. However, in the heavy snow and frozen ground, it was not easy to dig a foxhole. When heavy snowstorms moved in, the GIs had to hurry up and dig and it was slow work. Often, by the time a GI finished digging, the snowstorm had already blown more snow into his foxhole. If he were lucky, the GI would have dug enough to make himself a mini foxhole. One afternoon, Prater heard tanks in the distance and his Squad set to dig themselves foxholes as quickly as possible. They worked very hard and got nowhere; they could not break the ground at all. Soon, Prater's Squad discovered that they had been digging on top of an abandoned airstrip that was covered in snow!

Guard Duty

A necessary, but often undesired nightly task was that of guard duty. It would be done in pairs for two hours and then rotated. If there were no volunteers, then members of H Company would be "volunteered" by First Sergeant Whalen. The others slept in foxholes or in sleeping bags if the Company did not have to abruptly move during the night. The guards would keep their eyes open and try to stay alert. The rumors of Germans wearing American uniforms were very much on the mind of the guards. Guard duty was nerve wracking, as it seemed as if every tree or bush moved. One night Prater was on guard duty and he was looking at two small pine trees some distance away. At night, one's eyes can play tricks and it appeared to Prater as if the trees had moved. He and the other guard had their weapons ready, but there was nothing there but pine trees. Yet, behind any cover could be the enemy, just waiting to attack. The guards would move around and change positions to get a better view of the area. The guards kept their ears open too, listening for any approaching vehicles. The guards stayed close to the roads and in cover themselves, they did not want to get caught in the open of a crossroads. When shifts changed, those that had completed their guard duty huddled together in a foxhole, trying to keep warm. Fires were not permitted as they could alert the enemy to their position.

The Duties of a Messenger

Each infantry company had messengers; some moved swiftly on foot and some moved by jeep. Wells had left his squad buddies in Second Platoon to become his Platoon's messenger during the battles in the Ardennes. Wells would bring messages from the Company Commander to the platoon leaders, with information involving where a squad was to setup their machine gun. Wells would frequently scout far ahead of the

Company. During combat, he would bring messages from the platoon leaders or from sergeants about the situation at the front back to the Company Commander. Though he was only a messenger, the men on the front line expected Wells to know what was going on when he came back from the Command Post. Often, Wells would move undercover of darkness, alone on foot, or with a driver. He always ran the risk of capture or being ambushed and killed. Wells was selected to be a messenger because he was a farm boy and knew how to navigate by landmarks. His little town of Lyons, Indiana did not have street signs and so his background was a valuable tool for his duty as messenger. In some instances in the Belgian Ardennes, the Germans had moved street signs to confuse the Americans; this caused Wells few problems. One of the benefits of being a messenger was getting warm while at the Company Command Post, being offered the occasional cup of coffee, and having a good chance of laying claim to an extra pair of socks or gloves when some arrived.

Bed Check Charlie

A night spent outdoors in the frigid temperatures of the Belgian Ardennes was never complete without a visit from "Bed Check Charlie," a lightly armed German reconnaissance aircraft. Charlie would fly overhead in late afternoon, just before dusk to spot for targets for German artillery. After dark, it would linger around and would do little more than harass the infantry companies and keep the men from getting any sleep. Sometimes Charlie would drop a bomb or two, but not often. One night Charlie did succeed in bombing Division Headquarters. H Company got rather irritated with "Bed Check Charlie." Sometimes a GI would take a shot at Charlie with his M-1, but it never did much to get rid of the pest. One night, First Platoon got together and decided to do something about Charlie. One section got organized with their M-1s and fired together at Charlie. The first few rounds did little, but fire came in from one of the rifle companies in Second Battalion too. Charlie was hit and set ablaze. The aircraft went down in the distance and the pilot bailed out, but he was cut to pieces by rifle fire. That was the end of "Bed Check Charlie," or at least one of them.

A Cold Night in the Bulge

One night in the Ardennes, while the temperature was as frigid as ever, Lawson was in a foxhole with his buddy, "Hay Seed." They did not have any gloves, but did what many in the Company had done; construct a makeshift pair of gloves from cutting up a blanket. Their hands were so cold that they could not feel them. They huddled together to try to stay warm. Lawson tried to say something funny to his buddy, but his teeth were chattering so much that he could not be understood. They had to just sit in that cold foxhole all night and try to survive. Nearby, Slagle was lucky enough to be in an area where he could sleep in his sleeping bag; he kept his arms out in case he had to get up abruptly. Another GI was so cold that he zipped himself up all the way to his neck. In the morning, the GI woke up and struggled to get out. He dreamed that he was buried alive! The GI lit a cigarette and was visibly shaking; it had been a terrible dream.

An Icy Mountain

Early on the morning of 29 December, elements of the 83rd Infantry Division relieved Second Battalion, 291st Infantry. Later that day, the 2nd Armored Division finally confronted the 2nd SS Panzer Division, the lead unit in the German "Bulge" and virtually destroyed it. That afternoon, Third Platoon of H Company along with F Company boarded trucks and rode toward the north flank of Malmedy. They spent the night near Manhay and Grandmenil in reserve in the pine tree forest. On 30 December, Third Platoon of H Company continued to move with F Company to the top of an icy mountain. The mortar men pulled outpost duty and setup a roadblock along a road that moved up the mountain. They stayed there for nine days, expecting a German attack that never came. The weather was bitterly cold and heavy rain, snow, and hail came down. There were severe cases of frostbite among the men of Third Platoon as they braved the sub-zero temperatures, sleeping out in the elements.

Villers St. Gertrude- 1956   **Slagle at Villers St. Gertrude- 1956**

"Little Girl of Villers St. Gertrude" –1956   **"Slagle's Fort"- 1956**

Villers St. Gertrude, 75ᵗʰ Division Headquarters- 1956

Villers St. Gertrude

On the morning of 29 December, Second Battalion of the 291ˢᵗ Regiment, minus F Company and Third Platoon of H Company prepared for a move by truck. All other elements of the 75ᵗʰ Division were attached to other units at that time. Second Battalion was tasked with setting up Division Headquarters in the small town of Villers St. Gertrude, southeast of Brussels and about twenty miles away from Rochefort. Defensive positions were setup all around the town. It was here that First Platoon finally received some machine guns. First Platoon of H Company was setup in and around a large house at the top of a hill. The house commanded the surrounding area and was a good location for machine guns. Second Platoon was also setup in town. Villers St. Gertrude had a small church and several luxurious houses. The generous Belgian civilians offered their homes to the cold and hungry GIs. The Company kitchen truck had not caught up with H

Company and food was scarce. Division Headquarters also lacked supplies. The men made do with what few rations that they had carried.

Slagle's Fort

Second Squad of First Platoon was looking for a location to setup their machine gun. The large house had already been claimed. It was the warmest place to be and it filled up quickly. Sergeant Larson told his Squad to wait beside the house and he would look for some place for them to settle. Slagle noticed a small structure with an open back that no one had claimed. Slagle suggested that his Squad setup in the old icehouse, beside the large house overlooking the hill. Sergeant Larson quite agreed as the icehouse offered at least some shelter from the cold. The icehouse quickly became known as "Slagle's Fort." Second Squad setup their gun in "Slagle's Fort" with a clear field of fire. It was early afternoon and the temperature was barely above zero. They were so cold that conversation became almost impossible due to the chattering of teeth. Slagle found a cloth tarp hidden in a small space between the icehouse and the house. The Squad tore off pieces of the tarp to construct makeshift gloves, as they did not have any. Their next endeavor was to find something to eat.

The Little Girl of Villers St. Gertrude

As they were setting up in "Slagle's Fort," a little girl from the town appeared. She spoke a little English; enough to be understood. She was 13 years old, but looked much younger. She was very friendly to them and followed Slagle around as he paced back and forth to stay warm. She saw how cold he was and she ran off to her house and came back with a black velvet drape from her front window. Slagle fashioned it into a sort of cape and tied it around his neck to keep warm. Slagle gave her a candy bar he had tucked away in his pocket. The little girl would not leave his side and she stayed among the Squad. GIs had already setup in the girl's house in town and her family had moved into the cellar. Wells, the messenger, also met the girl and he gave her a chocolate bar from his rations and some magazines. Later, her parents invited him into the cellar where they were living and Wells did his best to communicate with them. Wells would point to a picture in Look Magazine and say what it was in English and they would name it in their language. In the morning, Wells was out relieving himself and heard a sound behind him, it was the little girl doing the same thing. Wells nearly wet his pants as a result; the same reaction that other GIs had when they saw Belgian civilians out in the open relieving themselves.

Slagle's Pot

The little girl of Villers St. Gertrude saw the poor state of the Squad held up in the icehouse: they had nothing to eat. She ran off and came back with a few potatoes for them. The little girl helped Slagle to get a fire going to cook with. Larson found an old crock pot and they melted snow in it over the fire. They put the potatoes in and managed to scrounge a few other rations to put in the pot: a can of beef stew and few other things. They sat down in the icehouse with their first hot meal in days. It did not taste very good, but it was hot and no one complained. Lawson joked that he thought he could now appreciate those soggy Brussels Sprouts that were so plentiful back in Wales. Other men in the Platoon smelled the stew and wanted some too. For a cup of stew, one had to contribute something from their rations to the pot. As they were eating, the Deputy Division Commander of the 75th Division, Brigadier General Mickle, arrived by jeep. He strode past the sentries on inspection then walked about. He stumbled upon "Slagle's Fort" when he smelled the stew cooking. He stopped in and said, "Sure smells good, I haven't had anything hot in a long while." The General then continued on his inspection. Slagle got up and handed over a cup of the stew to the General, who was speechless. General Mickle had a reputation for being a very tough commander of the Patton mindset. It is doubtful if any enlisted man ever offered him anything before. The General took the stew and thanked them.

Old Friends

As the Division Headquarters staff continued to arrive through the afternoon, Slagle spotted a few familiar faces: men from the Division Band. One of these men was Ray Brejcha. The members of the Division Band were tasked with M.P. duty and they guarded Division Headquarters. Slagle stopped and talked with many of his old friends from the Band. They had seen no combat, being well behind the front line, but they had heard it. As Slagle was walking back to his Squad, he spotted his Platoon Leader, Lieutenant Bergheimer, who was stumbling about. Slagle noticed Bergheimer was absolutely looped and was carrying an empty wine bottle. Slagle made himself scarce. Bergheimer stumbled around the house, barely able to keep himself on his feet. He threw up on the stairs and almost stepped in it. He then entered into the house on his hands and knees and shut the door behind him. Second Squad never saw their Platoon Leader again that day.

Good Deeds Remembered

The next morning, 30 December, Slagle woke up from a somewhat comfortable sleep in the icehouse and was walking through the snow around the big house, which became Division Headquarters. General Mickle called out to him and invited Slagle in for a cup of coffee. The General remembered Slagle, for giving him the cup of stew the day before. The General asked him his name, where he was from, and about his time in the Army. When the General found out that Slagle had intelligence training back at Camp Breckinridge, he told Slagle he could use a bodyguard. The hard-nosed General Mickle seemed quite friendly in private. Slagle returned to his Squad as Second Battalion prepared to leave Villers St. Gertrude for their move back to the front. The little girl of Villers St. Gertrude came out to say goodbye to Slagle and his Squad buddies.

The Duties of a Cook

Mess Sergeant Lyons had a big job on his hands during the rough winter in the Ardennes: he had to keep the men of H Company fed. This was no easy task when considering that each of the three platoons were frequently in different locations. The GIs each carried a mess kit with a utensil that served both as a fork and spoon. When food could not be brought to the men in the field, they had to eat C or K rations, which were not well liked. These contained foods such as processed cheese, ham, turkey, or stew and a chocolate bar. They were filling, but not tasty. Water would have to be added to the stew and snow had to be melted for that purpose. The Company cooks did what they could to feed the men hot meals. In the morning, before first light, the cooks made sandwiches and the cook's helpers brought bags of them to the front. For dinner, a good hot meal was made and brought up to the men at the front well after dark.

The Happy Cook

Corporal Casper sometimes brought food to the men in First Platoon. He always had a big smile even when there was no occasion for it. One cold morning, Staff Sergeant Slawson asked Casper if he had any coffee; the cook said something unintelligible and laughed. The men discovered why Casper was always so happy; he had a bottle of Cognac with him at all times! Casper was a drunkard, but he was a happy one and always performed his duty. Many of the men liked him, because he would always make it a point to bring them something they liked. One time Casper found a box of chocolate bars and he stuffed them into his pockets. One night after dinner, when some of the men from First Platoon were trying to get some sleep, Casper arrived and handed out chocolate bars. A near riot erupted, but Casper made sure he brought enough for everyone to get one. On another occasion, Casper filled up several bottles of cognac with water and left them out in the open near Bergheimer's foxhole. The Lieutenant saw the bottles and scrambled out of his foxhole, tilted his head back and slugged one down. The men of his Platoon laughed at Bergheimer's foul language when he discovered that his "cognac" was nothing but ice water.

A Cook's Nightly Journey

Every night, well after dark and sometime before midnight, the cooks would prepare their hot meal for the whole Company. Those not at the front were fed with ease. However, those men on the front line were often in a location where death could come at an instant. The cooks had to brave these dangers too, the same as any GI on the front line, in order to feed their Company. The cooks would prepare barrels of food and load them into the Company kitchen truck and drive as close up to the front as they could. When the starving men of each platoon lined up for their hot meal, one of the cook's helpers would serve them from the barrel that was almost as tall as a man. The hot meal was varied every day. The men that were held up in very dangerous positions, where the kitchen truck could not get to, had their meals brought to them in a covered container.

Enemy in Sight

On 31 December, as dusk approached, a German transport plane flew close overhead. In the distance, perhaps a mile or two away, it began dropping paratroops.

Slagle spotted the silhouettes of the parachutes in the dim light of dusk. He fired his M-1 Garand. Lawson said, "What the Hell are you shooting at, Slagle?" "Hay Seed," perhaps the best marksman in First Platoon got out his rifle and fired too. Before long, most of the Platoon was target shooting. The plane flew out of the area, having dropped its paratroops. Lieutenant Bergheimer organized a scouting party to locate any surviving paratroops: they were dropped well behind the American lines. The scouting party found the drop point. All the German paratroops were dead; full of holes. Their packs and equipment were scattered around the area. Packs of cigarettes were found and the scouting party picked off souvenirs including pistols, rifles, and bayonets.

The New Year

At the stroke of midnight, ringing in the New Year 1945, every artillery gun in 20 Corps fired three rounds into German territory for their New Year's Greetings to Adolf. The beginning of the New Year was very quiet for H Company. They were situated in Mont Derrieux, Belgium. The enemy in these first few days of 1945 was not the Germans; it was the bitter cold. The men of H Company had spent almost two weeks out in the elements and the effects of it were beginning to show. Some men were becoming ill from cold and fever, especially the men of the Mortar Platoon who were on that icy mountain for nine days. A few men were evacuated to the Battalion Aid Station due to frost bitten feet. Some of them never returned to H Company due to the severity of the frostbite. This led to a few promotions in the Company. None of the men of H Company would ever forget those harsh, frigid days of early January 1945. On 6 January, H Company reassembled and moved to Marteau near Spa, Belgium.

Patrol Duty

Lieutenant Bergheimer led a patrol ahead of Second Battalion's lines to locate the German positions. An artillery exchange had quieted down by afternoon and the German guns were silent. On the patrol, Slagle and Lawson spotted the frozen remains of GIs from the 106th Division; their rifles were facing east. Bergheimer used his binoculars and spotted the German forward observation post. He wanted to ambush them and take prisoners. Upon closer inspection, they saw no activity in the area. As they approached, they discovered that a shell had scored a direct hit on the observation post. A German

Colonel lay on his back, dead. Both of his eyes were wide open and his mouth agape. A subordinate was also dead. Slagle picked off the Colonel's binoculars, Nazi armband, and his ceremonial dagger. Bergheimer took the pistol as a prize. Bergheimer was disappointed that there were no prisoners to capture; he was bent on glory. A few weeks later, Slagle sent home his souvenirs to his younger cousin in New Jersey, who used them in a school play in the spring of 1945.

A Temporary Reprieve

On the afternoon of 7 January, Second Battalion arrived to Marteau and reunited with the rest of the 75th Division. While the weather worsened and blizzard conditions prevailed, the men of H Company moved into a warm shelter. Like in other towns they had passed through in Belgium, the inhabitants of Spa were very hospitable and welcomed the Americans as liberators. They offered their homes to the GIs. The officers slept in warm houses and the enlisted men crowded in barns with plenty of hay: it was much warmer than sleeping in the open. New clothes were issued, but there still was no winter gear. The men caught up on their meals. The Company cooks were kept quite busy, serving three hot meals a day. In the evening, the locals gave the GIs beer, wine, and schnapps. First Sergeant Whalen was invited into a home and came out with many bottles hanging out of his pockets. The three days spent at Spa were a welcomed and unexpected luxury to the men of H Company.

Searching for Quarters

Sergeant Hicks from the Mortar Platoon was the man tasked with locating sleeping quarters for the men of H Company. When the Company arrived to Marteau, Hicks began scouting for quarters. He could not speak French, but found a little boy who took him by the hand up a hill to a very large house that was almost a mansion. The mansion was beautiful and fully furnished. The town was battered from war, with few buildings still standing, but the mansion on the hill was fully intact. It had been occupied by Germans not long before and that was probably the reason it still stood. The officers got the bedrooms and the sergeants took whatever else was leftover; couches or chairs. The privates got what was left, the floor, with maybe a pillow; it certainly was better than sleeping in the blizzard outside!

The Blunder

While in the vicinity of Spa, the men of the 75th Division had an opportunity to take a shower for the first time in weeks. Each squad in each company was able to send a man to take a shower; the decision was made by cutting cards, with the man with the highest card winning the much desired opportunity for a shower. First Lieutenant Maxwell was the acting Executive Officer of H Company in First Lieutenant Goodnight's absence. Goodnight became ill and was diagnosed with appendicitis. He was sent to the Battalion Aid Station and then to a hospital to have his appendix taken out and he was gone for some time. Maxwell was the officer in charge of the shower detail. A truck arrived to pick up all the lucky GIs who had won a pass to take a shower. Maxwell was carrying a map and gave the driver directions to get to the showers. Ross was one of the apparent unlucky men who missed out on a chance to take a shower. Perhaps Ross was one of the lucky ones after all. A short time after the truck departed under Maxwell's watchful eye, it returned and the driver was quite sore with Maxwell. The driver took the directions given to him; these directions took him right into the German lines! The driver quickly turned around when he realized where he was and headed back. The men on the truck who thought they were the lucky ones with a shower pass ended up not being so lucky after all.

Obeying Orders

Division Headquarters was also located in the vicinity of Spa. Second Battalion was encamped not far away. The companies of Second Battalion took turns pulling guard duty. A secret meeting with many of the Allied Commanders was about to take place, unknown to any of the men of H Company. One evening, Slagle was pulling guard duty and it was very cold. He paced back and forth to keep himself awake and to keep warm. It was quiet and most of the men were sleeping. Suddenly Lieutenant Bergheimer stumbled out of his quarters: he was looped. He ordered Slagle to drive him into town immediately to get more liquor. Slagle protested: he had not been relieved of his guard duty. Bergheimer yelled at him and threatened to throw Slagle in the stockade for disobeying his direct order. Slagle refused his Lieutenant's order, profusely telling him that he could not leave his post without being replaced. Sergeant Larson awoke and wanted to know what the yelling was about. Though Larson was only a Sergeant, he was ten years older than Bergheimer. Larson spoke to Bergheimer in a tone as if he was speaking to a spoiled child. Bergheimer threw a fit and finally went back to his quarters. By then, many men were awake and wondering what was happening; Bergheimer was creating quite a scene.

Duty

Slagle was supposed to be relieved during the night, but he volunteered for more guard duty. The only thing keeping him from getting trench foot was the constant pacing he did through the night. Slagle took over for another guard near Division Headquarters in the early morning hours. Around dawn, Slagle was getting quite cold and was a sorry sight to see. General Mickle hung his head out of a window and spit out his toothpaste. He caught a glimpse of a battered looking man wearing a crumpled British field officer's coat, a black drape across his shoulders, and a long handlebar mustache. General Mickle said, "Hell Son, what Army are you with?" The General then recognized Slagle and invited him in for coffee. He had heard about what happened the night before with the private that refused to abandon his post without being relieved. General Mickle asked Slagle to serve temporarily as his bodyguard. That day, Slagle received a temporary transfer from H Company.

The Generals Conference

Late at night on 8 January, many of the Allied Generals met in a bunker somewhere near Spa, Belgium. Jeeps drove the generals to the secret location under cover of darkness. General Mickle, his driver, and Slagle arrived well after dark. The General went in and Slagle and the driver were to stay outside and wait for his return. The driver was tired and laid down beside his jeep to try to get some sleep. Slagle strode around, trying to stay awake. As the conference ended, the generals came out looking for their drivers. General Patton emerged and tripped over General Mickle's driver who was asleep on the ground. General Mickle apologized to Patton, but Patton's response was, "Let the man sleep, he's the only one worth a damn, he's driving you." Slagle then accompanied General Mickle back to Division Headquarters and then returned back to H Company.

The Death March

At 1700 hours on 9 January 1945, Second Battalion of the 291st Regiment left Spa to began a torturous march through heavy snow, icy winds, and below zero temperatures. The men still lacked their winter clothing. The heavy rains of autumn 1944 had saturated the ground, then the temperatures quickly changed to bitter cold and froze the ground, making it a sheet of glass. On top of this was about two feet of snow. Blinding snowstorms, resulting in whiteouts were another factor of the march. The snow came down so thick that one had to hold onto the shoulder of the man in front of him and hope he knew where he was going. Walking even a short distance through this terrain was tough, but Second Battalion had to march 22 miles in one night. The men of H Company had an even more daunting task before them: they had to carry their machine guns, mortars, and ammunition. The men marched on country roads under heavy forest cover. There was less snow on some of the roads due to the trees, but the slush that had become solid ice made for worse walking conditions. Some of the men slipped on the ice and injured themselves. One man in H Company broke his leg on the ice. Those carrying the machine guns and mortars began to lag behind. During the night, the icy winds picked up and blew snowdrifts around, causing more troubles for the march. At 0200 on 10 January, H Company made it to the assembly area at Basse-Boddeux, Belgium. Jeeps picked up many of the gunners and ammo bearers, who could not complete the march due to the added weight of their equipment. Prater, as with so many others in the Company and Battalion, bore signs of frostbite on his feet. The men that made this march commonly called it the "Death March."

Aftermath of the Death March

Due to the march, many of the men in H Company had trench foot and had to be taken to the Battalion Aid Station. One man in First Platoon took his shoes off and found his feet were black; some of his toes came off with the shoes. Others had to have toes amputated. Posnak from the Mortar Platoon was one of the men showing signs of frostbite. He and several others were taken to the Battalion Aid Station; Posnak was the only one in the group who made it back to the Company. Some men were so cold they could not feel their hands at all. No one could understand why they were not moved to the assembly area by truck, considering the distance and severity of the weather. No explanation was ever offered.

Relieving the 82nd Airborne

After the Death March of only hours before, Second Battalion was to make another march: to the Salm River to relieve elements of the 517th Parachute Regiment of the 82nd Airborne Division. On the afternoon of 10 January, the second march began with the Battalion arriving at the next assembly area, some seven miles away. When the Company arrived to the new designated area, they found out that they would have to make a third march to the Salm River. Most of the men were not in shape to make another march. No one had anything to eat or drink since the previous afternoon. The men were freezing, had wet feet, and were battling fatigue. The men of H Company would not be making a third march as trucks finally arrived to move them up to the front. There were not enough vehicles available to move the whole Battalion, so men crowded in what vehicles were available. Ten men were on a jeep, twenty men or more crowded the trucks: no one wanted to do any more marching. They moved six miles to an area near the Salm River. The men of H Company then got out of the trucks and marched to the front to relieve the 517th Regiment. The 82nd Airborne had been through a lot in the last few weeks and their appearance showed it. Yet, when H Company met up with men from the 517th Regiment, one of them said, "You guys look worse than us."

Preparing for the Offensive

As January progressed, the Germans began to lose any advantage they had. Their westward push came to a halt: they were now fighting to keep the ground they already took. The atrocities committed by the SS were very much on everyone's mind. The Malmedy Massacre, where the SS had gunned down 86 unarmed Americans was the worst atrocity of all. It happened not far from where H Company was. The Generals Conference of days earlier had determined that the Allies were now in position to begin an offensive, targeted at pushing the Germans out of Belgium altogether. The 75th Division was to take an active role in this offensive. In many areas in the Ardennes, the Germans had taken a beating. They were losing soldiers and equipment, but most of all, their fuel was running out. Hitler's Panzer Divisions could no longer proceed westward.

However, the Germans were far from defeated and the tenacity and viciousness of the SS kept the Wehrmarcht and Volksgrenadier troops in the fight. On 10 January, as the 82nd Airborne Division was relieved by the 75th Division along the Salm, there was no direct contact with the Germans. There was some scattered artillery fire coming from the direction of Vielsalm and Salmchateau across the Salm River.

Patrols to Salmchateau

Second Battalion of the 291st Regiment began to send patrols across the Salm River beginning on the night of 11 January to survey the German positions. The Germans were highly protective of their side of the Salm and the patrols were largely unsuccessful. Patrols from other units of the 75th Division also proved unsuccessful. More patrols were sent on the nights of 12 and 13 January with limited success. The Germans were determined to hold their positions. On the night of 14 January a German aircraft strafed a mess building near the Division Command Post, inflicting a few casualties. The Germans were apparently well aware of the 75th Division's presence and were conducting their own reconnaissance operations.

The Battle of Grand Halleux

"It was the worst day of my life."

-Henry H. Smith, Second Platoon, H Company

Orders to Attack

On 14 January, the 75th Division assembled as a complete unit for the first time. In the eyes of senior commanders, the Division was now ready for its first combat as an independent unit. Just before midnight, Second Battalion, 291st Infantry crossed the Salm River on a Bailey Bridge leading into the vicinity of Salmchateau and then they moved into the town of Petite Halleux. The Germans had withdrawn. That night, the G.I.s bedded down in some barns and slept in the hay to keep warm. On the morning of 15 January, by order of the XVIII Corps Commander, General Ridgeway, the 75th Division was to take Vielsalm and Salmchateau. It was to be a double envelopment with the 289th and 291st Regiments leading the attack, with the 290th in reserve. The 291st was to begin their attack at 0800 hours, five hours after the 289th began their attack.

The Fateful Advance

During the hours before dawn on 15 January, H Company moved into the town of Grand Halleux; the rifle companies preceded them through town. At 0730 hours, Second Battalion left the cover of woods and marched up a road to begin their advance across the snow covered cow pasture. Over two feet of snow covered the ground and the temperature that morning was hovering just below the zero mark. Their objective was to clear the Germans from the top of a hill overlooking the town of Grand Halleux, about 600 yards away over open ground. At first light, the Germans began firing their 88s into town. Smith from H Company's Fourth Squad from Second Platoon started to hear the 88 shells whistling close overhead and he hit the ground, then stood up to take a few more steps before hitting the ground again. It was this way all the way up the road to the line of departure. Once Second Battalion was organized into a line, G and E Companies advanced with F Company in reserve. H Company's Mortar Platoon was entrenched on several hillsides facing south toward St. Vith. Some of the mortar sections were able to fire their mortars to give the rifle companies some support. They also fired smoke rounds to screen the infantry advance. The shells hit the heavily wooded forest at the top of the hill. Sounds of timber splitting resonated and the German artillery was silenced. At first, it looked as if the mortar men had gotten the job done. H Company's machine gun platoons spread out by squad and moved up to an area just behind and around a small church that overlooked the battlefield. This small church became G Company's Command Post. H Company setup their Forward Observation Post at the crossroads, near a drainage ditch. The location offered a clear view of the German position. To the left of the machine gun platoons was a dirt road that led down to a larger church, which became the Battalion Aid Station. Behind the Aid Station was a road that led back to the Division Command Post. Prior to the attack, a messenger had arrived to H Company, ordering Slagle to report to the Division Command Post.

Pinned Down Under Fire

In the early morning hours prior to the attack, the First Section of the Mortar Platoon under the command of Staff Sergeant Modrezjewski slowly moved through the town of Grand Halleux; they were behind the rifle and machine gun platoons. During the march, PFC Hartranft said to Ross, "Today is going to be a rough day;" perhaps he knew a bit more about the situation than many of the younger privates. Garo, the Platoon Sergeant of the Mortar Platoon ordered his men to spread out as they moved up, in case of a German artillery attack. As the infantry advance across the snow covered cow pasture began, Modrezjewski's Section began to setup their mortars. Before they could be readied to fire, the Germans began to shell their position. First Section lacked any cover where they were setup and the Germans had a clear view of their exposed position. Garo ordered Modrezjewski's Section to take cover inside one of the buildings along the street. As they moved along the road and into the house, Ross saw his buddy Hartranft laying dead; shrapnel from one of the shells had taken half his face off as he had tried to fire his mortar. First Section was pinned down for the rest of the day, until evening, when the

German artillery ceased. Second and Third Sections of the Mortar Platoon were able to fire their mortars, but quickly ran out of ammunition as their ammo bearers were killed or wounded. Third Section had fired smoke rounds to screen the infantry advance.

The Advance of G Company

The rifle companies received their order to advance shortly after H Company's mortars had silenced. The snow was very deep and it was slow moving up that hill. The Germans were firmly entrenched on the hill in a thick forest of pine trees. The German infantry on the hill were flanked by many heavy machine guns. The Second Battalion infantrymen were wearing their olive drab colored uniforms, still lacking their winter gear: they were the perfect target for the Germans. The rifle companies made it to within fifty yards of that hill when heavy fire pinned them down in the open: there was no cover to be had. The Germans, wearing white snowsuits, well camouflaged against the terrain, fired submachine guns, rifles, and heavy machine guns. The men of G Company tried to return fire, but casualties mounted very quickly. Any man that raised up to fire was quickly hit. PFC Douglas Jenkins of G Company rose up and tried to fire his M-1, but was struck in the shoulder and ribs. He fell on his stomach with blood coming out his mouth. Jenkins laid flat on the ground and tried to calm himself. He looked to his right and saw a long line of soldiers lying across the field. They were all quiet and motionless. They were all dead or seriously wounded.

"Bloody Monday"

The attack was not going well for Second Battalion that morning. E and G Companies were pinned down and were already taking heavy casualties. H Company's Mortar Platoon had been targeted by the Germans and was being shelled: their fire was halted as their ammo bearers were pinned down and could not bring more ammunition. Private Luther Mason, a machine gun ammo bearer in Second Platoon found himself in a position where he was able to help out the Mortar Platoon. He braved machine gun fire and ran 500 yards over open ground and crossed the road to bring ammunition to the Mortar Platoon: he repeated this action three times that day. The Mortar Platoon took casualties. The machine gun squads were all pinned down, with Second Platoon taking casualties in their exposed position with little to no cover. First Battalion, attacking the hill from a position to the right of Second Battalion, was doing no better: they too were pinned down. Radio contact with First Battalion's Command Post was lost after it was shelled. The attack could not be properly coordinated. An American tank from the 3rd Armored Division emerged and tried to make it up to the area where the machine gun platoons were positioned, to provide support. The tank hit a landmine in the road and was destroyed. Men of Second Platoon used the tank for cover, as there was no other cover to be had in their area.

Some of H Company's machine gun squads were able to setup their guns and they fired on the German positions. Smith, the gunner of Fourth Squad of Second Platoon, led by Sergeant William Brannon was pinned down by heavy machine gun fire. His Squad had a small incline about the height of a curb to serve as their cover. He had to lay flat to avoid being hit. Smith had only a bayonet to dig with, but he did not even attempt to use it against the ice. Anyone who raised their heads or twitched would surely have been killed. 88 shells continued to whistle overhead of Smith's position. Some of the shells hit close to Brannon's Squad and the shrapnel from the blasts blew snow all over them. Second Platoon was very much out in the open and casualties mounted from shrapnel.

The Making of a Hero
Second Squad of First Platoon was pinned down toward the right side of the big church. Sergeant Larson took a chance and advanced to the cover of the church. The Germans began firing their heavy machine guns on Second Squad. "Hay Seed" told Lawson that he was tired of being pinned down. A moment later, Lawson witnessed quite the feat of soldiering. "Hay Seed" waited for a brief pause in the machine gun fire and then stood up, crouching and picked up his Squad's machine gun with its tripod affixed and made a run for it. Machine gun bullets grazed his shoulder just as he made it to cover, near Larson. Seconds later, a shell landed nearby and "Hay Seed" took shrapnel to his leg and side. A man from First Squad was severely wounded from the shell and cried out for help: he was all by himself, laying face down. The wounded man was some distance to the right of Sergeant Larson's position. "Hay Seed," with a blood soaked uniform and suffering from his own wounds, dashed out from cover and picked up the wounded man and carried him through the machine gun fire, back to the cover of the church. Lawson

watched these events with disbelief. Larson and "Hay Seed" managed to keep the wounded man alive.

The "Yellow" Lieutenant

For weeks, the men of First Platoon had thought their Lieutenant had a yellow streak. Second Lieutenant Bergheimer was never around when the sounds of combat could be heard: he would always find an excuse to have his driver take him to Battalion or even Division Headquarters. Somehow Bergheimer caught wind of what the men in his Platoon thought of him and he planned to do something about it. During the midst of the battle, Bergheimer came up to the front with his driver escorting him on foot. Somehow, they made it up to cover behind the small church. Bergheimer began shouting orders at his men that were all pinned down. His orders to advance under such conditions bordered on insanity. Suddenly, a shell flew overhead and came down well behind Bergheimer's position. He hit the ground and began shouting for help. It was probably the first shell Bergheimer had ever heard up close. His shouts turned to cries for help. Lieutenant Bergheimer, the loud mouthed, bully of a Platoon Leader had a breakdown on the front line. He was shrieking hysterically and in an absolute panic. He got up and moved out into the open and hit the ground again. He was directly in the German's line of fire and was out of his head. A young private from First Squad watched Bergheimer continue to scream and cry out for help. This young man was one of the men that Bergheimer had bullied at Camp Breckinridge. For some reason, the Private took pity on his Lieutenant. Under heavy machine gun fire and prodding from his Squad mates not to risk his own life, he moved up to Bergheimer's position and helped him to safety. Bergheimer was evacuated by his own driver, to the Battalion Aid Station; he had no visible wounds.

Looking for C Company

At the Division Command Post, frustration over the halted advance was mounting. Second Battalion's Command Post was shelled and radio contact was lost. Lieutenant Colonel Drain, the Commanding Officer of Second Battalion, had sent a messenger to Division Headquarters requesting permission to pull back and reorganize for a second attempt at taking that hill. The request was denied. The XVIII Corps

Commander, General Ridgeway was at the 75th Division Command Post and he would not permit a withdrawal: the hill had to be taken. Contact could not be made with First Battalion's Command Post either. General Mickle was present at the Command Post, listening to reports coming in about the stalled advance. He was not one for waiting around for anything and he called for a driver and for Slagle. They got in his jeep and went to look for C Company, who was leading First Battalion's advance. Slagle manned the jeep's .50 caliber machine gun. They drove behind the front lines, some distance behind the small church where Second Battalion's Aid Station was located. They moved up to an area somewhere near the front and well to the right of where First Battalion's position was thought to be. They drove over a high hill into a heavily wooded area and ended up in front of a German SS infantry company that had just finished eating breakfast. The cooks still had their pots and pans setup. The Germans ran for their weapons and Slagle opened fire from the jeep's machine gun, making a full turn. There were sounds of bullets clanging off pots and pans. Those not killed, dropped their weapons and ran for their lives into the woods. General Mickle shouted, "Good shooting Slagle!"

They finally found First Battalion's position and C Company who was pinned down. Part of C Company had taken a portion of the high ground and communications with them had been lost. General Mickle insisted on going up there in person to find out what happened. General Mickle and Slagle made it up to a trench at the top of the hill. No fire was coming toward the position at that time. General Mickle crawled through the trench and up to the position where the squad leader was positioned. Mickle's first comment was, "Why are you not clean shaven, soldier!" The Sergeant replied with quite vicious language, not realizing he was addressing the Deputy Division Commander. Mickle then went back down the hill to the position of the rest of C Company and told C Company's commander that the squad up on the hill was "In good spirits!"

Unintended Bravery

One of the sergeants from C Company that had made it up the hill was wounded. General Mickle ordered Slagle to load the wounded man's litter onto the back of the jeep and drive him to the Battalion Aid Station. Slagle did not get far, as German artillery had targeted their position. Slagle got out of the jeep, just as another shell came in very close.

He pulled the litter out and tripped over it, landing on top of the wounded man. The wounded Sergeant shouted, "Get off me!" General Mickle watched these events and said, "Look at that man, he is risking his own life to shield the wounded Sergeant!" Slagle actually had no intention of shielding the Sergeant; he had tripped! General Mickle wrote Slagle up for the Bronze Star. He might have deserved it from the General's point of view, but Slagle did not feel that he deserved it. Slagle made it to the Battalion Aid Station and returned to General Mickle's position. The General then ordered his driver to take him to Second Battalion's Command Post to see what could be done about the Germans on the hill above Grand Halleux.

H Company's Losses

In the midst of combat, Sergeant Hicks, from the Third Section of H Company's Mortar Platoon was running up and down the hill to the Forward Observation Post to patch up the telephone wire. Sergeant Bessner manned the radio to the Battalion Command Post. Staff Sergeant Lee, commanding Third Section was with Captain Haddock in the Observation Post, which had been setup in a drainage ditch. It was about two-foot deep and it gave Haddock a clear view of the German's position. Unfortunately, the Germans also had a clear view of Haddock's position. The Germans seized the opportunity and shelled H Company's Forward Observation Post. The map sergeant, Hoffman Wong was seriously wounded. First Lieutenant Leroy Wallis, commander of the Mortar Platoon was killed. Staff Sergeant Lee was killed. All the privates in the Observation Post were killed or wounded. One of the shells landed right on top of Sergeant Bessner with such force that it sent his helmet spiraling up in the air and it went down with great velocity across Captain Haddock's legs, severing them. Haddock laid bleeding, having lost both legs below the knee. No one could help him. After seeing the mortar attack on his Observation Post, First Lieutenant William Craig, commanding Second Platoon, called for a medic. H Company's medics were all pinned down, but Corporal Ed Coltrin, a medic from Second Battalion's Aid Station, was called up to the front and he made it to the Observation Post. Captain Haddock was bleeding heavily and Coltrin tied his belt and another man's belt around the stumps of Haddock's legs, keeping the Captain from bleeding to death. Coltrin rendered aid to the other survivors in the Observation Post too. Due to the constant shelling and machine gun fire, Captain Haddock could not be moved from his position until well after dark. After the death of

Staff Sergeant Lee, Sergeant Hicks took command of the Third Section of the Mortar Platoon.

Collapse of the Advance

After two hours, the advance up the hill was in shambles. Communications were lost altogether and each company did what it could, individually. G Company was taking the most casualties: they were pinned down in the middle of the cow pasture with no cover at all. Captain Druillard, the Commander of G Company climbed up to the church steeple room and surveyed the situation; it was grim. Druillard watched as his men were being slaughtered and he was powerless to help them. The men of G Company could not retreat, they could not advance, and they could not stay where they were. Death came from any decision made. E Company's advance was halted as well and their casualties mounted. H Company's casualties continued to mount, especially among Second Platoon that was caught out in the open with no cover. The Germans had successfully shelled the Mortar Platoon on the hillside where they were dug in and they too, took casualties.

Driving to the Battalion Command Post

General Mickle proceeded up to the front through heavy machine gun and mortar fire. It was no place for a Commanding General to be, but he would have it no other way. As they moved up the road to the small church where the men of H Company were scattered about, Slagle saw many of his friends laying dead. Sergeant Larson, in cover behind the church, spotted Slagle in the jeep and raised his rifle in salute. The jeep was parked behind the church with some cover from the artillery fire that continued to come in. Captain Druillard was spotted out in front of the church in a trench observing the remnants of his Company. General Mickle proceeded into the church and ran up to the little room inside the steeple. General Mickle made his inspection of the situation, telling Slagle, "I can see everything from here." Slagle told the General, "I think they can see us up here too." The Germans had indeed seen General Mickle's jeep approach the church and must have reasoned that the church was a target of opportunity. Artillery was directed at the church and a shell hit the front, below the steeple. The enlisted men in the church shouted to General Mickle that he must be evacuated; the General would have no part of leaving. Slagle grabbed General Mickle by the arm and forced him down. A few seconds later, a shell hit the steeple and killed two privates who were still up there. General Mickle and Slagle got out of the church and leaped from foxhole to foxhole until they found the trench where Captain Druillard was positioned. Druillard was bitterly angry and said to the General, "My men are being slaughtered!" General Mickle ordered his driver to take him back to the Division Command Post immediately to make an in person report of the situation to the Division Commander.

The Close of Battle

Heavy German fire poured onto First and Second Battalion throughout the day. G Company was virtually destroyed. H Company's losses continued to mount. By late afternoon on that fateful day of 15 January, the GIs had been in the field for many hours in the bitter cold. Those that survived had frostbite and many could not move themselves. As darkness fell, it was possible for the wounded to be moved to the Battalion Aid Station. As medics moved through the field, they heard the moans and cries of the dying. More than half the strength of E, G, and H Companies were killed or wounded. There were not enough medics and the able bodied men from each company did what they could to help their wounded. "Hay Seed" had been wounded more than he let on. His right side and leg was bleeding from the shrapnel wound, but he would not take the advice of his Sergeant and go to the Battalion Aid Station; he wanted to help his wounded buddies. "Hay Seed" finally went to the Aid Station, but only after he had loaded two of his wounded Platoon buddies into a jeep. That evening, Third Battalion moved up to the front and relieved Second Battalion.

Reorganizing

That evening, from a crouching position, Smith dragged his machine gun all the way back down the hill. As he passed by the knocked out tank, that a squad from Second Platoon had used as cover, he saw one of his good friends sitting waist up: the rest of him had been blown away. As Smith reached the road at the bottom of the hill, he got up to run and found he could not even stand up; his feet were nearly frozen. One of the lieutenants came out to meet Smith on the road and took the tripod to lighten his load. The battered remnants of Second Battalion moved back down the hill to regroup. At 0730 on 16 January, Third Battalion of the 291st Regiment advanced across the snow covered field, led by I Company. After taking their own heavy casualties, but being supported by Division Artillery, they succeeded in taking the hill above Grand Halleux. The Germans at the top of the hill were all killed or captured. Division Artillery had fired 1,887 rounds in support of Third Battalion's advance. 110 German prisoners were taken and a tank was knocked out during the double envelopment by the 289th and 291st Regiments.

The Casualties

Second Battalion had taken more casualties than any other unit in the 75th Division. "Bloody Monday" left Second Battalion in a weakened state. G Company had 30 men killed and 42 wounded. G Company was down to one weak platoon in strength. E Company had 18 men killed with 47 wounded. F Company that was in reserve had 3 men killed from 88 shells. H Company had lost its Commanding Officer, Captain Haddock and his staff. First Lieutenant Goodnight, the Executive Officer was out of action due to appendicitis and First Lieutenant Maxwell became the acting Commander of H Company. In addition to the men killed at the Forward Observation Post, an incoming shell killed Second Lieutenant Martin Ziegler as he tried to bring ammunition up to First Platoon. Private Zigmund Granat, PFC Dilbert Schueler, and PFC Carl Bruton were also killed. Eugene Finke, who had recently been promoted to Sergeant, was killed while leading his Squad from First Platoon. Many others were severely wounded or had trench foot. The Mortar Platoon was down to a strength of four squads from its original complement of six. Second Platoon that had been caught in the open had almost been annihilated: it suffered many wounded. First Platoon favored better, but still had its share of wounded and Lieutenant Bergheimer was temporarily out of action. Slagle left the service of General Mickle and returned back to his Squad. Second Battalion had little time to rest. Despite their horrendous casualties, they were back to duty two days later.

"Licking Our Wounds and Counting Our Noses"

In the morning of 16 January, the day after Second Battalion's fateful advance, the survivors were trying to get reorganized. Prater emerged from the house that he and others from his Section were sleeping in. He noticed that there was a mortar shell without its case lying in the courtyard. Lieutenant Colonel Drain walked out there to make a pit stop, but Prater was quick to warn him about the shell. That afternoon, the survivors of

Second Battalion were tasked with removing their dead for burial. Hicks had taken over as Staff Sergeant for Third Section of the Mortar Platoon. Hicks selected several men to go out into the field at Grand Halleux and recover their dead for burial. Page and PFC Francisco Key Palma were two of the men tasked with this duty. They could identify the dead sergeants and officers by the Army issued watches on their arms that were outstretched in the snow, where they fell mortally wounded. Page and Palma moved up and down the hill that afternoon, moving the frozen remains of the dead from Second Battalion. During the afternoon, they saw Lieutenant Maxwell, the Acting Company Commander. Someone asked Maxwell about H Company's situation; about their casualties. Maxwell responded, "We are licking our wounds and counting our noses."

The Battle of the Poteau Crossroads

To the Crossroads

On 17 January, at 1400 hours, Second Battalion left Grand Halleux. They bypassed Petit Thier and at 0315 had arrived at the crossroads town of Poteau, two miles east of Petit Thier. H Company had arrived a short time earlier than the rest of the Battalion. Second Battalion setup a perimeter defense around the town and a roadblock at the all-important crossroads. Poteau had been taken the day before by elements of the 290th Regiment. Some Germans were captured there, but most had retreated. Poteau commanded the crossroads that led to St. Vith; it was of prime importance to the Germans. In the early morning hours, under cover of darkness, Smith saw a GI who had three German prisoners to move through the woods and to his command post. The GI stopped and told the Germans to run, then he shot all three of them down. He did not want to move the prisoners through the woods in the darkness. The GI told Smith that the prisoners zigged when they should have zagged. The men of Second Battalion billeted in the houses and barns in town to try to get some sleep. There had been a major battle at Poteau back in December and many of the buildings were in ruins. There was plenty of hay in the barn and the men of H Company used it to keep warm and get some sleep. Smith and his Squad slept in the hayloft of one of the buildings. The Germans had left much of their ammunition behind in the houses and barns when they fled the day before. The loft where Smith was sleeping was full of 88 ammunition. Prater and men from the Mortar Platoon went to sleep on the ground floor of a small wooden shed behind the barn. Corporal Glen Johnson said, "We'll all be home by Christmas, this can't last for another year."

Incident at the Crossroads

Around 0300 hours, some of the machine gunners setup their guns to defend the crossroads. Any vehicle or messenger moving through the crossroads was checked. The snow was deep and the winds were icy. The temperature had gotten even colder, well below zero. Slagle was the sentry checking all the traffic moving into town. Lawson was manning a machine gun on one side of a stone wall, opposite Slagle's position. Messengers moved through the checkpoint and the Company kitchen truck moved into town to begin cooking for the next day. A jeep pulled up a few hours before sunrise with an officer, his driver, and two enlisted men in the back. The driver knew the password, but somehow seemed indifferent. He tried to joke his way out of any further questions. Slagle asked him a question about baseball that anyone would know. The driver did not know the answer, nor was he familiar with any of the famous American movie actresses. The driver was quickly getting agitated with Slagle. A safety clicked among one of the men in the back of the jeep and Slagle ducked behind the stone wall. Lawson had thought the driver shot Slagle and he opened fire on the jeep with his .30 caliber machine gun, setting it ablaze. The jeep exploded. The next thing they knew, Lieutenant Bergheimer, who had recently returned to duty, came running out to their position claiming his men had committed murder. Slagle and Lawson were thrown into the stockade. They thought for certain that they would be shot in the morning. Shortly before daybreak, Sergeant Larson came over and let them out of the stockade. After inspection of the charred remains of the men in the jeep, they proved to be SS soldiers dressed in American uniforms. The jeep had exploded as it was filled with demolition equipment. Papers were recovered from one of the bodies with a map and orders to destroy a bridge that General Patton would cross in the days to come.

The Ambush

H Company's cooks were very busy in those early morning hours before sunrise. They were preparing a hot breakfast for the men and were already working on lunch: pork chops. The smell of the food cooking woke up many a hungry GI Just after first light on 18 January, the Germans began a counterattack to take the vital crossroads at Poteau. Many of the men of Second Battalion had not even woken up yet. From a wooded valley below Poteau, the Germans fired their 88s. Shells fell throughout the town, setting many of the buildings ablaze. A shell hit the German ammunition in the barn and it caught fire and exploded. Prater awoke when a tank shell hit the wooden shed he was sleeping in. "Red" Hayes, the Mortar Platoon's medic and Corporal Johnson took cover behind a wagon in the shed. Strong jumped into a water trough that looked like a coffin and Ross took cover too. A mortar shell came down through the roof and killed

Johnson, while the others ran out of the shed and took cover behind a stone wall. The shed caught fire and burned down. The 88 fire pinned down the men of Second Battalion and they could not flee the town without being killed. The men of H Company began moving into foxholes outside of the buildings in an attempt to return fire. A Tiger tank came up the hill within 100 yards and began firing on the buildings, causing more destruction. The tank had an artillery spotter directing its fire. The Mortar Platoon was positioned on the edge of town near the road and they setup their mortars to fire at a range of 100 yards in an attempt to hit the Tiger. Buildings throughout the town were on fire. Slagle and Lawson cautiously moved along the side of one of the buildings to try to make it to one of the foxholes, but they did not get very far. Slagle spotted a wounded GI from G Company, who had been carrying a bazooka. The Tiger was moving around one of the buildings and was closing in on their position. Lawson loaded a shell and Slagle made a dash out from the cover of a building with the bazooka. Slagle took aim on the Tiger, as it was firing on a nearby building. Slagle scored a direct hit on the turret, but it bounced off with no effect. Then, the turret slowly turned in Slagle's direction. He and Lawson dropped the bazooka and made a run for it and made it to a foxhole, just before the Tiger opened fire. H Company's Mortar Platoon hit the Tiger and disabled it, but another Tiger came up the hill from the valley below and moved into the town.

An American tank destroyer had come up in an attempt to challenge the Tiger that was marauding through town, but German artillery quickly took it out. The tank destroyer was hit near the Battalion Aid Station and it ignited a stockpile of ammunition. Lieutenant Colonel Drain quickly arrived and personally supervised the removal of the tank destroyer and then helped to move the wounded out of the Aid Station that was set ablaze. Artillery shells rained down on the Aid Station, and Drain ordered Lieutenant Carroll Lundeen, who had assumed command of E Company after Grand Halleux, to get some men together and move the wounded to another building. Lundeen ordered Ross, Strong, and others from the Mortar Platoon to help move the wounded to safety behind stone walls that were about a foot thick. The wounded were later evacuated to a building at the back of town that had not been hit. The Tiger continued its push into town, unchallenged. Smith and Lambert from Second Platoon made their way toward a foxhole. Smith got to cover and watched as Lambert got into another foxhole just as a shell came down nearby. Smith's Squad gathered together and tried to make it to better cover as heavy artillery continued to be directed at them. As they passed by, Smith found his good friend Lambert, dead in the foxhole. Wells was in another foxhole and watched an ammo bearer carrying mortar shells run down the street and an 88 shell landed right on top of him. Wells got out of his foxhole and could find no remnants of the man.

The Withdrawal

Orders came in from Lieutenant Colonel Drain for the men of each company to withdraw from the town and into the woods for cover. There, they were to regroup for a counterattack of their own. The 88s had a brief pause between shells, enough time to make a quick run for it. In pairs of two, the GIs would make a mad dash for the woods. When it was their turn, Strong and Ross from the Mortar Platoon of H Company ran north up a hill towards the woods. Just before they got there a shell landed directly between them: it bounced ahead of them and exploded. Strong and Ross separated and ran in different directions and both safely made it to the woods.

All the while during this shelling of town at the crossroads, the cooks were still in the kitchen on the second story of one of the buildings! As artillery ceased in their immediate location, Slagle and Lawson decided to move through town and see what happened to the cooks, they could still smell those pork chops cooking. The Tiger was occupied with blowing up other buildings and the 88 shells were directed to the edge of town, firing on a few machine guns that H Company had gotten up. When Slagle and Lawson got into the kitchen, they found Corporal Casper drinking a bottle of schnapps and busily cooking, the other cooks had already fled. Casper refused to leave his kitchen. The Tiger apparently did not notice activity in the building and did not fire on it. Slagle could see the Tiger moving along the street below, but no one had any anti-tank weapons. Casper who was looped from the bottle of schnapps also noticed the Tiger. He had just finished cooking the pork chops and he took a very big vat of hot pork grease over to the window and when the Tiger was directly under it, he poured the grease onto the ventilation slits of the Tiger; a terrible smell emanated from it. The Tiger came to an abrupt halt: either it was damaged or its crew was dead. Lawson who was starving quickly took some pork chops. He and Slagle grabbed Casper by the arm and got out of the building. They ran past the Tiger and there was no sounds at all coming from it. After the Tiger had been stopped, it made it easier to evacuate the town. Prater and the men of

119

his Section walked on the road that led south out of town and reunited with Strong and Ross at the far edge of the woods. The rest of H Company was there too. Artillery continued to fall onto the empty town.

The End of Poteau

That afternoon, elements of the 75th Division put fire on the German's flank that was south of Poteau. The Germans retreated and 144 prisoners were taken. At 2000 hours on 18 January, Third Battalion of the 517th Regiment of the 82nd Airborne Division relieved the Second Battalion of the 291st Regiment at Poteau. Greetings were exchanged between many of the men of both Regiments; a mutual feeling of respect was evident. The 291st had relieved the battered 517th at Salmchateaux a few days earlier, now the 517th was returning the favor. The next morning, Third Battalion of the 517th Regiment had a fierce battle with the Germans that made a second attempt to take back the vital Poteau crossroads. The conflict was costly, with the Germans committing more Tigers into the battle. However, the 517th was ready for them and were victorious; they captured or killed the remnants of the German force that was positioned in the valley below Poteau. After the battle, there was little left of the small town of Poteau; most of the buildings were destroyed or badly damaged.

The End of the Battle of the Bulge

"Our greatest enemy in the closing days of the Bulge was the extreme cold. Every morning I woke up and was thankful that I still had feeling in my feet."

- Sergeant "Willard," First Platoon, H Company

Into Vielsalm

After leaving Poteau in the hands of the 517th Regiment, the men of Second Battalion, 291st Infantry moved into Vielsalm with orders to clear the town of Germans. As they approached Vielsalm, the men of H Company found that the Germans had retreated from the town, but left behind landmines scattered throughout the town. One of the prisoners taken hours earlier at Poteau was the same man who had laid the mines and he agreed to lead the engineers to the locations of the mines. Two of the older men in the Company, Sergeant Larson and Staff Sergeant Byrnes from Second Platoon were tasked with overseeing the operation. Vielsalm was cleared out and made secure. By the late morning of 19 January, Division Headquarters had moved into Vielsalm and the German prisoners were moved there too. General Mickle sent a messenger to H Company to again request Slagle's detachment.

Handling German Prisoners

General Mickle had selected Slagle as one of the men tasked with hauling prisoners from Poteau into Vielsalm. They were marched in a long line through the snow with several guards carrying M-1s behind them. The Volksgrenadier troops were quite polite and offered no aggression to their captors. Some spoke passable English and they were bitter about the SS retreating and forcing the Volksgrenadiers to have to screen their retreat and take the brunt of the casualties. The Volksgrenadiers were primarily old men and teenagers. The SS were very different. Slagle was guarding several SS privates and a captain. The SS men would not cooperate at all and frequently cursed their American captors. The SS Captain spit on Slagle and refused to march any more. Slagle hit him with the butt of his rifle and the Captain fell face down in the snow. He stood up with a bloody mouth and continued the march. When they reached Vielsalm, the prisoners were put into a secure location and were heavily guarded. The SS officers were brought into a house in Vielsalm for interrogation. Slagle was one of the guards during the interrogation phase. The SS officers were very spry, they did not miss a thing. Many of them spoke some English and would try to sweet talk their captors into letting down their guard. One SS officer succeeded in this task and managed to knock over his guard and escape the house. Slagle heard the commotion from another room and shot the man in the back just as he exited the house. After this incident, more guards were brought into the house to keep watch over the cunning SS officers. Slagle was in a room with two very young SS officers, one a colonel and one a general. Despite their ranks, they were probably only in their late 20s. The General, in perfect English asked when he and his men would get their weapons back so they could help fight the Russians.

Coffee and Doughnuts

After Vielsalm was fully cleared, the Red Cross moved in and setup in one of the buildings. Men from H Company heard that the Red Cross had coffee and doughnuts and the men rushed over to get some. Snow covered the ground and it was still bitterly cold. When they arrived, the men discovered that the Red Cross was *selling* coffee and doughnuts, not giving them to the troops. Also, the prices were far from cheap at nearly a half-dollar for a cup of coffee and a doughnut. A few of the officers went into the Red Cross building, but the enlisted men passed on it. Another building in town had an organization called the Salvation Army that had just setup. They had coffee and doughnuts too, only they were *giving* them to the troops at no cost. Staff Sergeant Slawson led his men to the coffee. Many men from H Company congregated around the Salvation Army's building to receive cups of hot tea with honey and milk or coffee from the nice English girls who staffed the kitchen. The GIs were also invited into the Salvation Army's building to warm themselves. An old man was baking doughnuts and the GIs got them fresh and hot. The GIs were very thankful to get warmed up, if only for a short time. As Lawson was walking out of the building with his coffee, a truck came into town loaded down with supplies. Lawson heard a loud shout from the back of the truck, it was "Hay Seed" who had just returned from the Battalion Aid Station. He had a big grin on his face and was glad to see Lawson. "Hay Seed" was still bandaged up from his wounds at Grand Halleux, but he was desperate to get back to his buddies. "Hay Seed" jumped off the truck and was welcomed back to his Squad.

A POW Incident

In Vielsalm, a rifle platoon from Second Battalion brought in a few prisoners; they were all SS men. Most of them were officers and were quite verbal about being held captive. Lawson, Cohen, "Hay Seed," and Staff Sergeant Slawson were standing beside a building as the prisoners arrived. A sergeant from the rifle platoon asked Slawson if he would tend to the prisoners and see that they were taken to the Battalion Command Post. It was early afternoon and Slawson had orders of his own. Slawson asked for volunteers to escort the prisoners. Cohen immediately volunteered. Slawson told Cohen, "They are to be kept alive for questioning, see that they all make it to Battalion." Lawson and "Hay Seed" stood near a building, trying to keep warm. One of the prisoners mumbled "Juden, Juden!" They identified Cohen as a Jew and started to mock him in German. Cohen, who could speak some German, shouted at them, but they continued to laugh. Lawson walked over and they shut up. Cohen did as ordered and marched the eight prisoners to Battalion. A half-hour later, Cohen returned with only two prisoners. Lawson asked what happened and Cohen said, "Nothing at all." Lawson persisted, "Where are the others?"

Cohen had pockets full of "loot" he picked off the SS prisoners. The two remaining prisoners were visibly terrified. One man got on his knees in front of Lawson. Both men had bloody mouths. As they were standing there, Staff Sergeant Slawson returned and demanded to know what had happened. No one said a word. Slawson repeated the question and Lawson replied, "They tried to escape and were shot." The story did not quite sit well with Slawson. He stared at Cohen and noticed his bulging pockets. Slawson did not accuse Cohen of anything, but he asked to see Cohen's rifle. He removed the ammo, except for two bullets and asked for all other ammo he had. Slawson said, "Son, none of us like the SS. Follow your orders." Slawson was a calm and understanding man, he was not hard to get along with. Slawson chose "Hay Seed" to escort the prisoners and he glanced at Cohen one more time before leaving; not a word was spoken. As soon as Slawson was gone, Cohen erupted in a tirade of swearing. He told Lawson, "They were SS! I shot them!" Cohen was very emotional and was acting irrational. Cohen threw down his rifle and got onto his knees. Lawson said, "I probably would have done the same thing." Cohen got up, looked Lawson in the eyes and said, "You might have, but not for the reasons I did."

Clear Skies

Days after taking Vielsalm, the skies finally cleared and the sun came out. The Allied Air Forces, who had been grounded for weeks, quickly took advantage of the situation. P-47 fighter-bombers of the US Air Force and Typhoons of the RAF wrecked havoc on the retreating Panzers. With little cover to be had, the Panzers became easy prey. General Mickle, his driver, and Slagle stood on a hillside above the town of Kesternick, watching formations of aircraft swooping down on the retreating Germans. Fires and smoke arose from seemingly everywhere as Hitler's once mighty SS Panzer Divisions were decimated. The tide of battle had turned decisively in the Allies' favor. The German's westward push, the great "Bulge" in the Ardennes was no more. The 75th Division had contributed their fair share and more to the outcome of this battle.

Threats from Above

In the closing days of combat in the Ardennes, the Germans sent up a few surprises. Some of the men of H Company saw what looked to them as a "missile with a man in it," flying very fast overhead. These aircraft, seen from a profile view, were Arado 234 jet bombers, out on reconnaissance missions. One afternoon, Slagle was digging a foxhole as one flew high overhead as American P-38s and P-47s chased it. The jet bomber blew out black smoke from its twin engines and sped off every time the American fighters got near it. A more menacing threat was the Messerschmitt 262 jet fighter that was often used to strafe troop positions and armored vehicles. One evening, just before dinner in the closing days of battle and well behind the front, Slagle and Lawson were manning the radio at the Company Command Post when a messenger arrived with orders for Slagle to immediately report to the Division Command Post, not too far away. Slagle went to get a replacement guard then walked to the Division Command Post. Lawson was also relieved. Along the way, Slagle passed one of his old friends from the Division Band who was carrying his clarinet and Slagle stopped him to ask about his friends in the Band and if they had played recently; they had a nice reunion. Slagle spent a little more time than he probably should have fraternizing with his buddy in the Band. Moments before Slagle returned to H Company, he discovered that an Me-262 had bombed the Company Command Post, where he had been. The guards that replaced Slagle and Lawson were killed. Music had saved his life, as Slagle told his Squad buddies that night.

Trench Fever

The men of H Company had been living out in the elements in the dead of winter for about a month with very little relief. Many of the men became ill. Colds, sore throats, and fevers became common place. The platoon medics would take those very ill to the Battalion Aid Station. These non-battle casualties continued to mount. Many of the men of H Company began to come down with a sickness worse than the common cold: Typhus or "Trench Fever." When Slagle returned to H Company from his duty with the Deputy Division Commander, he slept in the foxholes with his Squad buddies. Slagle felt tired and started to get ill. One morning he could not crawl out of his foxhole at all. One of his buddies pulled him out and took him to the Battalion Aid Station. Slagle was put in a bed under cover of a tent. The temperature was very cold and the sounds of artillery could be heard all around, signaling another advance by the 75th Division. Slagle had a high fever and was too sick even to sit up in bed. He clung to life, battling what was diagnosed as Typhus. Slagle went in and out of consciousness and overheard two medics making a bet over whether or not he would live. Several days later, Slagle awoke and felt better; his fever had broken. The first thing he saw when he awoke was a young nurse; the same one who had invited him to her parent's home for dinner in Evansville, Indiana back in the summer. Slagle said, "Either I am in Heaven or I am in the Aid Station." The nurse confirmed that he was indeed in the Aid Station. Slagle spent a few more days in the Aid Station being well looked after. Slagle then returned back to his Squad, after the end of combat in the Ardennes.

Hygiene

Living out in the elements for a month was a challenge even under ideal climate conditions, but doing so in the dead of winter was even more challenging. The men who had experience in the outdoors had a leg up on the city boys. The farm boys frequently knew how to take care of themselves. The men of H Company were quite dirty after spending a month in the field with only one shower back in early January. The mortar men's hands and faces were black from gunpowder. Yet, it was so cold that there was little perspiration. At 18 years of age or just a bit more, a lot of the GIs paid little attention to such things as hygiene and they had more important things to be concerned with. The men learned that to keep their feet free from frostbite, they had to change their socks. If he thought he had frost bitten feet, the GI was instructed to massage his feet to give them some warmth. Sitting too long was also a danger as poor circulation sped up frostbite to hands and feet.

Into St. Vith

As combat in the Ardennes came to an end, the men of Second Battalion, 291st Infantry moved on to St. Vith where they were able to take showers and get clean clothes. The men moved through town in troop trucks and there was a long line of traffic moving through the small country roads that were covered in snow. Slagle, Lawson, and "Hay Seed" were crowded together in the back of one of the trucks with the rest of their buddies. Slagle smelled fresh baked bread and they saw smoke coming from the second story of a building near the road. Slagle shouted to the cook who was looking at them from his kitchen window. Slagle held up a pack of cigarettes and without so much as a word exchanged, a trade was made. Slagle fixed his bayonet to his Garand, put the pack of cigarettes onto it and raised it up to the window. The cook took the cigarettes and attached a big, fresh loaf of bread to the end of the bayonet. Slagle broke off a piece of bread and passed it along to his buddies in the truck. When the men of H Company finally arrived to their assembly area, a hot water tank was setup and each GI took a quick hot shower and clean clothes were waiting for them when done. Lieutenant Smith, who temporarily took command of the Mortar Platoon, drove up and down the road in his jeep hollering at the GIs. The men of H Company spent a few days in a reserve area near St. Vith. They were located in an open area near to some woods and a few buildings, at the edge of town. The men finally got a chance to have some hot meals.

The "Bulge Busters"

From 19 to 24 January E, G, and H Companies were in Division reserve. They were near the front and still had guard duty and were living in foxholes, but they did not see combat. F Company was the only unit of Second Battalion to see combat in those last remaining days in the Belgian Ardennes as they had taken few casualties at Grand Halleux and could still function at near full strength. F Company was assigned to Third Battalion and L Company, that had also taken heavy casualties, was sent to Second Battalion in exchange. H Company had taken part in stopping the German advance across the Ouerthe River on 26 and 27 December, they had been through the terrible advance at Grand Halleux on 15 January, and a second unplanned engagement at the crossroads town of Poteau on the 18th. H Company was down to less than half strength. The remaining men were just trying to keep themselves warm and were thankful to be alive. By 24 January, the Battle of the Bulge had come to an end. About 600,000 American soldiers had pushed back the advance of over 500,000 Germans. Thus, had been the largest battle ever fought by American soldiers. Hitler's last gamble, his last great offensive had come to an end. In a month, the 75th Division was transformed from a green Division of kids into a veteran Division of men. The 75th Division had lost its moniker of "Diaper Division" and earned itself a new one: "Bulge Busters." The men of H Company had each earned their Combat Infantryman's Badges and their first Battle Star.

Unlikely Heroes

While history is not always kind to its heroes, it often is the result of historians failing to review all available materials. On 27 December, Second Battalion of the 291st Regiment had stood face to face with the focal point of the German westward "Bulge" and somehow stopped it. On that day, Second Battalion was the extreme end of the Allied line in that sector; there were no reserves. Many young boys became men during the fierce battle along the Ouerthe River. While the green troops of the 75th Division did not defeat the enemy during their first engagement, they desperately held their ground against overwhelming odds. They should have withdrawn, but they did not and this engagement played a significant role in the Allied victory that followed. Second Battalion was but one unit of the 75th Division that bravely battled the veteran soldiers of the German Army during those desperate days in the frigid Belgian Ardennes. While the men of the 75th Division might have been young and green going into their first combat, their actions proved to be nothing short of heroic.

Replacements and Promotions

On 23 January, H Company received its first few, much-needed replacements. One of these men was Private Galbreth who joined First Section of First Platoon to replace one of the ammo bearers who had left due to trench foot. A young man from Alabama arrived and also joined First Squad. He and Lawson had much in common and they instantly became friends. Also, Private Sotir joined Chisholm's Squad in Second Platoon as a replacement ammo bearer. Private George Bozovich arrived to First Squad of the Mortar Platoon as a replacement ammo bearer. Corporal Casper was promoted to Staff Sergeant and head cook. He was the man who had poured the vat of hot pork grease on the Tiger in Poteau. PFC Prater was promoted to Corporal to replace Johnson who was killed at Poteau. Many of the men of H Company were written up for medals by the men in their squads for their bravery during the Battle of the Bulge. Lieutenant Bergheimer wrote himself up for the Bronze Star for his so called participation at Grand Halleux. When First Lieutenant Goodnight returned, he revoked Bergheimer's Bronze Star and instead issued a Bronze Star to the young private that had braved machine gun fire to save Bergheimer's life: most of the men in First Platoon had written the young man up for it. First Lieutenant William Craig of Second Platoon received the Silver Star for his actions at Grand Halleux. Private Luther Mason, the ammo bearer who had crossed 500 yards of open ground at Grand Halleux (three times) to supply the Mortar Platoon with more ammunition, received the Silver Star. For his acts of bravery and selflessness in pulling his wounded Platoon buddies off the line at Grand Halleux, "Hay Seed" was awarded the Bronze Star. He also received the Purple Heart during his stay in the Battalion Aid Station. Staff Sergeant Slawson was also awarded the Bronze Star for holding together his Platoon on the Ouerthe River. Many other men in H Company were written up for Bronze Stars and those wounded in combat were given the Purple Heart.

A New General

On 16 January, Major General Faye B. Prickett, the Commanding General of the 75th Infantry Division was relieved of his command and replaced by Major General Ray E. Porter. The XVIII Corps Commander, General Ridgeway met with the commanders of several divisions that day. Ridgeway took notice of the casualties suffered by the 75th Division, with an emphasis on what went wrong at Grand Halleux. Ridgeway asked Prickett if he could do anything to help the 75th Division: Prickett said, "Just pray for me." After the meeting, Ridgeway took Prickett aside and told him that such a comment was damaging to morale. There was no excuse for it. The comment, coupled with Prickett's disastrous handling of his troops at Grand Halleux, cost him his command. Prickett was relieved on the spot and replaced with a more capable strategist in General Porter. The men of H Company were all glad to have a new Commanding General.

The Colmar Pocket

"The Colmar Pocket was worse than anything I went through in the Bulge, it was like the end of the world! We lost a lot of good men there."

- S. Phillip Lawson, First Platoon, H Company

No Rest for the 75th

On 25 January, the 75th Division was supposed to receive a period of rest after a very tough month of combat. However, the proposed rest was not to happen. On the afternoon of 26 January, H Company and the rest of the three infantry regiments of the 75th Division, boarded trains in Pepinster, Belgium bound for Luneville, France. The French First Army had been trying to push the Germans out of a region called Colmar, near Alsace, since September 1944. The area was very significant to the French, as it had long been a disputed territory between the French and Germans. The war had only further aggravated the dispute over this territory. The French were unsuccessful in their attempts to liberate Colmar and the US Army 75th Division was one of the units sent to support the French under the command of General Le Clerc. The two day long train ride was just miserable. The same "40 and 8" rail cars that had carried the men of H Company to the front in Belgium now were transporting them to a new combat area. There were not enough cars available and the men had to really stuff themselves aboard. The trains were so crowded that one could not move at all. Some men had to stand up, while others sat down on the bare floor. After sitting for such a long time, one could only stretch his legs by swapping positions with one of the men standing up. The conditions were so cramped that is was impossible even for one to try to light a cigarette; everyone just had to stay in their spot and wait for the trip to be over. H Company's Headquarters Platoon made this journey by truck. Wells as a messenger, was one of the men in the truck. There were about forty men in the truck and conditions were quite cramped in it too. The motor movement began at 0800 on 27 January, starting near Vielsalm and moved north of Trois

Ponts, south through Hotton, Marche, and Rochefort where H Company had met the tip of the German "Bulge" a month earlier. They moved through Sedan, France and saw the Maginot Line, Verdun, and St. Mihiel.

Preparing for Combat

The 75th Division regrouped as a unit in the assembly area of St. Mihiel at 1500 on 28 January. Under blackout conditions, they then moved by motor through Nancy, Luneville, St. Die, and across the Vosges Mountains to the town of Ribeauville, in the province of Alsace. The movement through the high Vosges Mountains was very difficult with heavy snow, icy roads, and more bitter cold that the men of the 75th Division had already become intimately familiar with in the Ardennes. The Division Command Post opened up at 0300 hours in Ribeauville. German mortar shells landed within fifty yards of the Command Post that morning. The 75th Division's second battle was about to begin. The 75th Division was to relieve the 3rd Infantry Division and their mission was to liberate a series of towns in the Colmar Pocket and to prevent the Germans from crossing the L'Ill River. The 289th and 291st Regiments were to lead the attack with the 290th Regiment in reserve. The 75th Division relieved the 3rd Division near Fortschwihr at 2330 on 31 January. The first duty of the 75th Division was to clear the Germans out of the town of Wihr-En-Plain on 1 February.

Actions of the 291st Infantry in the Colmar Pocket

The 291st Regiment assembled in the woods outside of Weidwihr on 30 January in preparation for an attack to the south on Fortschwihr, a heavily fortified town. The Germans had excellent cover in Fortschwihr and had plenty of heavy caliber weapons to defend themselves with. On 1 February, the 291st Regiment relieved elements of the 3rd Division. First and Second Battalions began a coordinated attack on Fortschwihr in the direction of the Rhine. Beyond Fortschwihr was the ancient walled city of Neuf Brisach that commanded the last remaining escape route for the Germans across the Rhine. The 291st Regiment took a very heavy shelling from the determined German defenders. The Germans committed everything they had to halt the 291st Infantry's advance and heavily shelled the 291st from their seemingly impregnable fortress of Neuf Brisach. First and Second Battalions pushed through the Colmar Forest on 1 and 2 February and attempted to attack Wolfgantzen on 3 February, when a German counterattack pushed them back. First and Second Battalions withdrew, circled back through the forest and made it to high ground above Wolfgantzen. First Battalion then seized Wolfgantzen on 4 February with a well planned attack and the battered up First and Second Battalions of the 291st Regiment then rested, while other elements of the 75th Division went on to seize the fortress of Neuf Brisach and thus, swept the last remaining Germans off of French soil.

Losing an Officer

In a wooded area on 31 January, H Company had been setup, preparing to move out towards Fortschwihr. Second Battalion was well behind the front lines at this time, but none the less was receiving sporadic artillery fire. First Lieutenant Craig, commanding Second Platoon of H Company had moved up. Craig had found a brightly colored walking stick and a top hat at some point while moving up to the Colmar area. Lieutenant Craig liked the walking stick and was strutting around with it. Craig was a good commander and a likable man, but he had a tendency to show off; he was somewhat vain. He had discarded his helmet in favor of the top hat, as H Company was not in front line combat. Many men in Second Platoon tried to persuade Craig to get rid of his hat and stick, but he would not. Artillery began to come in and Craig was caught out in the open in the middle of it. He was still wearing the top hat and strutting around with his walking stick. The bright color of the stick only helped to point out a target for the Germans to fire upon. As artillery came in Craig was strutting about with the stick, moving about almost as if he were trying to dodge the incoming shells. Lieutenant Craig was killed that day; his prized walking stick had cost him his life.

H Company's New Commander

When Captain Haddock was wounded at Grand Halleux on 15 January, command of H Company fell upon his Executive Officer, First Lieutenant Goodnight. However, Goodnight was also out of action due to appendicitis. First Lieutenant Maxwell was the acting Company Commander. On 31 January, a jeep pulled up near to the area where H Company was loosely organized in the woods. The men were in a sullen mood. However, this changed when Lieutenant Goodnight emerged from the jeep. Goodnight had recovered and returned to serve as H Company's new commander. The men were overjoyed to have him back. Goodnight was a draftee like most of the others in H Company and he understood their situation and they identified with him. Goodnight was very much a regular guy; he was approachable and friendly. If a man in the Company needed to talk to him, Goodnight was there for him. Goodnight was soft spoken, which was unusual for a man of his size. He was six foot tall and well over 200 pounds. He was an All-American football player in college and played Pro ball for a season for the old St. Louis Rams before being drafted into the Army. H Company's new commander was respected, liked; some might even say beloved by his men. Beyond the respect he was granted by his men, Goodnight was a very capable leader and had a sharp mind for split second decisions on the front line. Lieutenant Colonel Drain arrived to promote Goodnight to the rank of Captain on 31 January, on the evening before H Company was to go into action.

Long Awaited Equipment

The men of H Company were awakened at about 0200 hours by a truck that arrived, carrying crates of supplies. The men of H Company finally got their winter clothing that they lacked in the Bulge; they did not need it now. They received sweaters, a winter jacket, gloves, and boots; everything they needed in the Bulge, but did not have. They also received their weapons that they had lacked in the Bulge. Slagle got his personal M-1 Garand back; he had spent a lot of time getting it calibrated just to his liking and was glad to have it back. The weather was warming up rapidly. The ground was covered with about a foot of melting snow and the terrain was a sloppy mess and slow to trudge through. You could walk across a snow-covered field, only to sink down to the top of your boots. It was even more difficult to run through it.

Scouting Ahead

Before daylight on 1 February, Wells was scouting ahead of the Company. He left the cover of the woods where H Company had slept during the night. He discovered an open top bunker that faced Second Battalion's line of attack. Wells had a clear view of where to setup the machine guns. He was inside the bunker along the wall, nearest to the German position, looking toward them. As Wells was in the bunker, the Germans began their attack. Tiger tanks fired on Second Battalion and German mortar men went into action. A heavy artillery barrage was directed at the Americans. One of the mortar shells landed in the bunker with Wells, just behind him. The force of the explosion threw Wells into the wall of the bunker and knocked his helmet off. By the time Wells was able to get back to his feet and put his helmet back on, the shelling was slowing down. Wells quickly got out of the bunker and one of his buddies yelled, "Willie, you are on fire!" Wells said he could run fast, but not that fast. Another of his buddies again yelled that Wells was on fire. Wells took cover in the crater from a shell to check himself. Dempsey, Second Platoon's medic was alerted to Wells being wounded and he jumped into the hole and told Wells to get out of his overcoat. The back of his coat was full of holes and smoking. Dempsey started cutting through his clothes and found a hole in his left hip that went all the way through his body. Wells also had a hole through his left arm. Dempsey gave him sulfa pills and wrapped his wounds in bandages. Between the shells, Wells was carried to the Battalion Aid Station, setup in a bunker just behind the front line.

Wells' Departure from H Company

Wells was seriously wounded and due to the shelling, he could not be moved out of the Battalion Aid Station until nightfall. Wells was not bleeding too badly, as the hot steel shrapnel seemed to have cauterized his wounds. The only pain Wells felt was an area on his back near his hip wound. Dempsey removed a piece of shrapnel about the size of a half-dollar from there. Dempsey offered Wells morphine, but he refused it; Wells did not hurt too badly. He was wrapped in blankets that kept him somewhat warm. He could hear the constant artillery bombardment outside the Aid Station. After dark, Wells was placed on a litter and put on the hood of a jeep to be evacuated to another aid station further to the rear. Before they got far, the jeep carrying Wells passed a jeep with Sergeant Castanaga and they stopped. Wells told Castanaga he got a "million dollar" wound and was going home. When Wells arrived at the rear aid station, he was looked over again, his bandages changed and he was given more sulfa pills. Without asking, they shot him up with morphine, loaded him into an ambulance and sent him on his way to the Second General Hospital in Nancy, France, about three hours away. The ambulance was full of wounded and Wells passed out from the morphine. He awoke in the hospital and was taken off the litter and put onto a gurney with wheels in a long hallway, waiting in a line for surgery. Someone pushed Wells into one of the surgery rooms; it was full of wounded.

134

The Andolsheim Canal Crossing

After incurring several hours of heavy German artillery fire, and taking many casualties, Second Battalion, 291st Infantry began their attack at 0700 hours toward the Andolsheim-Neuf Brisach road, just as the 289th Infantry began their attack. The first obstacle was to cross the Andolsheim Canal. The Germans were in command of the town of Fortschwihr on the opposite side of the canal. The 75th Division's artillery had targeted Fortschwihr to soften up its defenses. H Company was given orders to support Second Battalion's advance with its mortars and machine guns. Staff Sergeant Slawson's First Section of First Platoon, was moving directly behind one of the lead rifle platoons in the attack, when they began to take heavy fire from the edge of town. Slawson ordered his Section to quickly rush across the canal. Mortar fire began to hit the area. A few of the riflemen were wounded during the shelling. The situation was becoming desperate. German machine guns opened up and snipers fired on the advance. Second Squad of First Platoon, led by Sergeant Larson was taking heavy sniper fire. Larson ordered his men to take cover behind a high stone wall. Slawson was ahead of their position, trying to help First Squad to get their gun into position to fire. The Germans spotted Slawson and opened fire on him. Slawson tripped in a rut on the road and injured his leg. "Hay Seed" saw his Section Leader go down and he was quick to take action.

"Hay Seed" left the cover where Larson's Squad was held up and ran through the open street. Lawson and Murza shouted for him to stay put, but "Hay Seed" did not listen. He ran through the street, incurring sniper fire, and stopped briefly to fire a few shots at a German machine gun nest on the second story of a house. While still in the open of the street, he threw a grenade into a house, killed the sniper hidden inside, and proceeded to Slawson's position. With Slawson across his back, "Hay Seed" made it to cover on the other side of the street. Slawson was not wounded, he had just twisted his ankle. The riflemen began to return fire on the Germans in town. A bazooka man took out a German machine gun that was holding up the advance and more Second Battalion troops crossed the canal. The Germans in town began to withdraw, but not without a fight.

Casualties on the Canal

As more riflemen were crossing the canal, Staff Sergeant Clarence Carroll's Second Section of First Platoon of H Company was preparing to cross the canal with their equipment. Carroll and "Kirk" had been very close friends since the summer of 1944. Carroll was a good leader and very well respected by his men. He was probably one of the most mature young men in the Company. As Carroll's Section prepared to cross, the German fire was beginning to slow down. One of the young replacements that had arrived to Carroll's Section the night before, was shot through the arm as he was crossing the canal. Carroll heard the shot and ran back across the canal to help the man. "Kirk" was in cover with Larson's Squad, when he turned to see what was happening. Carroll was trying to help the wounded young replacement to his feet, when a sniper shot Staff Sergeant Carroll in the neck. "Kirk" ran back across the canal and a few snipers took shots at him, almost hitting his feet. "Kirk" tried to help Carroll, but he was already dead. "Kirk" stood overtop of his dead friend, as if time had just stopped for him. Only due to shouts from his Squad, did he snap out of it. "Kirk" picked up the wounded replacement and took him back to safety. A few minutes later, "Kirk" crossed the canal again with several riflemen. When he returned to his Squad, "Kirk" was a very determined man; he was not the same after seeing his friend killed.

Snipers in Fortschwihr

As Larson's Squad was setting up their machine gun below a small incline and near to a thick stone wall, they discovered that a house on the opposite side of the street had German troops inside. Slagle and Lawson cautiously moved up to the front door. Murza and "Hay Seed" went toward the side window. Slagle kicked in the door and Lawson opened fire with his Garand on two German snipers who were caught reloading their weapons. The house was cleared and Larson entered and immediately ran upstairs. Through a window on the second story of the house, he spotted several other German snipers further in town. Slagle and Larson spotted German troops carrying a machine gun into a building further in town. Sergeant Larson ordered Slagle to find Captain Goodnight and report the positions of these snipers. By the time Slagle got out of the house, many more riflemen had crossed the canal and the sniper fire in the area of the canal had been silenced. Slagle found his Captain and made his report. There were no messengers available and radio communication had been lost with Battalion. Goodnight ordered Slagle to deliver his message to the Battalion Commander in person. While the 291st Regiment was attacking Fortschwihr, the 289th Infantry took the crossroads town of Andolsheim and proceeded to Appenwihr.

Worse than the Bulge!

By the night of 1 February, Second Battalion had taken Fortschwihr and they had little time for sleep that night. By dawn, Second Battalion began to take heavy artillery fire. The Battalion advanced through the shelling until 1400 hours when the Germans began a major counterattack supported by three Tiger tanks that moved up and fired into the rifle companies. The French First Army had a number of tanks available, but instead of committing a platoon of tanks to challenge the Tigers, they sent in one tank at a time; each one was quickly taken out. Sergeant Larson tried to move his Squad to cover to return fire, but they did not get far. H Company's machine gun platoons were pinned down, but had some measure of cover. The ground had some snow on top, but it was melting and it was possible to dig foxholes. Shells continued to pour down on H Company's machine gun platoons. It was far worse than anything they had seen in the Bulge.

Lieutenant Bergheimer ordered his Platoon to get their machine guns setup and into action. Lawson and Slagle tried to get their gun up, but heavy machine gun fire forced them to withdraw back to their foxholes. The GIs trapped in the foxholes could hear nothing but loud explosions, shells coming in, and heavy enemy fire. It was so loud that one could not hear the words of a man sharing the same foxhole. It was not even possible to raise one's head out of their foxhole for more than a brief few seconds. Bergheimer shouted more orders, then retreated in his jeep to the rear. As usual, Staff Sergeant Slawson assumed command. Lawson was in a foxhole with Slagle when a number of shells came in close. One shell landed dead in front of their foxhole and a huge burst of debris blew on top of them. Seconds later Slawson dove into the foxhole and said in his calm voice, "Is anyone hurt?" They were fine and Slawson quickly left the foxhole shouting, "Keep your heads down!"

Explosions were everywhere. Trees exploded with branches flying through the air in every direction. More shells landed very close to the foxholes and kicked up debris atop of many of the men taking cover. The artillery barrage was so thunderous and for the men trapped in foxholes in the midst of it, it was like the world was coming to an end. Some shells hit foxholes and killed or wounded its occupants. A shell came in and blew up one of First Platoon's jeeps. A shell hit a tree and the burst wounded PFC Gordon Woody from the Mortar Platoon. First Sergeant Whalen was there and he yelled for a medic. Ross was nearby and he tried to help Woody. Whalen said, "Get out of the way, get a regular medic." Woody had a shrapnel wound to the thigh, but it was not life threatening. Shrapnel from the shells flew everywhere, with some pieces clanging off of helmets. Late in the afternoon, the shelling began to slow down and the machine gun platoons went into action. A bazooka man from one of the rifle companies scored a direct hit on one of the Tigers and halted it. The riflemen of Second Battalion attacked the German position and were supported by H Company's mortars and machine guns. The infantrymen moved very fast and many of the Germans dropped their equipment and fled. The German counter-attack was repulsed. The fighting had been far more fast paced and intense than anything H Company had been through in the Bulge.

The Colmar Forest

By the afternoon of 2 February, H Company organized its squads and tended to its wounded and began to advance through the Colmar Forest that was full of dense cover for German infantry and machine gun nests. First Section of First Platoon moved rapidly, but was later halted by heavy fire coming from some brush directly ahead. A few men were wounded by sniper fire and First Section took cover. An 88 gun had zeroed in on their position and was firing point blank into them. Staff Sergeant Slawson, commanding First Section paid close attention to the timing between shells and told his squads to prepare to run straight toward the German position in pairs of two, between shells. A few Germans held a small hillside and directly below it was a measure of good cover. Second Section of First Platoon arrived and its staff sergeant, a newly arrived replacement who took over for Carroll, disagreed with Slawson. He instead ordered his squads to setup their machine guns and return fire. Sergeant "Willard," commanding Third Squad protested the order. The guns were setup and they immediately attracted German rifle and machine gun fire. The gunners had cover, but were running low on ammunition and the ammo bearers could not get to them.

Slagle was pinned down with Lawson and could not make it to his gun. "Hay Seed" took a big chance by braving enemy fire to setup their machine gun and he fired until he was out of ammunition. The irate Staff Sergeant of Second Section ordered an ammo bearer to carry ammunition to the setup guns. Within seconds of leaving cover, the ammo bearer was cut down by machine gun fire. The Staff Sergeant then ordered Slagle, one of the only men in his immediate area, to carry the ammunition. Slagle hesitated just for a second and a shell landed right on top of the Staff Sergeant. Slawson then took command of the Platoon and continued with his original plan. In pairs of two, the ammo bearers and others ran forward, just below the German position. They all made it. The last pair to make the run were Lawson and Slagle. Lawson was very shaken up and said to Slagle, "Are you sure we should do it?" Seconds later, they got up and ran for cover; they dove flat on the ground, just as an 88 shell hit the position they had just left. Had they waited a few seconds longer, they would have been killed. "Hay Seed" picked off the Germans above their position with his M-1 Garand. First Section continued its advance after suffering several casualties, including one dead staff sergeant.

Concerns

Sergeant "Willard" organized his Squad and prepared to move out. Cohen of First Squad and Lawson of Second Squad were talking. "Willard" said, "I have a bad feeling about this, I think we are going to be in for a tough day." Cohen was unusually silent. "Willard" took command of Second Section after his Staff Sergeant's death. Instead of feeling confident, "Willard" seemed indifferent. He usually was talkative and friendly. Staff Sergeant Slawson patted him on the back. They had been good friends since the days of Camp Breckinridge. Slawson was very quiet and serious as was "Willard;" they seemed to many of the others in the Platoon to be a lot alike. While Lawson stood by Slawson, Cohen, and "Hay Seed," "Willard" said, "What happened to our Lieutenant?" No one had seen Bergheimer since combat began. As they were talking, Bergheimer arrived by jeep and wanted to know the situation and about the casualties. Slawson asked Bergheimer where he had been. Bergheimer ignored the question and seemed satisfied with the situation. Slawson shrugged his shoulders after Bergheimer was out of view.

Murza from Second Squad said, "Our Lieutenant is going to get us all killed." The others all seemed to agree. Many of the men of First Platoon looked upon Staff Sergeant Slawson as their leader, even if he was not an officer.

Ambush in the Forest

That same afternoon, First Section of First Platoon was again ambushed. Heavy fire came from a position in the dense tree line. This time, they were able to setup their guns. A fire fight began and lasted until Second Section was able to move in and get setup. The conflict appeared to be a stalemate, with neither First Platoon nor the Germans willing to commit any risky action. First Platoon had sufficient cover that is until the Germans brought up what may have been a self-propelled gun. The heavy shell hit Fourth Squad point blank and killed them all. Lieutenant Bergheimer went back to request reinforcements. The next shell hit just in front of Third Squad's position, inflicting shrapnel wounds to many in the Squad. Two of the four machine guns were out of action. Sergeant Larson and Murza ran to one of the disabled guns and started firing into the German position. One of Slagle's ammo bearers was hit by shrapnel and it took his head clean off. The body continued running forward for a moment, until it collapsed. One of the men in First Squad screamed and was out of his head: he ran away and no one saw him again. Another shell came down right near Slagle's position and he and Lawson were momentarily deaf from the explosion. Debris flew everywhere and Slagle and the remnants of his crew stood up. He looked around and almost everyone was dead or seriously wounded. "Hay Seed" ran to Sergeant Larson's position and found him to be fine. Slagle snapped. He fired his machine gun into the German position, continuing until the ammunition was expended and the gun was too hot to handle. Smoke came up from the German position; something was hit and caught fire, likely the ammunition supply. The shelling stopped and there was dead silence; it was a surreal moment. There were no sounds at all from the German position and their guns were silent. Slagle looked around and saw so many of his buddies lying dead all around him.

Many of the men of First Platoon that were able-bodied got up and helped the wounded out of the area and to the rear. Some men were in shock and could do nothing. Cohen, who usually had a comment for every situation or a crude joke had nothing to say; he helped the wounded as best he could. Lawson's friend, the young replacement from Alabama had taken a direct hit to the face with shrapnel; most of his face was blown away, and he was wailing in pain. The sight of his mortally wounded friend left Lawson in a complete state of shock. Larson and Galbreth took another wounded man to the rear and Slagle, Lawson, and "Hay Seed" were the only three still standing there. Moments later, two SS soldiers emerged from the tree line, apparently thinking all the Americans to be dead. Slagle and his buddies took cover and stayed silent. The Germans began souvenir hunting among the American dead. In a moment of rage, "Hay Seed" fixed his bayonet to his Garand and leaped out from cover. Within seconds, "Hay Seed" had hit one of the SS soldiers in the face with his bayonet and as the second man reached for a pistol, "Hay Seed" impaled him. Lawson was in complete shock from the events that afternoon and stood staring at "Hay Seed" as he butchered the two SS men. Moments later, Slagle heard tanks coming close through the brush ahead. The three of them ran as fast as they could go out of the area.

A Terrifying Time

Slagle, Lawson, and "Hay Seed" ran in the direction where they had thought the survivors of First Platoon had gone. Somehow, they got lost and found themselves completely isolated, with Germans closing in from seemingly every direction. They were sure they would be killed or captured. Slagle urged them to lay flat on the ground and remain motionless. A patrol of Germans moved within a few yards of their position and did not see them. A jeep with German troops also moved through. In the far off distance, they saw an armored column moving up. Slagle led his buddies through the woods, very cautiously. Everywhere they moved they could hear voices and movement in the brush. They almost walked right into a German patrol, but managed to stay unnoticed. They found a small clearing inside the forest and ran through it. They were exhausted from running and stumbled upon two soldiers doing their business; they were H Company men! The men were from Headquarters Platoon and immediately recognized Slagle. They were taken a short distance to where Headquarters Platoon and the remnants of First Platoon were resting; evening was quickly approaching. Slagle reported what they had been through that afternoon to Captain Goodnight. The situation had become very disordered that afternoon and several platoons of riflemen from Second Battalion had become lost from their units and attached themselves to H Company. That night, the men of H Company slept in foxholes and were prepared for another confrontation in the morning.

Good Leadership

Shortly after sunrise on 3 February, Captain Goodnight was in the passenger seat of his jeep, going over a map when he heard vehicles moving not far away. Goodnight got out of the jeep, looked through his binoculars, and saw a number of German half-tracks and Tigers in a long column, moving toward the general direction of Second Battalion. He ordered his driver and the other jeeps in their group to move back and bring word to the rest of Second Battalion that the Germans were going to surprise them with a large convoy. First Platoon's machine guns were put aboard one of the jeeps. The situation was tense and the men were very concerned. Goodnight called all the men together for a pep talk. He told the men that they had to stop this armored column or at least slow it down temporarily; they had no anti-tank weapons. What Goodnight had were about 200 men with rifles: some were Garands and some were Carbines. All the men, including Goodnight, knelt down in the cover of the tree line, well hidden from the half-tracks that were coming up the road. Goodnight told them to aim at the driver's side door of the first half-track as it moved past them. As the lead half-track approached, Goodnight gave the command to fire; 200 M-1s opened fire at the same time. The half-track's driver must have received quite a surprise as the vehicle took a sharp turn off the road and drove straight into a tree and caught fire. Goodnight gave the command to fire on the second half-track and it swerved and hit the first one. The road was very narrow, really unsuitable for moving armor. Now it was blocked altogether with a burning half-track. German infantry support began to come up and Goodnight ordered a swift retreat. The 200 or so men all made it safely back into the cover of the forest; no one was wounded. Captain Goodnight's quick thinking had prevented what could easily have been a costly encounter for the 291st Infantry.

Preparing for the Assault

While First Platoon had its hands full moving through the Colmar Forest, the Mortar Platoon had moved swiftly through the forest, taking a different route. After reaching the edge of the forest with the fortified town of Wolfgantzen before them in the distance, Third Platoon setup their mortars. By 2 February, Third Platoon began firing its own artillery barrage into Wolfgantzen to soften up the German defenses for the inevitable infantry assault. The mortar men fired more shells on 2 and 3 February than they ever had before. They would fire nine consecutive shells, aimed at different trajectories to cover a much larger area and to inflict maximum damage to their target. Third Platoon was setup on the edge of a town and had good forest cover; the Germans could not target them. While they were in the midst of their duties, a lieutenant and two privates from the 275th Engineer Combat Battalion, attached to the 75th Division moved past Prater's Squad. They were walking along a little road through the woods. A few moments later the privates returned without their lieutenant; he had sprung a wire trap in the woods and was killed. The Germans had left many traps throughout the woods, it was a very dangerous situation. Ross walked through the woods and nearly stepped on a land mine. When he stopped and turned around, he almost stepped on another one! By 3 February, the mortar men received news that their mortars had been very effective and the infantry assault could begin.

A Tragic Loss

Second Platoon had been setup near the position of Third Platoon on 2 and 3 February. They saw little action, as their immediate area was rather quiet. Squads from Second Platoon setup their machine guns in several different locations to stop any potential German surprise attacks. Chisholm's Squad was to guard a crossroads on the edge of town and near the forest on 2 February. There was little activity in the area and the men of Chisholm's Squad were perhaps more relaxed than they should have been. Henry and Welch, the two men in the Company who were as close as brothers, shared a foxhole on one side of the road. Henry was the gunner of the Squad and Kravitz was the assistant gunner. Welch, the comedian of the group was an ammo bearer. Kravitz was in a foxhole a few yards away from Henry and Welch. As the situation was rather lax, Welch stood up in the foxhole just as a stray German shell landed right on top of him. Welch's head was literally blown off. It was a tragic loss for the Squad, the Platoon, and even for the whole Company. Welch was a friend to many, but especially to John Henry. Prater from the Mortar Platoon had seen the shell come down not far from his position and took the jeep over to see if anyone was wounded. Henry was not wounded physically, but emotionally, he was destroyed; he had lost his best friend. Henry was hysterical and could not be calmed down. He was pulled out of his foxhole and taken to the Battalion Aid Station, he was an emotional wreck and that was the last his buddies thought they would ever see of him.

The Spaghetti Incident

H Company's cooks would make a different hot meal every day. Perhaps the favorite meal of the Company was spaghetti. One night at Colmar, the cooks prepared a spaghetti dinner. The Company was not in any immediate danger on this night and everyone was able to enjoy their spaghetti supper. PFC John Nionakis, a former member of the Mortar Platoon who became a cook, brought the supper up to his buddies. Prater and his Squad reunited with their old buddy, Nionakis. Frequently, the men would eat their late supper, then go to bed. Prater very much enjoyed the spaghetti and ate more than his share. Shortly after, he climbed into his sleeping bag and went to sleep. It was necessary to tightly zip oneself up in the sleeping bag to keep warm. Prater found that he ate too much and just managed to get out of his sleeping bag in time! The same could be said for others in the Company that gorged themselves that night on a favorite meal. "Hay Seed" liked spaghetti a lot; it was his favorite. He always laughed as he at it, because the first time he ate it, he had asked his buddy Lawson if it was alive! Even on the front line, "Hay Seed" still found eating spaghetti to be quite amusing. The cooks were always looking out for the men in the Company. They would bring bags of sandwiches up to the men on the front line for lunch. For breakfast, the cooks were inventive. On one occasion, they made little solid doughnuts for the hungry GIs

In the Midst of an Artillery Barrage

On the afternoon of 3 February, the group led by Captain Goodnight had met a messenger from one of the rifle companies of Second Battalion, who was looking for their missing riflemen. Goodnight parted ways with the riflemen and assigned several men from Headquarters Platoon of H Company to fill in gaps in the battered squads of First Platoon, so it could operate with three weak squads. First Platoon moved ahead, coming near to the edge of the Colmar Forest, some distance away from Second and Third Platoons. First Platoon, with Lieutenant Bergheimer in command, made it to a roadway on the edge of the forest and German mortar men zeroed in on their position.

Shells landed throughout their area and the men took cover as best they could. Bergheimer ordered his Platoon to setup their guns and return fire on the Germans that were held up on the far edge of the town of Wolfgantzen, almost out of view. A thunderous mortar barrage landed just past First Platoon's position and Bergheimer again left to report the attack. Staff Sergeant Slawson took command and ordered the men to spread out and take whatever cover they could find. Slagle was standing near Sergeant "Willard" and two privates from Third Squad when a mortar shell landed almost dead on the Sergeant. Slagle was thrown off his feet from the explosion and landed face first on the ground; he knew he was hurt. The two privates were killed from the blast and Sergeant "Willard" had lost both legs above the knee, his left arm, and was riddled with shrapnel throughout his body. Half of his face was blown away, yet he was still alive and crying out for help.

The Duty of a Medic

Romano, First Platoon's Medic could not reach "Willard" as First Platoon began to take machine gun fire from one of the houses a short distance away. Slagle at first could not feel his legs, but managed to crawl using his hands to some cover, where he passed out, face down. Corporal Wendell Petersen, a medic from the 375th Medical Battalion that was attached to the 75th Division was moving with First Platoon that day. He saw the seriously wounded Sergeant and braved machine gun fire to pull him out of harm's way. Petersen and Romano tended to "Willard," who appeared to be a hopeless case. Petersen then braved machine gun fire again to pull Slagle off the line. Slagle was hit in the lower back with shrapnel and Petersen tended to him. Lawson saw what had happened to Slagle and thought he had been killed. Mortar fire hit the German position, fired by H Company's Third Platoon. The enemy fire stopped and Staff Sergeant Slawson ordered the men of First Platoon to get their guns up and return fire. The Germans in the edge of town retreated and First Platoon's wounded could be evacuated. Slagle was put on a litter and taken to the Battalion Aid Station. "Willard" was attended to by Romano, who thought the Sergeant had no chance of survival. His condition was beyond any imagination. "Willard" had shrapnel holes all through his remaining arm and across his chest and back. One whole side of his face was almost gone. Somehow, the shrapnel had not hit any major organs. Sergeant "Willard" was also taken to the Battalion Aid Station and then immediately evacuated further to the rear; no one could believe he was still alive.

A Failed Attack

Second Battalion continued to push through the woods on the afternoon of 3 February and began the attack on the town of Wolfgantzen. Air support from the USAAF and RAF did not come in as planned. Communications were in shambles and the attack could not be properly directed. There was such confusion, that some rifle platoons advanced, while others withdrew. Many squads were pinned down and were taking heavy fire. Several French tanks came up through the woods to support the advance; one hit a land mine and the others were hit by 88 fire. By late afternoon, Second Battalion was pinned down and took heavy casualties. After cover of darkness, the 88 fire silenced and Second Battalion withdrew from its advance, circled back through the Colmar Forest and regrouped for a second attempt at taking Wolfgantzen in the morning.

Assault on Wolfgantzen

By the early morning of 4 February, the engineers of the 275th Engineer Combat Battalion had cleared the mines from the narrow country road that led through the Colmar Forest. Second Battalion then prepared for its second advance on Wolfgantzen. More Germans had moved into the woods to leave booby traps, including anti-personnel mines. Lieutenant Colonel Drain arrived by jeep to see about H Company's casualties. Staff Sergeant Modrzejewski from the Mortar Platoon, Staff Sergeant "Stretch" Wilson from Second Platoon, and First Sergeant Whalen went to brief their Battalion Commander about their situation. Drain's jeep tripped an anti-personnel mine along the road and he, Modrzejewski, Wilson, and Whalen were all wounded and evacuated to the Battalion Aid Station. While on a patrol, Staff Sergeant Slawson spotted a group of Germans in the process of laying mines further along the road. He led his Section in an attack and all the Germans were killed or captured. In the afternoon, Second Battalion's rifle companies had surrounded the remaining German forces that were held up in the forest. In total, Second Battalion captured the remnants of three German companies in the forest that day. H Company then setup their machine guns and mortars in a clearing at the edge of the forest and bedded down for the night. On the morning of 5 February, word had come that Second Battalion would not make a second attack on Wolfgantzen. Instead, First Battalion attacked Wolfgantzen, supported by H Company. First Battalion's attack was well coordinated, as they had attacked the northern edge of town as opposed to the southern edge, where Second Battalion had previously attacked. The Germans were caught completely off guard and the 291st Infantry secured a nearly bloodless victory in taking Wolfgantzen.

Close of the Colmar Pocket

On 6 February, the 3rd Infantry Division had taken the Medieval Fortress of Neuf Brisach. That afternoon, Second Battalion, 291st Infantry moved to within sight of the Rhine near the town of Obersaasheim and were ordered to hold their position and await further orders. On 7 February, Messerschmitt Me-262 jets bombed H Company's position, killing and wounding several men in the Mortar Platoon. On 8 February, H Company moved into the town of Obersaasheim after the 290th Infantry took it over. Second Battalion, 291st Infantry continued to receive occasional shells from a German position across the Rhine. The men of H Company had much to eat at Obersaasheim with plentiful supplies of chicken and turkey. A wine cellar full of huge kegs of red and white wines was discovered in town and the Company had quite a celebration. By 9 February, the 75th Division had driven the last remaining Germans back across the Rhine and onto German soil. The German presence in France was forever gone.

Casualties in the Colmar Pocket

Second Battalion had suffered significant casualties in Colmar. H Company in particular had more than its share of men killed in action. First Platoon had fought its way through the Colmar Forest and was almost destroyed in the process. The men of First Platoon had been ambushed three times, but somehow they pushed the Germans back. First Platoon took 22 casualties during these ambushes and had lost the whole of Second Section. Staff Sergeant Slawson was awarded the Oak Leaf Cluster to his Bronze Star for his actions in holding First Platoon together, through some very tough combat. Second Platoon had lost Welch and Third Platoon had lost Staff Sergeant Modrzejewski to injuries. First Sergeant Whalen was wounded too. Following the Battle of the Colmar

Pocket, Captain Goodnight received the Silver Star for his actions. If it had not been for Goodnight, Second Battalion might well have been overrun by German armor. H Company went from a strength of 124 men going into Colmar down to a strength of 95 men; many of these men were wounded and in the Battalion Aid Station. H Company was operating at about half strength as they prepared to leave Colmar. Replacements were desperately needed and they were on the way.

A Period of Rest

Aftermath of the Colmar Pocket

After the Germans were driven from French soil in the Alsace region, H Company moved from Obersaasheim to Bischwir. It was a time of celebration for their victory. By 10 February the men of H Company found plenty of wine and food in the vicinity. The Division Command Post moved into town and with them came movie projectors and new films from America. It was the first leisure the men of H Company had enjoyed since back in the days of Wales in December. Also, the 75th Division Band performed for the first time since leaving the United States. This brief period of rest did not last long. The night of 10 February was wild. Guard duty was assigned as usual that night, but the guards were all drunk from the wine! In the morning, many of the men from H Company were suffering hangovers from the night before. On 11 February, Second Battalion moved by train to Luneville and the men finally got one thing they had lacked for so long: a shower.

Going AWOL

As H Company was aboard trains taking them away from the vicinity of Colmar, PFC Reynolds of Second Platoon smelled fresh bread baking and he decided to go buy some. There was a small village near the tracks and it was still populated, despite the combat in the Colmar region. The French were very thankful to have American GIs in their country and they were generous. Reynolds jumped off the train while it was stopped near the village. Reynolds rushed to the bakery and got some bread, but the train left without him! Going AWOL was a very serious situation and the punishment could result in being shot. Several days later, after H Company had arrived to its destination, Reynolds returned to his Platoon; he was not punished for having been AWOL.

Recovering from the Colmar Campaign

After the battles in the Colmar Pocket, Second Battalion, 291st Infantry was battered and in need of replacements. H Company was down to a strength of only 95 men, this number included all the replacements that arrived to H Company up to that time. In First Platoon, Second Section had been entirely lost; 22 men were killed in those series of ambushes in the Colmar Forest. Many of the survivors were severely wounded. Staff Sergeant Slawson was now to command the refitted Second Section. Third Squad was led by "Kirk," formerly a member of Larson's Squad. Cohen from First Squad was also moved to Third Squad and became gunner. Lawson was promoted to Sergeant and led Fourth Squad. "Hay Seed" became his gunner and Murza, another member of Larson's Squad, became assistant gunner. Thompson from Headquarters' Platoon became gunner of Second Squad. Galbreth, the only surviving replacement in First Section, became assistant gunner. Second Platoon had few casualties at Colmar, but the tragic death of John Welch had left a hole in Second Squad. After a week or more, John Henry who had lost his best friend Welch returned to his Squad. Henry was a good man and a great soldier. He was fully recovered when he returned. Henry was promoted to Sergeant when Chisholm was promoted to Staff Sergeant to replace "Stretch" Wilson who was wounded. Sergeant Henry was very well respected by his men. Kravitz moved up to gunner in Henry's Squad. In Third Platoon, Staff Sergeant Modrzejewski of First Section was wounded and Corporal Prater was promoted to Staff Sergeant to serve as Modrzejewski's replacement. PFC Strong was then promoted to Corporal and squad leader of First Squad to replace Prater. Small numbers of replacements began to trickle into H Company.

Attitude towards Replacements

Sergeant Lawson received a few replacements in his Squad after arriving to Luneville. Lawson had been through a lot in less than two months in combat and his attitude changed dramatically. He was just a farm boy when he first arrived to H Company back in the summer of 1944, now he was a combat veteran. Back then, Lawson was teased for his lack of an education and being only a simple farmer; no one teased him anymore. He had gained confidence in himself. When the first replacements arrived to H Company after the conclusion of combat in the Battle of the Bulge, Lawson welcomed them, especially the man from Alabama who Lawson shared much in common with. After the Replacement's death at Colmar, Lawson decided that he would never again get close with a replacement; he did not want to see any more friends killed. From the moment he was promoted to Sergeant, Lawson looked upon all replacements as being completely different from any veteran soldier. This, however was not an exclusive attitude towards all replacements. Staff Sergeant Prater of Third Platoon received many replacements in his Section and he treated them as any other. Many of the replacements earned their spot and some respect in their new squad after being in combat with the veterans. However, this was not an easy task as there were many established cliques among the squads who were not content with accepting new members.

Visiting

On 12 February, Second Battalion, 291st Infantry received its first true "rest" period since arriving to Europe. They moved out early in the morning back behind the lines through the Vosges Mountains. H Company was billeted in the small farming village of Rambeville, near St. Die. Third Platoon slept in a barn and were instructed to clean their weapons in preparation for their next combat. Staff Sergeant Prater and his Platoon buddies walked through the village that had less than 500 inhabitants. They came up to a farmhouse and spoke to the people in the yard; Prater and his buddies were invited inside. Corporal Strong could speak some French and helped them to get acquainted with the Thiebeau family. There was the father, mother, and two daughters; their son was sent to southern France to avoid conscription into the German Army. Prater had a "D" chocolate bar in his pocket and with milk from the Thiebeau's farm, Prater made chocolate milk for all of them. They sat around the kitchen table, visiting, and trying to speak only French. Prater and Strong played cards with the daughters and frequently visited the farmhouse during their stay in Rambeville. It was a nice and relaxing time for them between the battles.

Back to Where it all Began

After an enjoyable three-day rest in Rambeville, Second Battalion, 291st Infantry was back on the move. On the morning of 15 February they moved by truck to the town of Deinvelliers and then boarded a train. They were headed back to where their journey had first begun back in December: Tongres, Belgium. The men of H Company were billeted in the town of Millen, near Tongres and there was some familiar scenery. Some of the men of First Platoon visited a barn they had slept in on Christmas Eve 1944. Lawson found his duffel bag buried in a pile of hay inside the barn where he had left it. He was amused to find a chocolate bar among his belongings. For Lawson, it was also an emotional time, other duffel bags were also hidden away in the hay, bearing the names of many men who were killed in the Battle of the Bulge and at Colmar. Some of these men were Lawson's close friends from the days of Camp Breckinridge; even if he was not best friends with all of them, he at least knew all of them. Lawson got up, reburied his duffel bag and walked out of the barn. He paused, taking one last glimpse at the hay stacks he and many of his now dead buddies once slept in trying to keep warm on the terribly cold nights of winter.

Slagle's Recovery

Slagle spent about a week in the Battalion Aid Station after his wound in the Colmar Forest. At first, he thought he would be permanently paralyzed, as it was some time before he regained feeling in his legs. His wound was significant, but it could have been a lot worse. Slagle had shrapnel removed from his lower back, but much of it was too deep to be removed. First Sergeant Whalen was also in the same Aid Station with minor wounds from the anti personnel mine that Lieutenant Colonel Drain's jeep had hit. His wound was more along the lines of a scratch and the doctors at the Aid Station did not believe it warranted a Purple Heart. If Whalen could not have one then he thought no one else should either. One of the doctors pinned the Purple Heart on Slagle while he was in bed; Whalen promptly removed it and would not include it in his records. Whalen left the Aid Station in time to rejoin H Company before they left France. After his surgery, Slagle made a miraculous recovery: he was not expected to walk again. He had a tender back for some time and was not in shape to return to H Company before they left. Lawson had thought Slagle was killed at Colmar. The last time Lawson saw Slagle he was laying face down and was not moving. After Slagle had been taken to the Battalion Aid Station, a messenger had arrived to H Company requesting Slagle to report to General Mickle at the Division Command Post. The messenger was told that Slagle had been killed.

Back from the Dead

About a week after his surgery, Slagle was released from the Battalion Aid Station. The first man he saw was one of the runners from the Division Command Post who was quite shocked to find Slagle alive. He told Slagle that H Company was long gone and that he should report to the Division Command Post for orders. Slagle had found out that the Division Band had been performing for many days in the Colmar region and he attended a show and reunited with his buddies in the Band. He then came into contact with General Mickle who temporarily assigned him as an MP to guard the Division Command Post. Slagle was given office duty, functioning as one of General Mickle's assistants when he was not needed for guard duty. The General liked him and treated Slagle well. Slagle remained with the Division Band when they moved back to Tongres, Belgium and then into Holland.

Holland: Operations on the Maas

Into Holland

After the weekend spent in Tongres, Belgium, H Company moved into Holland. The 291st Infantry Regiment arrived on 19 February and relieved the Canadian 6th Parachute Infantry. The 291st setup their Regimental Command Post at Heijthuisen. H Company arrived to defensive positions along the west bank of the Maas River. The Germans were on the other side in plain view. H Company's Command Post was setup near the little town of Haelin. There were a few barns and farmhouses and a tavern on a long, narrow road that led into the center of town. The tavern had previously been a British billet and their machine gun emplacements were several yards in back of the tavern. The British machine gun had a greater range than the American 30 caliber water-cooled gun that H Company was equipped with. On 20 February, the 75th Division Headquarters was setup in Panningen, Holland. The 75th Division fell under the command of the VIII Corps of the British Second Army commanded by Montgomery and was tasked with nightly reconnaissance patrols across the Maas River.

Chaiklin's Journey

Harris Chaiklin from Bridgeport, Connecticut finished high school in June 1944. Through high school, he had worked full time for his uncle, who operated a forerunner of the supermarket. The store was arranged into different sections with an operator running each one. Chaiklin candled eggs, worked with cheese and helped wait on long lines of people who used ration stamps and tokens to get their allotment of dairy products. Bridgeport was a factory town with many ethnic groups. The Depression hit the city particularly hard. His father lost the little soda fountain candy store that he ran. Divorce soon followed. Chaiklin lived on Welfare, moved frequently, lived with different relatives, attended many different schools, and had short stints in a foster home. This left him with a spotty education and borderline delinquency.

Chaiklin turned 18 in June and knew he would be drafted at some point. So he decided to enlist and in September 1944 he arrived to Fort Devens, Massachusetts. After a week of getting shots and taking tests, he boarded a train for a two-day trip to Camp Croft, South Carolina, for what was to be 17 weeks of Basic Training. He was assigned to a heavy weapons company. At Camp Croft, the 17-week Basic Training Program was shortened to 14 weeks because the Battle of the Bulge had increased the need for replacements. One incident that stood out during his Basic Training revolved around taking the test to qualify for Officers Candidate School. He and three others took the test. When the other three men received orders and left for Fort Benning, Georgia, Chaiklin was left waiting. He made an appointment with the Captain in charge of his training unit. The Georgian officer leaned back in his seat and said, "Jewboy, you are going to the ETO."

After a one-week furlough home, Chaiklin went to his next assignment: Fort Meade, Maryland for the decision as to whether he would go to the ETO or CBI. It was the ETO and in late January he arrived to Camp Shanks, New York. Shortly before leaving for Europe, Chaiklin received a leave pass and went to New York City and spent most of his time around Times Square. At one point he went into Jack Dempsey's Bar in Times Square. Replacements were under orders not to say anything about where they were stationed or what they were doing. Apparently, it was a secret only to the base commanders, but not to the bar patrons. When Chaiklin walked in, one of the patrons said, "You are going overseas, have a drink." Chaiklin did not leave the bar until it was time to return back to Camp Shanks.

On the bitterly cold night of 31 January, Chaiklin boarded the Wakefield, which before the war was a civilian liner called The President. It was a fast ship and required no escort. The ship docked at the port of Liverpool on 8 February. From there, Chaiklin began his long journey to catch up with the 75th Division. The arrival was not without humorous elements. A riot among the longshoremen was almost caused by tossing oranges over the side. There were also somber warnings of things to come. As the troops disembarked they passed lines of wounded Canadian soldiers, many on stretchers, waiting to be loaded onto a hospital ship next to the Wakefield. As the arrivals passed by, many of the Canadians gave a thumbs up and said loudly, "Giv'em Hell Yank!"

Chasing the Division

After Chaiklin arrived to England, there was rapid movement until he reached the front. First there was an overnight ride to the Port of Southampton. Chaiklin was introduced to warm, sweet tea laced with canned milk by the wonderful Salvation Army ladies whose warmth more than made up for the strange tea. Arriving by dawn, the replacements boarded an LST and left as soon as it was filled up to capacity. They sat down on oil covered floors of the LST and crossed the English Channel arriving to Le Harve. Chaiklin moved to the train station at Yvetot and boarded a "40 and 8" and moved across France. The commanding officer aboard the train told the troops not to buy any wine from the French farmers: it might be horse urine! Chaiklin first stopped in Givet on the French border with Belgium. The next day he went into a small town in Belgium. There he was able to buy French Fries in a newspaper cone. It proved to be the last semblance of decent food Chaiklin would get for several days.

A Little Bit of Excitement

H Company had arrived to Haelin late at night on 18 February and was immediately assigned to cover patrols on the Maas River. At night, the machine gun platoons moved through the small town of Buggenum, cautiously moving through houses, taking what cover they could. Machine gun fire was hitting all around their positions. The Germans knew where the British were billeted and had targeted their former positions, not knowing that they had been abandoned. H Company returned fire and there was a significant firefight. The Mortar Platoon was tasked with guard duty and were also receiving heavy machine gun fire near their positions. There were no casualties in H Company that night, but it was a wake up call to combat after ten days away from any direct combat operations. That first night was not to be equaled; each night to follow was quieter.

Chaiklin's Arrival to H Company

Chaiklin arrived to the Division Command Post at Panningen, Holland on 20 February. General Mickle gave a pep talk to the replacements that were lined up in a loose formation, telling the young men that he expected them to come back with their chests covered in medals. The replacements then boarded trucks to move to their new units. By the next day, Chaiklin had moved to the Regimental Command Post. The replacements then were loaded on trucks to be moved to Second Battalion at Roermond. During the move from Regiment to Battalion, the trucks were strafed by German aircraft and the heavy weight champion boxer from Camp Croft, also a replacement to H Company, panicked, ran across a field and was cut down. A jeep from Battalion took H Company's replacements to a position near Haelin. Here the final assignments were made and Chaiklin was assigned to Second Squad of First Platoon. Chaiklin and a couple of others got into a jeep to take them to the Platoon. As the jeep pulled up to the tavern where the Squad was billeted, they were met by heavy shelling. Sergeant Larson quickly said, "Junior get out of the way and don't try to be a hero."

Within a couple of minutes, and through artillery fire, jeeps arrived from the Maas carrying Second Lieutenant Bergheimer and squads from First Platoon. They had just completed a firing mission on the Maas. The Germans were still targeted on the old British positions so the jeeps returned into fire rather than escaping it. One of the jeep drivers, a Pole shouted, "This god damn war is all the fault of the Jews." Chaiklin had moved his finger toward the safety lock on his rifle. The rifle was empty because in a Belgian "repple depple" someone had shot himself in the toe and all ammunition was taken away. Sergeant Larson stepped in and said, "Junior, get out of the way." As things died down, Bergheimer noticed Chaiklin and asked who he was; Chaiklin identified himself. At this point, Chaiklin had not eaten much of anything in three or four days. He asked, "When do we eat?" Bergheimer exploded as usual: "Here I am fighting a god damn war and this son of a bitch asks when do we eat!?" Chaiklin had arrived to the Squad with his heavy duffel bag full of clothes and other issued equipment, including a gas mask. Schooled in the army rule of being accountable for everything one signed out for, Chaiklin was worried when the veteran platoon members began to take some of the clothes. Larson smiled at him and told Chaiklin he could keep whatever he could carry. Thus, Chaiklin was introduced to the world of Combat Loss Reports.

When the shelling ended, Chaiklin got settled and that night with his Squad, he went to the Maas to provide cover for a patrol. As a replacement ammo bearer, Chaiklin quickly learned that the expected two boxes of ammo he had to carry had became four. It was standard to tie two boxes together with a cloth belt and carry four boxes. That night there was intermittent artillery fire from both sides of the Maas, but none of it came close to First Section's guns. Chaiklin's first night on the line was a memorable one. He had to cross a cold, muddy field with foot deep furrows. He also had difficulty digging his first foxhole.

Replacements in a Distinguished Squad

The Second Squad of First Platoon was entirely different than only a few weeks earlier. Gone were Slagle, Lawson, "Hay Seed," and Murza. Only Bert Larson remained as Sergeant. Thompson had been transferred from Headquarters Platoon to serve as gunner and Galbreth, the one time replacement, now a combat veteran himself, served as assistant gunner. Galbreth was a large and strong man of few words; he was silent as stone. Pedro, a Mexican was also a replacement ammo bearer; he carried a guitar with him and was an overall friendly guy. Larson had changed little through the battles in the Ardennes and at Colmar; he was still level headed and cool under fire. Larson remained very much a father figure to the young replacements that arrived to his Squad, in particular to Chaiklin. Sergeant Larson treated Chaiklin as a human being, something few others had done for the young replacement.

Life in Holland

The men of H Company found Holland to be a beautiful change in scenery from where they had previously been. The weather was getting much warmer and they were all glad for that. The Dutch Underground had many soldiers in the area and they were friendly and generous to their American Allies. The Dutch had been treated roughly by the Germans, who had taken away everything from them. The Dutch wanted American cigarettes and a friendly barter system was the result, with the Dutch trading eggs, chickens, and freshly made pies to the Americans in exchange for cigarettes. Kravitz and men from Second Platoon gave many food items from their rations to the thankful Dutch civilians. The Dutch helped to provide valuable intelligence in the form of maps and personal knowledge of the area to the leaders of the nightly patrols. In a rear area, the riflemen of Second Battalion, 291st Infantry were instructed in boat training. Rubber boats had been delivered for use in the nightly crossings of the Maas. Six men with weapons could fit into the boats. One major concern in the area were minefields that were left behind by the Germans. Lieutenant Colonel Sanders, the Deputy Commander of the 291st Regiment was killed when he tripped a mine.

Daytime Activity along the Maas

H Company operated primarily at night along the Maas. On 19 and 20 February, the machine gun platoons setup their guns near the riverbank at night to cover the patrols. As dawn approached, they would move back through Buggenum and into Haelin to get some sleep in the barns or farmhouses. By first light, the Germans would send the occasional mortar shell in H Company's direction. It was more of harassment than anything else. H Company's Mortar Platoon would also send the occasional shell into German territory. Often, the Germans would cautiously move out into the open and lay out in the sun. Conditions were rather lax on both sides of the Mass; at least in the beginning.

Guard Duty on the Maas

While the machine gun platoons were actively involved with covering for the patrols, the Mortar Platoon had lighter duty. The mortar men stayed in another part of the town of Haelin that was relatively quiet, except for an occasional artillery shell coming in, or one fired at the Germans by Third Platoon. In teams of two, the mortar men also moved up to the shoreline every night and positioned themselves in foxholes for rotating guard duty. They were watching for German patrols that might cross the Maas. One night, Ross and a replacement, Private John Scaduto who had arrived at the end of the Battle of the Bulge, were setup in a foxhole on guard duty. Scaduto saw Ross' head bowed and thought he was falling asleep; he nudged Ross and whispered, "Floyd, don't go to sleep!" Ross was in fact not asleep, but praying silently. He told Scaduto that he was very much awake and waiting for any Germans that might show up.

A Night in the Aid Station

Every night, after the guns were setup, the ammo bearers would help the infantrymen carry the heavy rubber boats to the river for the riflemen who were going on patrols. At night the temperature was in the 30s or 40s, but the ground did not freeze. However, the field was muddy, forming a texture something like soft concrete. It was hard even to walk on, yet the men had to carry the boats across it. This nightly task was exhausting and after it Chaiklin would move with his Squad to the shoreline to cover the patrols. One night Chaiklin's feet got wet and he ended up at the Battalion Aid Station because he did not have an extra pair of socks to change into. The doctor at the Aid Station was a pediatrician in civilian life and he gave Chaiklin a talk about the need to keep his feet dry. It was the same lecture heard by all the original members of H Company who had been through the bitterly cold winter in the Ardennes.

Preparing for a Patrol

Every night, the rifle companies of Second Battalion would send patrols across the Maas River on reconnaissance missions. One afternoon, Sergeant Lawson made an in person report to his Platoon Commander, Lieutenant Bergheimer, about the status of his Squad. Two of them were in the Battalion Aid Station recovering from dysentery and "Hay Seed" was stricken with a high fever and was also out of action. Bergheimer lost his cool and started swearing at Lawson. A messenger arrived to request a patrol from H Company that night. The messenger probably had mixed up his orders as patrol duties were intended for the rifle companies, not H Company. However, without any hesitation, Lawson volunteered his Squad. Bergheimer grumbled as usual and finally agreed. Later that afternoon, a messenger delivered Lawson a map, sketched out by Bergheimer detailing where they were to scout on the other side of the Maas. That evening as the machine gun squads set up to support the patrols, Lawson briefed his Squad. Two men were replacements, having just arrived days earlier; this was to be their first taste of combat. One of the replacements was a short and stout Armenian who was very outspoken; he sold rugs in civilian life. The only other veteran in the group was the assistant gunner, Murza who had been with the Company since Breckinridge. He was not a courageous man at all, in fact all he wanted was to survive the war and return to his job as a musician in Philadelphia.

A Patrol across the Maas

As their rubber boat slid off the shoreline, the men were very nervous, but none so much as Sergeant Lawson. He had been in the shadow of others since his first introduction to combat in December and he was out to prove that he was a competent leader. It did not take long to reach the other side of the Maas. However, they had a problem: Bergheimer's map was wrong; there was no clear spot to beach the boat. They had to move further to the south and their map did not show this area. They managed to hide the boat and go ashore without difficulty and were trying to ascertain their position. Lawson smelled cigarette smoke and told them to lay down flat on the ground in the brush. A German soldier with a rifle slung over his shoulder strode past them and toward the shore. They watched as he cautiously smoked and strode back to his original position. They noticed what looked like a bunker with several men in it. They heard German voices, then silence. Lawson and his Squad were trapped, they could not return to their boat and if they moved, they would be killed or captured. One of the replacements, the Armenian started to panic and Lawson grabbed him by the throat and whispered to him, "Calm down son, we will get through this." Time was quickly passing by and Lawson knew he had to do something. He pulled the pin on a grenade and threw it toward the river and it exploded, making a big splash and a lot of noise. A German shouted and machine gun fire opened up all around, then it became quiet again. The same sentry came out of the bunker and cautiously strode by again, this time looking around. Another German joined him and both of them walked right up to the shore. Lawson whispered to Murza to throw his grenade toward the water, far from their position, while Lawson moved toward the bunker. Murza threw the grenade some distance away, to the north and fire came down again. Both Germans quickly strode right past Lawson's concealed Squad and moved to the north; in the direction Lawson's Squad was supposed to have gone.

Sergeant Lawson motioned for his Squad to remain hidden and he crawled toward the bunker. Lawson heard no sounds at all, the two Germans had apparently moved some

161

distance away to scout for what they must have thought to be an American patrol landing to the north. Lawson reached the bunker and saw a German officer in the bunker, alone. He was using a flashlight to make some notations on a paper. Lawson hit the officer with the butt of his rifle and knocked him out. Lawson stuffed all the papers into his pocket and dragged the unconscious soldier back to his Squad's position. Murza whispered that the two German sentries did not return. Lawson told them to get up quickly and run for the boat. They got it out of its hiding spot and into the water. A German machine gun opened up near them, but apparently could not see them. Shouts were heard. An American machine gun opened up in response and bullets were flying all over the area and hitting the water. Murza grabbed the Armenian who was in shock and got him aboard the boat; they also put the unconscious German officer aboard too. They were about halfway across the Maas when heavy fire hit the water all around them. The Armenian panicked and started screaming. Lawson shouted, "Shut the Hell up and start rowing or I am going to shoot you!" They made it back to the American lines, some distance to the south from where they had started. It was close to 0300 and they were very late. A squad from Chisholm's Section of Second Platoon was setup nearby and they shouted to Lawson for the password, which he knew. The squad leader asked Lawson what happened and why there was suddenly so much activity. The squad leader helped Lawson and his group to get to cover. Lawson's Squad returned to First Platoon's area just before sunrise.

One Angry Sergeant

Lawson was absolutely furious with Lieutenant Bergheimer. His map was wrong and the patrol could easily have cost them all their lives. Lawson searched the German prisoner, who was in and out of consciousness; he probably had a concussion from the rifle butt to the head. The German officer proved to be a cartographer and in his coat were a number of maps, detailing the positions of German machine gun nests and bunkers on the other side of the Maas. The prisoner was taken to the Battalion Command Post for interrogation. Lawson found one of the jeep drivers and ordered him to drive him to Bergheimer's location, a few hundred yards from the front. Lawson walked into the Platoon Command Post and found Bergheimer lounging around, looking rather comfortable. Captain Goodnight was standing in the corner of the room, apparently speaking to Bergheimer, who paid little attention, continually stroking his beard.

Bergheimer was rarely clean cut; he usually had a dark, two day's growth of beard. Lawson said to Bergheimer, "Sir, your map almost got me and my Squad killed!" Bergheimer blew his cool and swore at Lawson, who stood his ground. Lawson recounted his story, with emphasis on how lucky they were to have made it back. He mentioned the captured cartographer and the maps; this made no impression on Bergheimer, who replied, "So, you failed then. Get the Hell out!" Captain Goodnight stood by and listened to all of this and said nothing. Lawson strode off, even angrier with his Platoon Commander. Seconds later, Captain Goodnight caught up with him and in his soft spoken voice said, "Sergeant, I am going to see that you get a medal for this." Goodnight patted Lawson on the shoulder and walked back to Bergheimer's Command Post.

Incompetence

That same afternoon, Sergeant Lawson and his Squad had just awoken from some sleep in the barn. It was very quiet and a rather nice day. Lawson took a few steps out of the barn and a shell landed not far from him with the blast knocking him to the ground. It proved to be just a stray shell, but more were coming in towards a specific target. Lawson got one of the drivers to take him to the Platoon Command Post. Lawson shouted, "Lieutenant!" with no response. He then went into the farmhouse and found Bergheimer laid out with an empty bottle of Cognac beside him. Apparently Bergheimer had a rather not so pleasant chat with Captain Goodnight. At that point, Lawson decided that his Platoon Commander was utterly worthless and decided to instead locate Staff Sergeant Slawson who had often taken command in Bergheimer's regular absence. Slawson rode up in a jeep, from somewhere to the rear; he had seen the shells coming in and ordered everyone to take cover. Slawson asked where Bergheimer was and Lawson said, "He's taking a nap, I think he had a tough day." Slawson, who was not known to show much emotion, produced a smile.

Meals on the Maas

As the machine gun squads were tasked with supporting the patrols during the night, they would usually return to their sleeping quarters by dawn. There, the men would be given hot meals, brought to them from the Company Kitchen in containers. In addition to these meals, the men of H Company had the opportunity to barter for eggs, chicken, and pies. Also, some of the men were living on a farm with cows; the farm boys and city boys were quickly distinguished. The farm boys milked the cows and drank the milk, with no difficulties. For the farm boys, it was a warm reminder of home. However, the city boys often tried to drink the unpasturized milk too and they were not used to it and it made them sick. Symptoms of diarrhea and cases of dysentery swept through the squads. Many men became severely ill and had to be carried off to the Battalion Aid Station. Some men were so sick that they were absent from duty for days.

Trading with Allies

Just to the left of H Company's position on the Maas, were the Canadian paratroops. They were friendly and men from H Company would often go over to them and trade rations or stories. One morning two desert rat tanks pulled up outside the tavern. Chaiklin traded his rations for British beef stew that he thought tasted good. Chaiklin chatted with one of the tankers who said he had been in tanks for six years through the campaigns in Africa. The tanker was gray haired and looked visibly older than Chaiklin; the tanker was 26. Sergeant Lawson had met some of the British soldiers as well and exchanged greetings. He had never had hot tea with milk and honey before and was offered a cup. Unfortunately, this was in the afternoon under clear skies. The Germans shelled their position and Lawson and a member of his Squad took cover with the British troops. Lawson asked why they were not actively preparing to return fire and was told that the British were having their "High Tea" and would soon return to their duties. Lawson left the area and never again returned to chat with the British.

The Rhine

"The night of the crossing was like all the fireworks in the world you could imagine!"

Bill G. Prater, Third Platoon (Mortars), H Company

Mortar Platoon Crossing the Rhine

Middle: John Scaduto
Bottom Right: Ira Posnak

Front L-R: Jim Strong- Boyce Turner- ?,
Top: Bill Prater- George Bozovich- Charles West

L-R: **Bill Prater- Jim Strong**

L-R: Bill Prater - John Scaduto

166

Bottom Left: Elton T. Page   **John Scaduto- John Malarich**

New S/SGT: Bill G. Prater

167

Moving Through Holland

By 3 March, H Company completed its duties along the Maas and prepared for their next move. H Company assembled near the tavern at Haelin and boarded trucks and moved to a little town called Neustadt on the German border. A nice Dutch family billeted the Company on their farm overnight. The next morning the men of H Company crossed into Germany and moved back through Holland. Trucks then took the Company to Venlo, Holland and to Arcen. Around the little town of Arcen, the men of the Mortar Platoon discovered many booby traps along the road and the combat engineers disabled them. The town was empty with the exception of a few German soldiers who were left behind for garrison duty; they surrendered without a fight. By dusk, the situation was unknown and more German soldiers could have been held up in the town. As a precaution, the Company remained on the outskirts of town and slept in trenches. The next day, the men of H Company moved into the town of Arcen; it was completely abandoned. They cleaned up a big house and slept there for three nights; there was no significant activity to report. On 8 March, H Company moved to Budberg, Germany and setup in a barnyard and slept in a farmhouse. While H Company was continuing to move, Slagle was still with Division Headquarters, assigned as an MP and bodyguard to General Mickle. He was traveling with his buddies in the Division Band.

Just Like Home

On 9 March after leaving Budberg, H Company moved up by truck to Hocht, Germany, about a mile from the Rhine. Ross from Second Section of the Mortar Platoon walked up a dirt road and towards a farmhouse. There were a few houses in the area. As Ross walked up to the house he encountered a German Sheppard, took care of the dog, and banged the door open. There were a few families visiting in the house and Ross shouted at them to get their possessions and get out of the house. The families were sent back to the village H Company had just moved through. In the vicinity of Hocht, H Company dispersed by platoon and by section and lived in the surrounding areas, which were primarily working farms with barns and large farmhouses. For the farm boys in H Company, it was like a homecoming. They could milk the cows every morning and have fresh eggs for breakfast. There were horses all around the area too; many men took up horseback riding. There was little for H Company to do for about two weeks other than

168

enjoy the leisure of farm life or its hard work, depending upon the perspective of the individual. Their primary duty was to setup their machine guns and mortars to halt any potential German patrols during the night.

Footsteps in the Attic

Staff Sergeant Slawson, commanding Second Section of First Platoon setup quarters in a large farmhouse. He and the Company Translator, Siegfried went into the house and met the inhabitants. There was a mother and two young daughters who looked very scared. Through his translator, Slawson told the mother that his men would be occupying the house, they were free to stay if they were quiet and kept out of the way. Slawson asked where the woman's husband was and she said he was a soldier and she had not seen him in a long time. Slawson took the jeep and moved off to Battalion to make a report. Sergeants "Kirk" of Third Squad and Lawson of Fourth Squad moved their men into the house. It was quite comfortable and well furnished. Lawson walked upstairs and saw the bedroom and a guestroom; both were fully furnished. The Sergeants shared the guestroom, the mother and daughters stayed in the bedroom, and the privates took over the large living room and a side room. There was a small attic that Lawson climbed up and looked in. There were a lot of old pieces of this and that and a few large trunks; nothing of particular interest. The men had dinner in the house; the mother cooked for the whole Section. She seemed nervous, but was cooperative. When Lawson went upstairs after dinner, he opened the closet in the guestroom and found men's clothing inside; Lawson found it peculiar. Some men were sent out on guard duty that night, but Lawson stayed in the house.

During the night Lawson thought he heard footsteps coming from the attic and he went up to see what it was. Before he even got up, Cohen rushed up the stairs and by the time Lawson got up to the attic, Cohen had a German man on his knees with his Garand pointed at the back of his head. The German had apparently hid himself in a trunk. Cohen escorted the man out of the house and forced him to kneel down outside. Just as Cohen was about to pull the trigger, the man's wife pleaded on her hands and knees not to kill her husband. Cohen smiled and ordered the man to stand up; he had soiled his pants. Cohen escorted the prisoner to the Company Command Post just before sunrise; the prisoner did make it there unscathed. The woman and her two children were taken from

169

the house in the morning and sent to Battalion to be removed from the general area of operations.

The Cheese Incident

While living in the farmhouse, Lawson took advantage of some luxuries. He went to the hen house each morning and got fresh eggs for everyone's breakfast. He milked the cows too. However, the greatest luxury he discovered came from the cellar. Lawson found several blocks of cheese wrapped up in cloth; it was like finding gold. The men of Second Section divided up the cheese and each had some. It smelled terrible, but few complained. Cohen told everyone that he knew quality cheese and this was some real exotic German cheese. Later in the evening, Lawson was sitting on a couch in the house and others in the Section were playing cards. Suddenly Cohen got up and ran to the window. Lawson laughed and said, "Cohen, did your big mouth get you in trouble again?" When Cohen said nothing and stayed with his head hanging out the window, Lawson got up and walked over to him. Cohen threw up out the window and was too sick to even talk. He was taken to the Battalion Aid Station. "Hay Seed" was holding his stomach and looked sick too. By morning, most of the men were taken to the Battalion Aid Station and were lying on stretchers. They all had nausea and diarrhea. While laying flat on the stretcher, Cohen shouted, "You idiot Lawson, you made us eat bad cheese!" Lawson replied, "I thought you were the cheese expert?" A shouting match between the two continued until one of the doctors told them he would knock them both over the head if they did not cut it out. A day or so later, some of the men felt better and returned to their duties. Cohen got up and threw up all over himself. Lawson laughed at him and said, "The real men are going back to duty now." Lawson made it about two steps before he too got sick on himself. Cohen and Lawson spent another day and night in the Aid Station arguing. The doctors were greatly relieved and cheered when both men finally returned to duty.

Too Much Comfort

While the farmhouses that H Company captured and moved into offered surprising comfort, not everyone was satisfied. Some men had lived out in the elements for so long that such luxuries were no longer important to them, but this was not always the case. Staff Sergeant Prater moved into a well-furnished bedroom and shared a luxurious feather bed with his buddy Malarich. They slept in their clothes, still on alert should they be called to duty unexpectedly. Prater slept wonderfully in the soft bed, but when he woke up in the morning he found Malarich sleeping on the floor. Malarich said that he could not stand to sleep in that soft bed after sleeping on the ground for the last many months. Kravitz, the gunner of Second Squad, Second Platoon had moved into another farmhouse with his Section. The civilians were ordered out and Kravitz was glad to be living in a house for the first time in four months.

Mortar Men on the Rhine

Staff Sergeant Prater, commanding First Section of Third Platoon had setup his observation post in a farmhouse, about 200 yards from the Rhine. The mortar sections had dug their mortars into the front yard of the barns they were living in, half a mile from the Rhine and were waiting for orders from their staff sergeants. The mortars were readied to fire when needed. Prater observed mortar fire coming from a barn on the German side of the Rhine. German fortifications were clearly visible from the farmhouse and both sides had clear view of the movements of the other. Prater climbed up a ladder to the top of the barn and knocked out a shingle so he could spy across the river and see the German movement to and from their fortifications. He had captured a German binocular periscope and he set it up on top of the barn. First Section's mortars were lined up on about ten different targets so that Prater, from his vantage point could order fire by target number. The gunner then could automatically set the sight on the stake that aimed the mortars. Prater saw the Germans hidden well behind their fortifications. When the Germans appeared in an open courtyard, Prater would call the target number and fire would be put down on the Germans. It is unclear if the shells claimed any Germans, but it did at the very least, create a disturbance that kept the Germans in cover and away from making any mischief.

Counter Fire

One day while directing fire on the German fortifications across the river, Staff Sergeant Prater took notice of the Germans setting up an artillery piece beside a barn. It was a 105 mm gun that was firing at a low trajectory, like a rifle. From his location,

Prater could see the shell come out of the muzzle, but not where it landed. While watching for German troop movements, Prater watched as a shell landed just in front of his observation post. Moments later a shell hit just behind his position. Prater hurried down the ladder and his radioman was there waiting for him. The radioman said, "Let's get out of here!" The next shell that came in hit the barn and Prater and his men got out just in time. That same afternoon, Staff Sergeant Flud's Third Section was also positioned in a farmhouse and was taking fire from the German side of the Rhine. Flud's mortars were readied to fire smoke rounds to screen the nightly patrols across the Rhine. Flud was wounded by shrapnel when a shell hit the main level of the barn. Posnak and the others moved into the basement and waited for the shelling to conclude.

"Farmer Page"

Page was also in Staff Sergeant Flud's Section and was enjoying life on the dairy farm. The German family that owned the farm was permitted to do their daily chores on the farm during the day and at night they were told to stay in the cellar. The GIs were free to do as they wanted on the farm. Page, who grew up on a farm, wanted some fresh meat and he killed a pig and cooked it up; it tasted like ham. While they were at the farm, one of the horses was about to give birth and the German family asked "Farmer Page" to keep watch over it. One night, the horse was in labor and the German family was not allowed out of the cellar. Page went into the cellar and told the old man about the horse. The farm owner and his daughters, with Page escorting them out of the cellar, successfully birthed the colt. "Farmer Page" had put his knowledge of farm life to good use even while in the Army.

On the Farm

Third Section of the Mortar Platoon had other notable incidents while on the farm. PFC Francisco Key Palma was from California and he was a bit older than most in the Company. When he had a drink, he became wild and uncontrollable. Corporal Cook could not do anything with him and Palma ended up being transferred out of the Squad and eventually became the Platoon Leader's bodyguard. Palma did however perform another task in his Platoon: he became the official taster of drinks and the Platoon discovered plenty of drinks. The Germans were known to poison liquor as they withdrew from areas and someone as experienced with drinking as Palma did perform a credible task in keeping his buddies safe. While a group of men from Third Section, including Page and Palma argued in the farm yard one afternoon, a stray mortar shell came in. The shell hit an apple tree and the shrapnel hit the "liberated" P 38 pistol that Palma had on his hip. The shrapnel bent the side of the gun! There were cattle on the farm and many of the GIs tried to round them up. "Red" Hayes, the Mortar Platoon's Medic was one of the men that was rounding up the cattle.

Writing Home

While on the Rhine, the Men of H Company had much free time on their hands. Besides enjoying the fresh milk, eggs, chicken, and sleeping in houses, they had time to write letters home for the first time in a long while. Many of the men wrote home to tell their families a little about what had happened to them. One could not write names of locations as that could be dangerous if the mail was intercepted by the Germans. Mail would first be censored by the Platoon Commanders and then by First Sergeant Whalen. The city boys wrote the most and Cohen wrote frequently. Sergeant Lawson would have written a letter home, but he was not much of a writer, with only a 6th Grade education and besides, no one in his family was literate. He decided instead to send a picture home. In one of the magazines that were circulated among the Platoon, Lawson found a big picture of President Roosevelt. During the worst days of the Great Depression, Lawson's family had gathered together on a neighbor's farm where they had a radio and listened to FDR's "Fireside Chats." Lawson's Father always wanted to see a picture of FDR and that is just what Lawson sent home. Kravitz wrote to his girlfriend, Thelma. They had contrived their own code words before he shipped out to the ETO. "Chocolate Pie" was England and "Hamburgers" was France. Kravitz had successfully sent letters home to Thelma as often as he could.

Ray Brejcha

Bandsman Captures German with his Clarinet

Slagle moved with Division Headquarters and the Band while H Company was on the Rhine. The Division Command Post was setup in an area near Lintfort, to the southwest of H Company's position at Rhineberg. The Band had put their instruments away after Holland and were back to their secondary role of MP duty. One morning Brejcha, one of the Band's Clarinet and Alto Sax players, got up from the barn he was sleeping in and went off to do his business. Brejcha, as an MP carried his M-1 Carbine. As he walked a short ways he saw standing at the far end of the street and beside a barn, a German soldier with a rifle slung over his shoulder. Brejcha pulled the bolt on his Carbine and caught the German's attention, who threw up his hands to surrender. Brejcha called for his buddies in the Band to wake up and help him with the prisoner. The 75th Division's Newspaper, "The Mule" ran a story the next morning with an article entitled, "Bandsman Captures German with his Clarinet." The author must have mistaken some details or assumed that a bandsman was unarmed as Brejcha was indeed carrying a Carbine that morning.

The Band at Rhineberg

On the outskirts of Rhineberg, The Division Band was sent to perform for the troops, well behind the front lines. Prior to this event, one of the Band members was killed. Brejcha received a note from a messenger that stated, "Ray, your friend George Lorenz was killed today." Joe Cook was the 75th Division Band Leader and they setup a band stand near one of the aid stations on the outskirts of Rhineberg. Medics and infantrymen gathered around to hear the Band perform songs from Glenn Miller, Artie Shaw and others. Even though they were well behind the front lines, artillery fire could be heard during the concert. Corporal Petersen, the medic that had saved Slagle at Colmar was in attendance for the Band performance and he reunited with Slagle. They became good friends. Petersen had a camera and he took pictures of the Band members. Slagle was not in shape to play the sax and he sat by and watched his buddies play. Brejcha was playing the clarinet during the performance and in the middle of a song, German artillery hit a crossroads not too far away. Infantrymen scrambled off and the Band quickly dispersed. One of the musicians standing behind Brejcha dropped his instrument and fled; the instrument cracked Brejcha in the head and left him with a sizeable gash.

Police Duty

Following the incident at the crossroads, the Division Band members were recalled to MP duties and were tasked with patrolling a town near Rhineberg. Murza from Fourth Squad of First Platoon of H Company was given orders to be transferred back to the Division Band and he reunited with Slagle, whom he thought was dead. The casualty in the Band had freed up a spot for Murza. The Band moved through the town; there were no incidents and the civilians were friendly. There was little to do in the town but take in local cuisine or pull guard duty. A truck carrying Coca-Cola came up and nearly caused a riot among the GIs that had not had one in months. Someone in the Band had a camera and all the men in the Band were photographed in and around town. The Division Command Post moved up and the bandsmen were tasked with more routine guard duty.

Rhineberg, Germany   **Robert O. Slagle   Mike Murza**

Night attacks on the Rhine

Every afternoon and before dusk, "Bed Check Charlie" would fly high overhead and spot targets for German artillery and especially for German aircraft that would attempt to make a bombing run at night. The Germans were desperately trying to knock out the remaining bridges over the Rhine. Hitler's mad scheme of buying himself more time was for naught. Staff Sergeant Prater had a good view of one of the remaining bridges over the Rhine from his observation post. At night, German aircraft swooped down and tried to bomb the bridge; the result was a fantastic display of anti-aircraft fire. The whole sky was lit up with anti-aircraft fire; from the mortar man's perspective it was like all the fireworks in the world going off! Whenever a German aircraft came near the bridge, the firing would commence and there would be tracer bullets flying everywhere. The German aircraft were not shot down, but the fire forced them to veer off from their intended target. "Bed Check Charlie" would continue its flights into the night; it did little more than harass GIs who were trying to get some sleep.

A Machine Gunner's Nightly Duty

The men of First and Second Platoons moved out of their farmhouses at night and up to a series of dikes before the shoreline of the Rhine. The machine gunners setup on one of the dikes. They supported patrols moving over the Rhine every night. Their function was to provide covering fire in case one of the patrols got into trouble. Not all of the machine gun squads were up at the shoreline; some were further back, observing for German patrols. First Platoon encountered a German patrol one night. The Germans walked right into their machine gun and they suffered casualties. Two prisoners were taken and both looked very scared. During the night, the Germans would periodically send up flares to illuminate the sky and try and attempt to reveal the positions of the Americans. Smith from Fourth squad of Second Platoon would stand perfectly still like a tree to avoid attracting the German's attention.

The Almost Fatal Pit Stop

Chaiklin had first arrived to H Company in Holland with another man, Pete Pontes from Hartford, Connecticut. Chaiklin and Pontes had formed a sort of bond as many GIs did who hailed from the same locale. Pontes was crafty and quite a card shark. On several occasions, Chaiklin had watched him cheat. Pontes knew Chaiklin saw him do it too. Chaiklin was not going to say anything, considering Pontes was much older and stronger than he was. Chaiklin would not get into a card game that had Pontes in it. One night when the Section was moving up to the Rhine to support the patrols, Chaiklin went off for a pit stop and the Section went on without him. He tried to find them, but got lost and realized that he must have passed them somehow. He ended up on the Rhine and

177

turned back. Chaiklin did not stop until he heard the click of a safety going off. Pontes asked for the password in his very soft-spoken voice and Chaiklin did not hear it. Chaiklin was very lucky.

Suffering from Bad Leadership

One day, while on the Rhine, the men of H Company were to be inoculated for Typhus. Chaiklin was on guard duty in the farmhouse that served as First Platoon's Command Post. This duty consisted of sitting by the field phone to await any calls. A call came in from Lieutenant Bergheimer who said something along the lines of, "The Platoon needs shots, send the first ten men at 1300 and the rest at fifteen minute intervals." Chaiklin relayed Bergheimer's orders and watched as the first squad came in. They moved along the farm's field fence that was covered on one side by dense hedges. The Germans clearly saw this movement in broad daylight and shelled the squad; there were casualties, one of them being severe. After the incident, Bergheimer called and chewed out Chaiklin, telling him, "I told you to have them infiltrate." Chaiklin could not remember the exact words and did feel the casualties were his fault. Sergeant Larson reassured him. As Chaiklin calmed down, he reviewed the situation and concluded that there was no way to infiltrate; the squad had moved over open farmland. The incident was yet another case of Bergheimer's general lack of competence. A man of his age and apparent experience should have concluded the great risks of the orders he gave. Instead and as always, Bergheimer laid the blame on his subordinates.

Attitude before the Crossing

As the men of H Company awaited the inevitable event of crossing the Rhine and into Germany, many different opinions arose. Cohen was very forceful with his opinions. He was going to cross the Rhine, head straight to Berlin and put a bullet in Hitler's head, or so he told everyone who would listen. Despite his comments, Cohen was very nervous. Lawson had his own reservations about crossing the Rhine. He told his friend "Hay Seed" that he could not understand how he had come through all these battles without so much as a scratch; he was sure that his days were numbered. Sergeant "Kirk" said that he thought the war would soon be over after the crossing; but he later said it was wishful thinking on his part. Others were anxious about the crossing, wanting to get it over with.

Overall, crossing the Rhine was a big event and everyone had their own personal thoughts about it.

The Great Crossing

On the afternoon of 23 March, H Company received word that they were to support the Rhine crossings. The Mortar Platoon moved up behind a levee on the riverbank and dug emplacement pits for their mortars. Second Platoon was dug into the side of a hill, several hundred feet above the river bank. First Platoon took up its positions right along the riverbank at the end of one of the dikes. At the stroke of midnight, the American guns opened up to support the crossings. 52 artillery battalions with 672 artillery pieces fired over 378,000 shells at the German side of the Rhine; it was the largest artillery barrage in history. H Company's Mortar Platoon began firing just before 0500 and was instructed to continue firing until all of their ammunition was expended. The artillery was deafening; no GI had ever heard such intense artillery fire before and no one ever would again. The machine gunners were firing tracer bullets across the Rhine to guide the crossings.

The machine gun ammo bearers from First Platoon were continually sent up to the gun crews at the front to bring them more ammo. The ammo bearers left the farmhouses and walked across the farm fields and over the slight man-made rises that resembled dikes. Chaiklin was one such ammo bearer and after delivering his ammo, just prior to H-Hour, he returned to the Platoon Command Post. Lieutenant Bergheimer ordered those not at the front to dig in. Chaiklin entered into the stone outbuilding of the barn. It had plenty of hay inside. Chaiklin was there with several other men, including Staff Sergeant "Stretch" Wilson. Chaiklin heard a lot of noise outside; the beginning of the artillery barrage, and he thought he was missing something. "Stretch" told Chaiklin, "Be happy you are here." After First Platoon completed its firing, the men returned to the Platoon Command Post. One of the men was a big loud mouth and claimed he would get a Purple Heart for a pinprick he received from one of the American shells that exploded nearby. Sergeant Lawson's Fourth Squad was setup at the front, but he had different orders. Lawson had a radioman assigned to him and they were sent up towards a bridge in the area and were told to watch for German aircraft and report them to an Anti-Aircraft gun crew that was positioned in the area. Lawson spotted several German fighters that flew low overhead, but the anti-aircraft fire was so intense that they could not come anywhere near the bridge. Lawson reported what he saw. One of the fighters attempted a second pass and tried to hit the bridge. Lawson watched as fire hit the aircraft and it streamed flames as it flew out of the area.

The mortar men were dropping the shells down the tube of the mortar as fast as they could. They fired more on that one night than at any other point in the war. The paint on the barrel of the mortar began to smoke and it got so hot that it could not be touched. The barrel of the mortar began to glow a cherry red! The mortar men got nervous about dropping the shell in and having it explode before it would hit the firing pin. There was very little if any counter-battery fire in the 291st Infantry's sector; the Germans must have had one fantastic wake up call on the morning of 24 March! The Third Section of the Mortar Platoon was tasked with firing smoke rounds across a bridge to the south of the crossing point, in an effort to divert the German's attention away from the true crossing point. The 30th and 79th Divisions passed through the 291st Infantry's positions and began the Great Crossing of the Rhine. By first light, thousands of Allied troops had crossed the Rhine and were rapidly progressing through German territory.

Pontoon Bridges

From 24 to 28 March, H Company was setup to defend a pontoon bridge that was being setup in their sector by men from the 275th Engineer Combat Battalion. The engineers would take small boats out on the river to work on the bridges. The speed by which the bridges were built was amazing to the men of H Company, who watched from the riverbank. It only took about three days to complete. As soon as it was complete, units began to move across the bridge day and night. The Germans were long gone. Sergeant Larson's Squad was setup to guard the bridges being built. One afternoon Chaiklin laid on his back and watched a massive American bomber formation fly high overhead; he counted 750 aircraft. These bombers were on target to bomb the Ruhr Valley, just beyond the Rhine. By March 1945, the German Luftwaffe could put up very little opposition to the large numbers of Allied bombers routinely pounding targets all across Germany. The German fuel shortage was now at critical levels. German aircraft had been unsuccessful in destroying the bridges across the Rhine and the Germans took such desperate measures as to attempt to hit the bridges with V-1 and V-2 rockets; these were far from accurate. Chaiklin heard the rockets flying overhead and could see them trailing fire into the night.

H Company Crosses the Rhine

By 28 March, it was the 291st Infantry's turn to make the crossing. They crossed on several different pontoon bridges and went in different directions once across the Rhine. Second Battalion, 291st Infantry crossed in the wake of all other elements of the 75th Division; they brought up the rear. Troops were marching in two columns on the bridge's treads. In the middle of the river, the Division Commander, Major General Porter was in a jeep with a war correspondent standing next to it. It was quite an impressive sight. Once they had crossed the Rhine, H Company dug in on the other side and assumed defensive positions in case of a German counter-attack. The Mortar Platoon was among the last units to make the crossing; their jeeps full of mortar shells followed them.

Bandsmen on the Rhine

By late March Slagle had recovered from his wound at Colmar and wanted to get back to his buddies in H Company, but could not find any means to get back to them. He was restless at the Division Command Post and wanted to get back anyway he could. By mid-March, Slagle had been moved again to Headquarters' Special Police Platoon and was overseeing incoming traffic to the Command Post; it was not to his liking. When he was in the Deputy Division Commander's makeshift office, Slagle asked him if there was anyway that he could get back to H Company. General Mickle was willing to grant him passage and signed his orders. Slagle went on a troop truck bound for what he was told was Second Battalion, 291st Infantry's position. Unfortunately, he was instead sent to First Battalion's sector near Duisberg, Germany. By 28 March, elements of the Division had crossed the Rhine. Slagle was stuck with D Company. He knew no one there and wanted out. No trucks were going in the direction of Second Battalion and Slagle could do nothing but wait patiently. D Company had little activity in their sector and Slagle spent much of his time in a local tavern. He enjoyed the food and was learning a bit about German culture. He met a girl there and got acquainted with her family. The Germans in the area were quite peaceful and actually generous to their American occupiers. The Germans in town invited American GIs to dinner every night.

Returning to H Company

On 29 March, while H Company was dug in along the German side of the Rhine, a jeep pulled up with Slagle in the passenger's seat. Slagle was directed to Second Lieutenant Bergheimer's position, inside of one of the farmhouses. When Slagle walked in, he saw three familiar faces: Bergheimer, First Sergeant Whalen, and Sergeant Lawson. Lawson had a joyous reunion with Slagle, whom he had thought was killed at Colmar. Whalen was not pleased to see Slagle; they had last seen each other in the Battalion Aid Station after the battle in Colmar, where Whalen had taken away Slagle's Purple Heart. Bergheimer shouted at Slagle and demanded to know why he had gone AWOL. Slagle explained what had happened to him and how he ended up at the Division Command Post. Slagle was told that the Platoon had been restructured after Colmar. Lawson had been promoted to Sergeant in Slagle's absence. Slagle asked if he could return to duty as part of Lawson's Squad. Bergheimer raised his voice again and told Slagle to get lost; to go back to Division, he was unwanted. Slagle stood up to Bergheimer and said, "Sir, I will return to duty now." Bergheimer shouted, "Who the Hell do you think you are?" Slagle pulled out his written orders that were signed by General Mickle and handed them to Bergheimer. Whalen and Bergheimer stood wide-eyed and said nothing. Slagle said, "Sir, I will now return to duty with your permission." Lawson and Slagle walked off together with no words from their superiors. Slagle was glad to be back with his buddies in First Platoon.

Cooking on the Move

By 30 March, H Company began a series of rapid advances through German territory. The Company moved to the outskirts of the town of Dorsten and billeted themselves on another farm. The whole area was abandoned and the GIs found dozens of chickens in the yard. The men were hungry and the farm boys knew all about chickens. Lawson and "Hay Seed" killed some chickens, skinned them, and began passing them out to others in the Platoon to cook. Many men tried to cook chickens or rabbits in their helmets. Ross also caught some chickens and was beginning to prepare chicken stew in a pot he found. The men assumed they would be billeting in the area overnight and took their time with cooking. Just after Ross got his stew started and it was beginning to get warm, a jeep pulled up and an officer told them that H Company was to move into the town of Dorsten. Ross took his pot of stew that was still warm and brought it with him to Dorsten, where he found a stove to cook it on. The Company had plenty of chicken to eat that night. A supply of champagne was found in town and those that drank had plenty to drink before turning in for the night. While moving through the Ruhr the liberated diet also had some variability. There was fish from a pond on the farm. The fish were collected by using a grenade to stun them. Another time a pig was slaughtered.

Friendly Fire

On the farm in Dorsten, the men of Second Squad of First Platoon began to clean their weapons. They were sitting in a circle and talking, when Sergeant Larson's nephew, a jeep driver with the 375th Medical Battalion, arrived to visit his uncle. Larson was fooling around with his nephew when somehow his pistol went off. His nephew was hit and was taken to the Aid Station. The men in Second Squad were very upset and nervous over what would happen to their Sergeant. A month later, the men in the Squad were called into the office of the Regimental Commander, Lieutenant Colonel Robertson to be interviewed about what happened. It was only an accident, Larson had not tried to shoot his nephew, but his men had to officially testify to that.

On the Move

On 31 March at 0300, the men of H Company were awakened and ordered to prepare to move out immediately. Second Battalion, 291st Infantry was to attack an area on the outskirts of Dorsten. Many of the men were still drunk from the champagne they drank only hours earlier. As they reached their target, they found no resistance; the Germans had withdrawn. Second Battalion captured a synthetic rubber plant. It had been bombed in August 1944 and was no longer operational. Upon inspection, the machinery was found to be in rusted condition; no one had been there in a long time. On the outskirts of the town, Second Battalion discovered two slave labor camps. One contained over 3,000 Polish laborers who were living in terrible conditions with limited food. Many of them were very sick. The Germans had run off and abandoned the camp as Second

Battalion approached. In an area nearby, Staff Sergeant Prater was among a group that discovered a small slave labor camp containing primarily old people. The lock was shot off and the people were told they were free and could take any clothing or food they wanted from the town.

Halting the Battalion

On the afternoon of 31 March, Second Battalion continued its rapid move through German territory. They moved ten miles on foot and met no resistance. Carrying the machine guns, mortars, and ammunition for both, bogged down H Company and they had to stop and rest for a short while in several places. Second Battalion had moved out of the vicinity of Dorsten and into an area near the small town of Sickingmuhle. A creek stood in front of the town and it had to be crossed. F Company moved to the north to flank the town and E Company was to cross the creek and move into town. H Company was to support the attack. As E Company approached the creek, panzerfaust fire came from a small stone farmhouse that commanded the bridge over the creek. E Company and sections of H Company were pinned down. Panzerfaust shells continued to be fired and Second Battalion's advance was entirely halted. Slagle was pinned down just behind E Company and he tried to get a clear shot at the Germans in the farmhouse, but was unable. Larson's Second Squad of First Platoon was to the rear of the column, taking cover in a slight depression. They heard that snipers and panzerfausts were responsible for the holdup. Air-Support was called in and a British Typhoon aircraft opened up with its cannon, 500 yards behind Larson's position. The Typhoon hit the farmhouse and halted the panzerfaust activity. G Company that had been in reserve, flanked the stone farmhouse and captured a few Hitler Youth members who were responsible for holding up Second Battalion's advance.

Attack on Sickingmuhle

After seizing the farmhouse that commanded the creek crossing, E, G, and H Companies crossed Sickingmuhle Creek and entered the town. H Company supported the rifle companies as they began to clear out the few remaining homes in town. The Germans responded with rifle fire, but they were quickly pushed into a retreat and were captured by F Company that had maneuvered into town from the north. A German 88

184

was hit by mortar fire from H Company's Third Platoon and its crew killed. Riflemen of G Company overran another German gun and its crew killed. By dusk, the town had been secured. Sickingmuhle was in rubble from the Allied bombings of only days earlier. The American bombing raids were highly successful in destroying whole towns. The GI witnessed the after effects of this devastation first hand. H Company rested in the clearing outside of the burned out town. Only a handful of buildings were still standing and in any shape to serve as sleeping quarters. H Company split up into platoons and slept in the remaining buildings. During the night, they began to receive a few shells and intermittent shelling continued through the night, with no casualties.

Into the Die Haard Forest

On 1 April, Second Battalion, 291st Infantry continued their rapid succession of movements into the Die Haard Forest, which had been a German National Park. Second Battalion encountered a few German snipers that were picked off by the rifle companies. Four 88 mm and two 75 mm guns were overrun with their crews killed or captured. In an area of dense foliage, Sergeant Lawson thought he heard some movement and ordered his Squad to halt. Slagle moved up to one corner of the brush and "Hay Seed" took the other side. Five very young German children in Volkssturm uniforms put their hands up and surrendered. They had no weapons and were visibly terrified. Lawson handed them some food from his rations and sent them back under guard to the Battalion Command Post. The prisoners were probably no more than nine or ten years old. There were few such incidents in the forest and the Battalion moved very quickly. By dusk they had reached a lavish German manor on the edge of the forest. There were several beautiful homes, including guesthouses. The rifle companies of Second Battalion continued on to a small village nearby and H Company billeted in the homes.

Sleeping in Luxury

Cohen of Third Squad of First Platoon rushed into one of the houses. Sergeant "Kirk," his Squad Leader was not far behind. Cohen took everything of value he could carry including a collection of very old antique knives. "Kirk" got himself an old pistol, a beautiful antique. The home was the most beautiful and luxurious house that any of the men had ever seen. Cohen found a featherbed and jumped in and threw his boots off.

Men of Second Section poured into the house and were amazed by what they found inside. The latecomers had to sleep on chairs or on couches, both were very comfortable; there was not an uncomfortable spot in the whole house. Cohen walked all around the house looking for anything of value to "liberate." What he was doing made no sense to his buddies, there was no way he could carry much of it off. Lawson and "Hay Seed" stood in awe inside the house; both coming from very humble beginnings, they had never seen anything like it. Lawson said, "So this is how the rich live." Third Platoon stayed in the main house, which had belonged to a German sportsman-hunter. In the morning, it was time to move out and Cohen decided that he was not going to leave anything of value for rear-area units and definitely was not going to allow some wealthy German to return home and reclaim his valuables. Cohen took his rifle butt and smashed up mirrors, antiques, anything of value that could be broken. While others did not criticize Cohen for laying waste to German property, they could not bear to look at what he was doing to such a beautiful home.

Scouting for Targets

Staff Sergeant Hicks, who commanded Second Section of H Company's Mortar Platoon was moving up as a forward observer with one of the rifle platoons. Ross had volunteered to carry the heavy radio backpack. They moved along a two-lane road and came to an embankment with an overpass across the road. There was a farmhouse near it and they thought they saw a German scurry into the house. Staff Sergeant Hicks radioed to his Section to fire on the farmhouse. The first salvo fell just ahead of the house; the second fell just short of it. The third salvo scored a direct hit on the farmhouse. The duty of clearing the farmhouse and its immediate areas were left to Second Battalion's riflemen. Hicks and Ross continued on to scout for more targets of opportunity.

Nearing the Canal

By 2 April, Second Battalion had moved to within sight of the Dortmund-Ems Canal; a route that led straight into the heart of the German industrial center in the Ruhr Valley. It was the 75th Division's objective to clear out the Ruhr Pocket of German resistance and to encircle Dortmund: the center of industry. H Company encountered no resistance along the canal and moved into farmhouses in view of the canal. The Germans had retreated across the canal before Second Battalion had arrived. There was little activity of importance on the first day in the area. On 3 April, H Company separated by platoon and moved into a series of small family homes. Third Platoon moved into an artist's house near the canal. The Company had thought they would be crossing the canal by the night of 3 April, but orders did not come. On 4 April the 289th Regiment moved into the area and relieved the 291st Regiment, who was sent back to stay in farmhouses. Elements of the 289th Regiment were to cross the canal on the night of 4 April and scout ahead. As the men of H Company remained in the area, an all-black platoon moved through and crossed the canal. It brought out much commentary from the men of H Company.

Encountering Resistance

During the night of 4 April, the 289th Regiment encountered some resistance in the area of the Dortmund-Ems Canal. By 5 April, orders changed and the 291st Regiment relieved the 289th and was to lead the attack over the canal on 6 April. A few German troops could be seen on the banks of the Ems, opposite H Company's position. Some of the riflemen of Second Battalion fired at them and they moved off. Slagle was pulling guard duty with Lawson and he saw on the other side, partially hidden by brush, a German officer squatting and reading a newspaper. Slagle took aim with his M-1 Garand and fired a shot straight through the newspaper. The German got up with his pants around his ankles and ran off into the woods. It appeared as though all German resistance on the other side of the canal had withdrawn by evening. On a canal bridge to the south, the 290th Regiment prepared to cross as well. Combat engineers were busily constructing more pontoon bridges to move tanks and vehicles across on.

Resistance Near the Canal

The Germans put up significant resistance as Second Battalion began to probe the immediate area near the canal. Staff Sergeant Prater commanding First Section of Third Platoon of H Company had moved up as a forward observer with riflemen of G Company. One of the riflemen had his canteen shot and the water poured out on him; he thought for a moment that he had been hit. Prater took cover with Malarich, his gunner, in a bomb crater as German shells came in. A shell exploded nearby and they heard the shrapnel whistle, then pop. A piece of the shrapnel hit Malarich on the leg. Malarich grabbed his leg and said, "I've been hit in the leg." Prater checked over Malarich and he was fine. They looked around in the bomb crater and saw a piece of shrapnel that measured about 3 x 2 x 1 inches and it was lying in the dirt and smoking. The flat side of it had hit Malarich on the leg, but it did not even break the skin. Malarich was a very lucky man, he could have easily lost his leg from the jagged edges of the steel shrapnel.

The Actions of a Forward Observer

Staff Sergeant Prater continued to move up with riflemen of G Company to scout for targets for his Mortar Section. At one point he was very close to the front and helped two wounded riflemen out of a ditch. Prater scouted the area around the Dortmund-Ems Canal and his position was just 30 or 40 yards away from the enemy, which were entrenched on the other side of the Ems. He spotted German troops moving about in the trenches and some of the riflemen would take an occasional shot at them. The shots were ineffective as only the tops of the German's helmets could be seen. Prater called in for mortar fire and the Germans withdrew from their trenches. Prater also called for his Section to fire smoke to cover rescue attempts in moving out the wounded riflemen on the front lines. Considerable sniper fire came from buildings close to the canal that had not yet been cleared. As Prater moved with his radioman through an open field near the canal, he spotted a field bunker that was thought to be a storage cellar. Prater thought that he might find something good to eat in it. As Prater and his radioman entered, two young Volkssturmers came out with their hands up. Two prisoners were taken without even trying.

A Cook's Adventure

During the night of 5 April, orders were issued to cross the Dortmund-Ems Canal at 0445, before dawn and after the men had been given a hot meal. Earlier in the evening, there was little to do and many drinkers in the Company got loaded on the plentiful supply of wine in the area. This was the case of H Company's kitchen truck driver; he had several drinks and was looped. The task of moving the truck up to H Company's position to feed the men then fell on the shoulders of the assistant driver. He was a small man, ten years or more older than most in the Company. He had been with H Company since Breckinridge, but his vision was too poor to be a soldier; he wore thick glasses and often wished he would get at least a small taste of action. He had performed the rather mundane duties of a cook's helper during the battles in the Ardennes and at Colmar. In the early morning of 6 April, the assistant driver got his taste of action.

The assistant kitchen truck driver got the driver into the passenger's seat; he was out cold. The assistant then drove his truck, under blackout conditions, in the direction of the Dortmund-Ems Canal. It was raining very hard that night and with no lights and his poor vision, he managed to get lost on the road. He took a wrong turn, but then thought he was back on the correct route. The rain came down heavier just as he came within sight of the canal. He pulled up close, but saw no one around. He decided he must have taken a wrong turn after all. As he was about to pull away, two men came out of the brush carrying rifles. He thought they looked like officers and assumed one of them was Captain Goodnight. The men waved and walked up to the truck. Just as they got up to the front of the truck, he saw that the men were in SS uniforms! It was dark and raining heavily; it was hard to see anything. The Germans realized their mistake as well and one man raised his burp gun. The assistant driver made a split second decision; he had no weapon handy and was not going to become a casualty. He hit the gas and ran over both of the Germans. He backed up over them again, hearing the clunk of the tires hitting their helmets and he rushed out of the area. He was scared and had an adrenaline rush, somehow he made it to H Company's position, just a little late. The driver awoke with a bad headache and asked if he missed anything. His assistant replied, "Not a thing."

The Ruhr Pocket

"By April, we thought the war was all but over… we never imagined that we would fight our toughest battle against some of the most decorated veterans in the German Army."

-Sergeant "Kirk", First Platoon, H Company

Dortmund-Ems Canal- H Company crossed this foot bridge

Tommy Thompson- Albert Galbreth (1ˢᵗ Platoon)   **Castrop-Rauxel, Germany**

Middle of picture: Capt Owen L. Goodnight Jr- Castrop-Rauxel, Germany

Crossing the Dortmund-Ems Canal

On 6 April, Second Battalion, 291st Infantry was awakened at 0430 and given a hot meal. H Company's kitchen truck had arrived and the meal was being prepared in one of the German homes along the banks of the canal. The men of H Company were fatigued from the constant movements over the past few days and the overall lack of sleep. The heavy rains had continued through the night and into the early morning hours. After completing their meal the men prepared to move toward their destination of the town of Castrop-Rauxel. G Company led the advance across the Dortmund-Ems Canal on a small wooden footbridge. F Company moved across next with H Company following them. A few rifle shots were heard in the distance, but the heavy rain had masked most of the sounds. Sergeant Lawson led his Squad and he was carrying his machine gun's tri-pod as "Hay Seed" had overloaded himself with ammo. Slagle was carrying the machine gun. As they neared the end of the footbridge Lawson heard a bullet fly right past him and a second one hit him in the shoulder, knocking him off his feet. His helmet fell off and he dropped the tri-pod due to the sharp pain in his shoulder. He managed to get back on his feet and put his helmet back on as a third bullet hit his helmet just above his eyes; had his helmet not been on, he would have been killed. Lawson was flat on his back with a terrible pain in his head; he thought he was going to die. Men scurried across the bridge to seek cover as a few more rifle shots came from the direction of dense woods, where Germans had been seen in previous days. Men from Second Section of First Platoon put Sergeant Lawson on a litter and prepared to carry him back across the canal and to the Battalion Aid Station. "Hay Seed" looked him over and said, "It's not too bad, you are going to be alright." Lawson was given a shot of morphine and blacked out on the litter.

Sergeant Larson, commanding Second Squad of First Platoon proceeded across the canal just before sunrise without incurring fire. First Section was some distance behind the Second Section, who by then was already attached to G Company. Chaiklin had a very difficult time trying to walk across the slick wooden planks of the bridge while carrying a heavy load of ammo. The infantry advance into the vicinity of Castrop-Rauxel had already begun. It was a fast paced move, stopping only to briefly organize with a section of H Company's Mortar Platoon, and a section of machine guns attached to both G and F Companies. First Battalion was attacking to the left of Second Battalion's route with the battle order structured so that the two battalions would meet after having taken

193

the town in a double-envelopment maneuver. Plans are subject to change and the battle in Castrop-Rauxel would prove to be anything but a "by the book" engagement.

Entering Rutgers

By the beginning of the attack, sections of H Company were well spread out and following close to the attacking rifle platoons. H Company's machine gun sections were on a quick move, with orders to fire on targets of opportunity. First Section of Second Platoon under the command of Staff Sergeant Chisholm was the lead machine gun element in the attack; they followed G Company's Second Platoon on the right. Third Platoon of G Company attacked on the left with the Second Section of Second Platoon of H Company following it. First Platoon of G Company rode tanks behind its two attacking rifle platoons, followed by the Second Section of First Platoon of H Company under Staff Sergeant Slawson. Third Section of H Company's Mortar Platoon under the command of Staff Sergeant Galway also followed the tanks (Galway was promoted and replaced Staff Sergeant Flud after he was wounded on the Rhine). As they reached the outskirts of the small town of Rutgers towards their objective of Castrop-Rauxel they began to encounter increasing sniper fire and 120 mm mortars. Most of the houses were two story homes and were very old. Castrop-Rauxel was an ancient town that dated from the 9th Century. As the attacking platoons moved through Rutgers, sniper fire came from seemingly everywhere and mortars landed in front and behind of the rifle platoon's position. The situation was quickly worsening.

Encountering Elite Troops

The German troops in Rutgers and in Castrop-Rauxel were among the finest troops in the entire German Army during World War II. They were from the 2nd Fallschirmjager (Parachute Infantry) Division. They were battle-hardened veterans and many of them had been in combat since 1939. By April 1945, they were down to regimental strength, but they were not to be treated lightly. Their last major combat was against their American counterpart, the 101st Airborne Division during the D-Day landings. The 2nd Fallschirmjager Division had orders to fight to the last man. Also in the towns were Volkssturm, "Citizen's Army" troops which were little more than old men and boys handed a rifle and told to fight. Many of them did not even have a uniform and instead fought in their civilian clothes. Most of the Volkssturmers did not want to fight, but were shot if they tried to surrender. The towns of Rutgers and Castrop-Rauxel had been heavily bombed and in the rubble, there were plenty of hiding spots for snipers. Further in the town of Castrop-Rauxel was a major railroad that carried coal from the mines and chlorine gas tanks away from the plant in town. SS troops controlled the railroad and they too were experienced soldiers.

House to House Combat

G Company's First and Second Platoons met heavy resistance inside of the town of Rutgers. Snipers fired on them from the front and to the flanks. The men of G Company took cover along the sides of houses and entered the houses to confront their occupants. In some houses they found terrified women and children, while in other houses they met the enemy face to face, often resulting in combat in close quarters. Phosphorous grenades were thrown into many of the houses to induce the surrender of their occupants. The men of H Company were not far behind G Company and once the riflemen cleared houses, machine gun squads would enter the houses and setup their guns to support G Company's advance. The Third Platoon of H Company also continued its movement and prepared to ready their mortars to fire when orders came. When snipers were located, groups of two or three riflemen would pursue them. In several instances, the snipers would retreat and lead the riflemen into an ambush. It was a terrible situation and the German Fallschirmjagers were a highly motivated enemy. Despite the support G Company received, the advance began to collapse with men of both G and H Company seeking cover from the incoming sniper fire.

A Breakdown of Communications

Sniper fire began to claim casualties among the men of G Company. First Lieutenant Ripley commanding Third Platoon of G Company was shot by a sniper and laid wounded. Second Platoon of G Company had lost contact with F Company to the right of their position. Captain Druillard attempted to contact his First Platoon and the tanks by radio, but was unsuccessful. Debris and railroad tracks had halted the advance of the supporting tanks. The only route forward for the tanks was a highway on the outskirts of town and it was covered by German Tigers that were well-entrenched in cover in

Castrop-Rauxel. Panzerfaust crews were also operating in the area. By noon, Second and Third Platoons of G Company had made it up to the railroad yard in Castrop-Rauxel and to the main track. Second Platoon and Second Section of First Platoon of H Company were moving up in close support. As they attempted to move through the railroad yard, sniper fire became intense and the men of G and H Companies sought what cover they could find. There were a number of trains on the tracks and SS troops were in the process of loading cargo aboard them. The SS troops aboard the trains were quick to take action. 20-mm fire poured down from the train's defensive guns. Communication was lost between platoons and between sections.

Slagle's Run

Sergeant "Kirk's" Third Squad of First Platoon took cover inside a house near the train tracks. 20-mm fire followed them right up to the house and then halted. The men of G and H Companies spread out and began to return fire. Second Platoon of H Company crossed the main track and reached the other end of town, encountering no resistance. Second Section of First Platoon could not follow; they were pinned down. Suddenly, snipers began to open up on Second Platoon from an upper floor of a building. They were pinned down, but had some degree of cover. The radioman, Sergeant Ramirez took fire and his backpack was damaged and unusable. Slagle, who had taken command of his Squad after Sergeant Lawson was wounded, saw that Second Platoon was in a position to clear the path ahead, but there was no way to contact them. Slagle carefully observed the area and the locations of the German troops. Through heavy rifle, mortar, and machine gun fire, Slagle dashed out from cover, fired a few shots at a German machine gun nest, and climbed a chain link fence near the railroad yard. Slagle ran about 100 yards through enemy fire, unscathed and linked up with Second Platoon that was heavily disorganized. He shouted, "Go! Go!" and the men of Second Platoon climbed over the rail tracks and charged into the German line. They knocked out a machine gun nest and several snipers. Second Platoon moved rapidly through the town with Slagle leading them. No one was wounded.

After Slagle's move, fire targeted his Squad's position and the rest of the men could not follow. "Hay Seed" took command of the Squad and led them forward to a small area of cover below the main track. 120-mm mortars landed all around the tracks. SS troops got out of the train with their burp guns and fired on the Americans. "Hay Seed" ordered his Squad to lay perfectly flat and not to move so much as an inch. "Kirk's" Squad got their machine gun setup in the front window of the house and opened fire on the SS troops that had gotten out of the train; he accomplished little, but attracting heavy fire from German anti-aircraft guns that had been depressed to fire on troop positions. "Kirk" ordered his men to take down the gun and seek cover at the back end of the house. A quick inspection revealed that the house was filled with German machine gun ammunition and mortar shells.

Trapped

Sergeant "Kirk's" Squad began to take heavy fire from depressed 40-mm anti-aircraft guns. The front of the house was blown away. The men in "Kirk's" Squad were terrified. The Germans knew that they had ammunition in the house and had targeted it. "Kirk" did not know what to do and he was in a terrible situation; there was no means of escape. Seconds later German fire hit the ammunition in the house, setting it ablaze. The mortar shells exploded and threw the men of Third Squad against the wall of the house. Amazingly, none of them were wounded; they just had the wind knocked out of them. The house was on fire and filled with smoke. Sergeant "Kirk" yelled for the men to get out of the house, while they still could. They ran out of the house and through sniper fire to some cover behind another house. "Kirk" was in shock and suffering from smoke inhalation. Cohen, also suffering from the smoke, tapped him on the shoulder and said, "We are missing two." Sergeant "Kirk" quickly noticed that two of his young replacement ammo bearers did not make it out of the house. "Kirk" saw that the house was engulfed in flames and he was too shaken up to do anything. Captain Goodnight arrived by jeep to their position and was surveying the situation.

The Heroics of Captain Goodnight

Sergeant "Kirk" could barely raise a voice, still coughing from the smoke. He staggered to Goodnight's position and pointed to the burning house, just managing to get out a few words: "My men are trapped inside." Without any hesitation, Captain Goodnight leaped out of the jeep and ran through sniper fire and made it into the burning house. A part of the roof caved in and explosions could be heard from the German ordinance inside. Seconds later, Goodnight emerged from the house with the two ammo bearers slung over his broad shoulders. All three of them were black from the smoke. As rifle shots rained down upon his position from snipers on the other side of the street, Goodnight ran back to the cover of the house where "Kirk" and his men were being checked out by Romano, First Platoon's medic. The two ammo bearers that Goodnight rescued were unharmed, just suffering from smoke inhalation. "Kirk" was in awe of the heroic scene he had just witnessed. Goodnight stopped for a moment and told them that they were needed and to get back to duty as soon as they could. Goodnight got back in his jeep and moved up toward the railroad tracks. "Kirk's" Squad rested for a while, tried to calm themselves down, and prepared to move up. Though they were all very shaken up, they did not have the luxury of time to contemplate how lucky they all were to still be alive. A few moments later they moved up to the tracks and joined up with Fourth Squad that was about to make a move.

Pinned Down

"Hay Seed," now commanding Fourth Squad had been pinned down for sometime from machine gun fire. It had quieted down and he told his men to move up. They made it only a few feet before another machine gun opened up on them. Once again, they laid flat on the ground. By this time "Kirk" and Third Squad had linked up with them and they moved as a Section. Staff Sergeant Slawson was behind their position and his jeep could not move up due to the sporadic artillery that continued to come in. "Hay Seed" was laying flat on his back and put his hand on a grenade he was carrying. The machine gun fire began to slow down; a few short bursts, then nothing at all. "Hay Seed" reasoned that the Germans had run out of ammunition, but he was not willing to take a chance and find out. A German "Potato Masher" stick grenade was tossed over near their position and it produced a loud explosion. No one was hurt. The German grenades lacked the "punch" of their American counterparts. More grenades were tossed over, but fell far behind their position.

"Hay Seed" whispered, "I want everyone's grenades now!" "Hay Seed" tossed four or five grenades over the railroad embankment and then fell flat down again. They heard a few Germans shout, the grenades exploded, then dead silence. There was no activity at all from the Germans on the other side of the embankment. "Kirk" suggested that it might well be a trap to lure them out into the open. After several minutes, they heard footsteps coming towards them from the German position. "Kirk" pulled out his pistol as an SS officer walked right over to their position with his hands up. The German had blood trickling from his ears, nose, and mouth; his eyes were red with blood. The German was trembling and emphatically shouting that he wanted to surrender. The grenades that "Hay Seed" tossed had landed directly in the midst of the German machine gun crew, killing them all. The SS officer evidently had been standing in close proximity to them. The prisoner was taken to the Battalion Aid Station for treatment; he lived.

Advancing Under Fire

Riflemen from G Company picked off the snipers that were held up in the control tower in the railroad yard. They were partly responsible for holding up Second Battalion's advance. With the area cleared, Second and Third Platoons of G Company proceeded with their advance. More house to house fighting resulted, with snipers fleeing many of the buildings. Riflemen from G Company ran after the snipers and the advance again slowed down. Due to continuing sniper fire, G Company moved up by means of clearing one house after the other and using the houses as cover. It was a slow, but successful process. One could not walk directly through the streets without attracting a volume of sniper fire. Second Section of First Platoon of H Company had reached the outskirts of town and setup their machine guns to defend the highway that the tanks were to move up on. G Company regained contact with C Company that was on their left and by 1700, the southern outskirts of town had been reached.

Losing Officers

First Lieutenant Craig arrived as a replacement to command Second Platoon of H Company prior to the crossing of the Dortmund-Ems Canal; he had no connection to William Craig who was killed at Colmar. Lieutenant Craig had no combat experience prior to arriving to H Company, as he was a replacement fresh from the United States.

Craig acted as a forward observer for Second Platoon in Rutgers and had moved up with one of G Company's rifle platoons. He was caught out in the open by German artillery and was killed. Lieutenant Craig had moved up too far; a risky move and a clear sign that he lacked actual combat experience. (Craig was killed shortly before Slagle had linked up with Second Platoon in Castrop-Rauxel). H Company's Mortar Platoon also received a replacement lieutenant prior to the advance into Rutgers and Castrop-Rauxel. He also took a chance by climbing up a fence near the railroad embankment in Castrop-Rauxel. The more experienced combat veterans of the Mortar Platoon advised him against it. A sniper killed the lieutenant. H Company had lost two platoon commanders in one afternoon.

A Call for Mortars

Third Section of Third Platoon of H Company, under the command of Staff Sergeant Galway, had moved up to support G Company's advance. They stayed some distance behind, prepared to support the advance with their mortars when ordered. Galway was a rugged man and a tough soldier. Periodically, Captain Druillard would request the mortar men to target German anti-aircraft guns and 20 mm cannon that were positioned to fire on G Company's advance. The mortar men did some good, but they too had attracted the German's attention and received counter-battery fire. They were forced to withdraw further to the rear and setup again. They were positioned just below a hillside and had an excellent field of fire. They remained in this position for most of the afternoon, firing when the order came to them.

Cognac

In the midst of the battle in Rutgers and Castrop-Rauxel, First Sergeant Whalen had been driving around in his jeep. Despite a battle going on, he was in desperate search for a drink. After many months in Europe, alcoholism had claimed Whalen. He could not live without it, even while on duty. As Galway's Section was setup below the hillside, Whalen's jeep pulled up and he rushed over to their position. Page had routinely stashed a jug of cognac aboard the trailer that carried his mortar and ammunition; there was just enough excess space available from expended shells. Whalen walked over to Page and asked, "Where in the Hell is the Cognac!?" Page went to the trailer and pulled out the jug of cognac and handed it to his First Sergeant. Whalen took a drink of the cognac and walked back to his jeep and took off over the hill. Seconds later a German mortar, likely aimed at Galway's Section, hit Whalen's jeep. First Sergeant Whalen was seriously wounded and taken to the Battalion Aid Station. Whalen survived, but this event ended his days with H Company.

Castle Bladenhorst

After crossing the Dortmund-Ems Canal, F Company had moved to the right of G Company's position and took heavy fire from a structure surrounded by woods. F Company surrounded the structure and attacked. Castle Bladenhorst was a fortified strong point and its defenders inflicted heavy casualties to F Company, who requested air-support, but it did not arrive. Heavy fire came down from the castle and pinned down the men of F Company. First Section of First Platoon of H Company that had been in reserve was called up to support F Company's attack on the castle. Sergeant Larson's Second Squad followed the rifle squads to the castle. As they crossed an open field, they began to see some of F Company's casualties lying on the roadside. The dead were covered with ponchos. The combat at the castle had concluded by this point and Larson's Squad did not have to setup their gun. Larson and his men crossed the narrow walkway to the entrance. Castle Bladenhorst had a moat surrounding it, but at this point it did not have water in it. Artillery fire could be heard in the distance, from the battle that was raging on in Rutgers and Castrop-Rauxel.

The Million Dollar Wound

Larson's squad moved around the castle to the courtyard in the back and then moved into a room on the lower level of the castle to seek cover from the sporadic artillery fire that was coming in. There were many GIs in the room, some from H Company and some from F Company. While they were in the room, they heard prisoners being brought in. Chaiklin and a few others went out to see them. As the prisoners dropped their equipment, the GIs began to go over it. Chaiklin spotted a pistol and was hoping that it was a Luger, but it was instead a Walter P.38; still a nice prize. Second Lieutenant Bergheimer showed up and saw Chaiklin take the pistol and he smelled loot. Bergheimer took the pistol away from Chaiklin and ordered him into the castle with the rest of First Section. Bergheimer was alone in the courtyard with a few prisoners. As Chaiklin made his way into the castle, he heard shells come down in the courtyard. Several German prisoners were killed and Bergheimer was hit in the butt with shrapnel. Bergheimer shouted for help. He was put on a stretcher and loaded into an ambulance that arrived to take him to the Battalion Aid Station. No one was sorry to see him go. That sorry excuse for an officer, that bully of a Lieutenant, who had been with H Company since the summer of 1944 had concluded his days with the Company. At the Battalion Aid Station, Bergheimer was given the Purple Heart for his wound. However, his doctor later put a surprising note on his record. Bergheimer's Purple Heart was revoked as his doctor noted that his wound was "self-inflicted." Though shells had come down in the courtyard near Bergheimer's position, he still was out there alone. Perhaps Bergheimer's reputation had finally caught up with him. Regardless, Second Lieutenant Bergheimer's "million dollar wound" had taken him away from H Company.

Ahead of the Advance

Earlier in the afternoon, Slagle had linked up with Second Platoon and took command, as Lieutenant Craig had been killed. After clearing several buildings of snipers and taking out several machine gun nests, Slagle left the First Section of Second Platoon to defend an area in the railroad yard, so that the rest of G Company could move through without difficulty. Second Section continued to advance through Castrop-Rauxel, until they began to take direct fire. 20-mm mortars, machine gun, and sniper fire forced them to spread out. Slagle had intelligence training back at Camp Breckinridge and had some command training; he knew what had to be done in this desperate situation. Some of the sergeants began to argue with Slagle over what should be done. Slagle shouted, "Follow me!" As mortar shells zeroed in on their position, Slagle led the men of Second Section to a church, deep in Castrop-Rauxel. They were actually far ahead of G Company's advance and due to the confusion, could not locate any other American soldiers. Sniper fire came from every direction as they entered the Lutheran Church. The men took cover inside.

Home

Slagle approached the altar in the church and had a strange feeling that he was home. He felt like he had been in the church before and for some reason, he felt as if he knew the town; he had never left the United States until he joined the Army. Slagle told the men that he would lead them to a safe location in town. One of sergeants argued with him and questioned how Slagle could possibly know anything about the town. Slagle sounded so confident, that the men followed him. They exited the Church, just as it was getting dark. One squad followed Slagle into an ancient house across the street from the church. The other squad entered another building in town and took cover in a hayloft. German troops were beginning to move up under cover of darkness and tanks could be heard nearby. A counter-attack was underway. As Slagle and the squad entered the house that had little more than a five-foot tall doorway, they looked for cover, and found none. Slagle found an attic door and he ordered the men to get up there. Slagle shut the door just as a German soldier entered the house, but did not think to check the attic. Slagle and the squad lay in hay that might well have been centuries old. It was dusty and smelled horrible. It made them sick to their stomachs. Through a small slit in the roof, Slagle saw the positions of the German Tigers in town and saw the troop concentrations; all vital intelligence to Second Battalion's advance. The men remained in the attic all night.

A Battlefield Commission

Just before sunrise, Slagle decided to try and make a mad dash for the American lines. They climbed out of the attic and down into the house; they saw it was full of German ammunition. Slagle heard voices outside, but it did not stop him. He ordered the men to run out of the house, carrying their machine gun and tri-pod. There was a group of Fallschirmjagers standing beside the house and were smoking. They were either caught off guard or altogether too stunned to respond as not a shot was fired. The other squad of Second Section caught up with them. Only a few rifle shots were heard and long after they had made it out of the area. Slagle led the men back through the railroad yard that by then had been cleared. While a battle was raging on in another part of town, Slagle found Captain Goodnight and reported to him the position of the German Tigers and the concentrations of German troops in town. Goodnight had lost all of his platoon commanders the previous day and Slagle, being one of the most senior PFCs left, received his battlefield commission of "acting" Second Lieutenant to command Second Platoon.

Darkness Halts the Advance

By 1730, the tanks made it up to the highway outside of Castrop-Rauxel. F Company had taken Castle Bladenhorst and G Company's advance through Castrop-Rauxel was steadily progressing. As darkness fell, Second Platoon of G Company was ordered to scout ahead and probe the enemy's defenses; Third Platoon followed close behind them. H Company's First and Third Platoons were setup to cover the advance. The platoons from G Company moved out into the darkness with no opposition. Radio contact was lost and a messenger returned to inform Captain Druillard that they had seized several houses, meeting no resistance. The remainder of G Company prepared to follow in the wake of the tanks, but the tanks were being refueled and could not navigate the rugged terrain undercover of darkness. G Company reorganized as a unit and moved uneventfully through Castrop-Rauxel.

"Then… All Hell Broke Loose"

After passing through a roadblock that had been established to organize traffic, G Company was suddenly fired on from all directions. German machine guns opened up. The men of G Company scrambled off for whatever cover they could find. Panzerfaust crews destroyed the roadblock and sent its defenders into ditches along the highway for cover. All Hell broke loose and a period of immense confusion followed. The German Fallschirmjagers sent up two flares to illuminate the area and the men of G Company froze in place. Sniper fire came down on the men who moved, but luckily no one was hit. As the flares died out, G Company withdrew to a defensive position, however part of the Company was fired on by a scouting party from C Company from First Battalion that had just arrived in the midst of the German counter-attack. First Lieutenant Allen, G Company's Executive Officer took cover with four riflemen in a ditch. They withdrew back to the outskirts of Rutgers. The Germans had succeeded in halting Second Battalion's advance, but only temporarily. Several men were wounded as fierce machine gun fire was directed at G Company's platoons. By morning, G Company had reorganized in Rutgers and found several men missing, including their Executive Officer. G Company sent out a patrol and captured two Germans who recounted that it was a platoon from the 2nd Fallschirmjager Division that had caused all the trouble.

The Looped Advance

The men of H Company, less Second Platoon were together in Rutgers. The First Section of First Platoon left Castle Bladenhorst in the afternoon after the artillery had died down. They arrived to Rutgers by dusk and setup their guns in houses. The Mortar Platoon was setup in and around an auto repair shop where they discovered cases of Vermouth, wine, and Cognac. After many of the men drank their share and more, they moved off to houses in town to sleep, but they had little time for sleep. The counter-attack on G Company, just a short distance ahead had awakened the men of H Company. By 0300, the men of H Company were called out from their positions and ordered to move up to support G Company. Some of the men were absolutely looped from drinking just hours before and they still marched off to combat. As his Squad crossed the line of departure, Chaiklin saw that some of the riflemen had forced two recently liberated slave laborers to carry a heavy casket of wine slung between a pole on their shoulders.

Bunkers

In Castrop-Rauxel, there were a series of underground bunkers that led through town. Many of the German troops had used them as an escape route. The men of Second Battalion spotted the bunkers on the right side of the road as they advanced. There was a factory complex in the area and artillery began to come in and hit several hundred yards ahead of the bunkers. G Company was attempting to clear out some stiff resistance near an entrance to the factory. A small SS contingent held good cover and was stalling G Company's advance with rifle and mortar fire. Sporadic shelling began to come in. Slagle was leading Second Platoon and they were just a short distance behind a rifle platoon. Sergeant Ramirez took point and scouted ahead to look for a good position to setup their machine gun. Ramirez had been with H Company since Breckinridge and was an experienced soldier in all respects. He saw some rubble from a blown out building just ahead and thought it would be a perfect position to setup. He turned to wave to Slagle to move up. A second later, a mortar shell came in and blew Ramirez against the wall of a building. He was covered in blood and his pants were smoking. One of his legs was blown clean off from the shell. Slagle and Second Platoon 's Medic, Dempsey picked up Ramirez and carried him to safety. Ramirez was shot up with morphine and carried to the aid station. More shells began to come in and Second Platoon took cover.

Sergeant Larson's Squad from First Platoon of H Company, was further to the rear and they took cover in four or five bunkers. Chaiklin took cover in the stairway of one of the bunkers as shrapnel was whizzing about. Suddenly, people appeared at the bottom of the stairway. The bunkers were full of slave laborers from one of the factories. Likely, they had used the underground tunnels to escape from the factory. A horrible stench arose from the bunkers. As soon as the artillery slowed, Larson's Squad moved on. The men of H Company were well spread out as they advanced under sporadic artillery fire.

Countering the Fallschirmjager's Attack
The night before, while Slagle and Second Section of Second Platoon of H Company were held up in the attic of a house, far ahead of Second Battalion's advance, a few men from G Company were also pinned down in a house. It was dark and a Sergeant and three privates from G Company were held up in a house with Germans all around their position. They could not make it back to Rutgers without being killed. They heard German voices all around the house and decided that it must be a surprise counter-attack. The Sergeant had a radio with him and he radioed Second Battalion of the situation and identified the location of a concentration of Germans in his immediate area. The Sergeant continued to relay target coordinates by radio and H Company's Mortar Platoon went into action. Fire was put down on the Fallschirmjagers whenever the Sergeant called for it. The mortar fire halted part of the Fallschirmjager's advance and forced a portion of the advance into retreat. The Sergeant and his men made it safely back to Rutgers in the morning to rejoin G Company.

Second Battalion's Regrouped Advance

By first light, the German counter-attack had been repulsed and Second Battalion, with G Company in the lead, continued their advance. G Company had reorganized its platoons and with H Company's machine guns and mortars in support, was prepared. The tanks had arrived and the First Platoon of G Company along with the Second Section of First Platoon of H Company rode the tanks. Two tanks moved up with a tank destroyer in support. Sergeant "Kirk" and the men of Third Squad had recovered from their close call from the day before. Second Platoon was setup on the second story of houses along the road to support the advance. First Section of First Platoon was moved into houses along the road, also to cover the advance. H Company's mortar men were setup on the outskirts of Rutgers, awaiting the order to fire. C Company attacked from the left of G Company's position at 0700 and began the attack. The tanks with their infantry support made it onto the highway on the outskirts of town and cleared the area of the roadblock that German panzerfausts had destroyed the night before. Just after the roadblock, the Fallschirmjagers opened up with rifle fire on the tanks. The riflemen and machine gunners jumped off the tanks and took cover in the houses along the highway. The tank destroyer took a direct hit from a Tiger and was set on fire. The other two tanks withdrew back into Rutgers. Without tank support, First Platoon of G Company and the Second Section of First Platoon of H Company were pinned down.

Bravery under Fire

Three men from First Platoon of G Company leaped off one of the tanks, moved to the rear of one of the houses, and surprised a German gun crew, who were about to fire a 120 mm mortar. The Germans were killed and a thermite grenade dropped into the barrel of the gun. Sergeant Bond had led his Squad into a garage for cover. He ran back onto the road, braving fire and pulled the four tankers out of the burning tank destroyer. He led them to safety with his Squad. The Second Section of First Platoon of H Company had moved into a large house along the road to seek cover. "Hay Seed" heard movement in the basement and several German Fallschirmjagers opened fire. "Hay Seed" tossed a grenade into the basement and slammed the door; all became quiet after it exploded. Sergeant "Kirk" opened the back door of the house, looking for a way out of the area as the front of the house was taking concentrated rifle fire from the other side of the street.

"Kirk" took one step out the door and a panzerfaust shell flew right past him. The panzerfaust crew had missed their target and tried to withdraw to load another shell. "Kirk's" Squad cut them down with rifle fire. The area behind the houses appeared to be clear and the whole Section withdrew from the house. They moved just a few yards and were confronted by several Fallschirmjagers who were moving up to the front. As both sides were completely unprepared, hand to hand combat resulted. The Germans were killed, with the exception of a German Lieutenant that got off a shot at "Hay Seed," grazing his face. The Lieutenant was knocked to the ground by the men of "Kirk's" Squad, his pistol taken and he was taken prisoner. Cohen struck the Lieutenant in the face with the butt of his rifle. "Hay Seed" was very lucky, he had a bloody face, but was not seriously wounded.

"That's Captain Goodnight!"

Second Section of First Platoon began to take fire from the upper level of a house as they tried to withdraw back to Rutgers. "Hay Seed" spotted the sniper's position due to the shine from his scoped rifle. With one bullet expended from "Hay Seed's" Garand, the sniper was hit and toppled down from his hiding spot. They made it back to the main road that had been cleared earlier in the morning only to find that a squad of Fallschirmjagers had moved into the area. Panzerfausts targeted their position and "Hay Seed" told everyone to separate and take cover. A panzerfaust shell hit the side of a house as "Hay Seed" was running for cover; he ran right into the shrapnel and fell to the ground. The heavily armed German squad continued to fire. Captain Goodnight pulled up in a jeep, moving up the road that was thought to have long since been clear. The Germans fired their panzerfaust at Goodnight's jeep, narrowly missing it. The jeep pulled up to cover behind a house. Cohen shouted, "That's Captain Goodnight!" Goodnight quickly moved up to their position and was told that "Hay Seed" had been hit by shrapnel and might have been killed; no one could get to him. In a split second decision, as the Fallschirmjagers opened fire with their burp guns, Goodnight ran out into the open. He threw a grenade at the Germans who were amassed together beside a house and then took a running dive behind cover of a house on the other side of the street. The grenade killed several of the Germans and disrupted their fire. Goodnight moved up alone and pulled "Hay Seed" off the line and back to cover with the others. "Kirk's" Squad opened fire on the remaining Germans, who dropped their weapons and fled. "Hay Seed" said he was

208

fine and it was nothing that would keep him off his feet and he refused to go to the Aid Station. With all the men of Second Section crowding around their heroic Captain, Goodnight told them to put their machine guns in his jeep and to follow him on foot.

Severely Wounded

Staff Sergeant Slawson had been caught up in the firefight and reunited with his Section just as they moved from Rutgers, back into Castrop-Rauxel. Captain Goodnight, with Second Section of First Platoon following his jeep on foot, arrived to some cover; a war-ravaged house on the outskirts of town. Though several German shells landed not far from their position, Goodnight was standing tall and showed no emotion. He ordered Slawson to send "Kirk's" Squad up to support a platoon from G Company that was moving up. "Hay Seed" though clearly wounded, still led Fourth Squad; he had a pained expression on his face. As a few artillery shells came in, they took cover. "Hay Seed" was in mid speech when his voice became muffled and his words became incoherent. A moment later his head slumped over his shoulder. Goodnight pulled off "Hay Seed's" jacket and found that his whole left side from hip to shoulder was full of shrapnel wounds and his clothing was soaked in blood. Cohen and "Kirk" put "Hay Seed" into the jeep and Captain Goodnight ordered his driver to take "Hay Seed" to the Aid Station. The Armenian in Fourth Squad, the same man that had panicked under fire on the Maas, always had a shrewd comment. He told Sergeant "Kirk" that now maybe he would get a promotion to Sergeant too. The Armenian thought a lot about himself. "Kirk" whispered very quietly to the Armenian: "If you say one more word I will ring your neck!"

Clearing Castrop-Rauxel

By late afternoon on 7 April, the second day of the advance, the Germans were finally pushed back. Third Section of H Company's Mortar Platoon under the command of Staff Sergeant Galway had fired over 150 shells into Castrop-Rauxel in support of G Company's attacking platoons. Buildings had been targeted, Fallschirmjagers and SS troops hit by shells, and German artillery pieces with their crews hit. Squads from G Company continued to relay target coordinates to Galway's Section throughout the day. The Tigers that Slagle had spotted the night before withdrew from the town. The Fallschirmjagers made one last weak counter-attack in late afternoon, only to screen their own retreat. As the fighting began to conclude, Castrop-Rauxel's Mayor approached some of the men of H Company. He was holding a white sheet tied to a broomstick and was followed by two aids. He pleaded with the men of Second Battalion not to shell his town anymore as it was full of chlorine gas tanks. The combat in Castrop-Rauxel was over and Second Battalion, 291st Infantry was victorious in their efforts to mop up the town. It was fierce and intense combat for those men that were caught up in the middle of the battle. Some of the veterans of the Battle of the Bulge and the Colmar Pocket noted that combat in Castrop-Rauxel was more intense than anything they had been through before. For those units that were not at the front, it did not seem like a particularly big battle.

As G Company moved through the town, they captured many Germans of military age, who were dressed as civilians; most had probably dropped their uniforms in favor of civilian clothes when they realized that resistance was futile. The men of Second Battalion had faced some of the finest soldiers in the German Army and defeated them. Upon inspection of the miles of boxcars located in town, it was discovered that Second Battalion had deprived the Germans of hundreds of tons of military equipment. The loss of the highly valued synthetic fuel tanks aboard the trains was a major blow to the German Luftwaffe, who needed it to fuel their jet aircraft. Large quantities of Chlorine gas tanks were also found aboard the trains; likely headed to concentration camps. Second Battalion's actions on 6 and 7 April had delivered a significant blow against the German's last ditch effort at resistance. It was but one of many such blows dealt by units of the 75th Division in the Ruhr Pocket.

The Aftermath of Castrop-Rauxel

By the night of 7 April, the men of Second Battalion began to celebrate their victory. Liquor could be found throughout the town. For those that drank, they had all they could drink and more. By 8 April, the men of H Company moved into houses on the edge of town. The machine gunners setup their guns in preparation for a German counter-attack, but there was little chance that one would come. Casualties from combat on 6 and 7 April were relatively light when considering the severity of combat and who the enemy was. F Company had lost almost a whole platoon in seizing Castle Bladenhorst. G Company lost a few men and had several more wounded. H Company had lost the lieutenant commanding the Mortar Platoon and Lieutenant Craig from Second Platoon. Lieutenant Bergheimer with his "million dollar" wound was gone from the Company, as was First Sergeant Whalen who also was wounded. Sergeants Lawson and "Hay Seed" were both wounded and in the Battalion Aid Station. The respect for Captain Goodnight grew, especially from the men of Second Section of First Platoon that had seen combat beside him in Castrop-Rauxel.

Genes

On the morning of 10 April, just as Second Battalion was moving out of Castrop-Rauxel towards their new objective of the town of Witten, Slagle saw the church and the house he had led Second Section of Second Platoon through on the night of 6 April. He went back into the house, still having a strange feeling of "home" and that he had been in the town before. Slagle "liberated" from the house a geography book and a Family Bible both dating from the early 18th Century. Years later, when Slagle became fluent in German, he discovered that the Family Bible he took belonged to his ancestor a Von Schlegel, who founded the Lutheran Church in Castrop-Rauxel back in 1683. The house that Slagle hid in, belonged to his ancestor! In an issue of "Stars and Stripes," Slagle read about other German-Americans in the US Army who had similar experiences of feeling like they were home, upon entering Germany. Slagle believed that memories must in some way be passed on in one's genes; that is the only explanation he could offer for his personal experience.

2LT Robert O. Slagle after combat in Castrop-Rauxel

Clearing the Ruhr Pocket

H Company convoy move to the South after Castrop-Rauxel

Moving South

After clearing Castrop-Rauxel, Second Battalion, 291st Infantry continued its rapid move to the south. They moved south of Dortmund to a town called Witten. The remnants of five German divisions continued to operate in the area, but at limited strength. Most of the German forces were operating at only battalion strength. The last elements of the 2nd Fallschirmjager Division had fled Castrop-Rauxel and regrouped for a fight to the end. As Second Battalion moved through the German countryside, they saw how devastated the German forces were. They passed by horse-drawn carriages that had been hit by American artillery. Half-tracks and tanks were abandoned due to a lack of fuel and their artillery was also disabled. The Germans were in full flight from the rapidly advancing Americans.

The Devastation of War

Second Battalion moved through bombed out German towns. The destruction was incredible to see and beyond anyone's imagination. The Allied bombing campaign had been a great success. Buildings were blown wide open. Kravitz and the men of his Squad saw a bank that had been bombed. Bags of Deutchmarks were lying in bundles for anyone to take; some of the men took some as a souvenir. The civilians that had survived the bombings peered out of the rubble after it was clear the Wehrmacht had left the town. There was very little resistance during the concentrated move to the south. The combat experienced in Rutgers and Castrop-Rauxel from snipers hiding in the rubble of houses was not to be found again. Civilians frequently hung white flags of surrender from the remaining windows of their houses. It was becoming clear that these were the final days of the Third Reich.

South of Dortmund

As Second Battalion continued to move south they moved around the outskirts of the industrial town of Dortmund. They found in the midst of the rubble of bombed out buildings, a few that still stood intact. The Allied bombing campaign had spared a few buildings that were of interest to the Allies. A Bayer drug administrative center was left standing as the Allied Expeditionary Force claimed they wished to use it as a headquarters building. Next to it, stood a large synthetic oil plant that was also spared. It was of scientific value to the Allies as the Germans were known to be pioneering many new technologies. The oil plant had recently been in operation. Despite the dire state of Germany by April 1945, munitions production had actually increased many times over the levels it had been in previous years. Production was moved underground where bombing raids could not stop it. Bombing railroads and in particular, destroying train engines was the key to finally crippling production.

"Seven Lootin' and Five Shootin' "

The men of the 75th Division had their own slogan as they moved through Germany, "Seven Lootin' and Five Shootin'." As the remnants of the Germany Army were in headlong retreat, the GIs took it upon themselves to "liberate" souvenirs from the towns they moved through. In H Company, many of the older veterans were after booze. The veterans of the Battle of the Bulge and Colmar had seniority in their units and they got first pick whenever there was loot to be had. The replacements, who were mostly younger and less experienced, often were restricted to watching. Saul Cohen had a talent for locating loot. He never kept any of it; he would trade it for other goods. The quest for German pistols was another great prize to be had if one could be found. Staff Sergeant Galway of the Mortar Platoon found himself a Walter P. 38 that he carried on him. Others took Nazi flags and armbands as souvenirs. Even German officer's caps made a nice souvenir. Anything with a swastika on it proved to be tempting "loot" to the GI.

POWs and a Pit Stop

German troops began to surrender in droves as Second Battalion moved through the Ruhr. Often, there would be so many Germans trying to surrender that there were not enough men available to guard them. On one occasion, after leaving Castrop-Rauxel, Sergeant "Kirk" walked off the marching path to relieve himself and was approached by about twenty Volkssturmers that wanted to surrender. They tried to hand him all of their rifles! They apparently were hiding in the woods from the SS troops who would have shot them all if they surrendered in their presence. The Volkssturmers were old men and teenagers; they had no desire to fight anymore. An old Volkssturmer caught "Kirk's" eye as he looked pale and sickly. The man was in his 70s and had been on the march for a week with almost nothing to eat. "Kirk" handed him some canned meat from his rations and the old man bowed and almost kissed his feet. "Kirk" had to leave the Volkssturmers and call out for assistance in moving them. They waited patiently and made no effort to run away or even to move from where he left them; they stood by the side of the road as if they were waiting for a bus. Cohen and several men from Slawson's Section arrived to guard the prisoners. One of the prisoners, a lieutenant handed his pistol to Cohen and pointed to Cohen's canteen; the man had nothing to drink in days. Cohen, impressed by the prized pistol, gave the German a drink from his canteen. Most other prisoners taken gave their captors no trouble at all. One Volkssturmer even got on his knees and thanked one of the privates for taking him prisoner and not shooting him. The riflemen of Second Battalion frequently escorted prisoners in a long line, marching back from the front.

Into Witten

As Second Battalion moved into the town of Witten, they expected to encounter snipers and resistance, but found none. They saw a burned out factory in town and a fenced in enclosure behind it. The men of H Company marched up to this area to see what it was. They found a large slave labor camp, populated primarily by Russians and Poles. The SS guards had long since fled and abandoned the laborers. The slave laborers were in very poor shape and had not eaten much in a long time. The conditions of the camp were horrendous; the people were treated as if they were not even human. GIs sprayed them with DDT to eliminate lice. Captain Goodnight arranged for a chow line to be setup to feed the laborers a thin soup, to get them back in shape to eat solid food again. Solid food was fed to those in shape to eat it. A problem resulted when trucks moved in to collect the laborers and take them off for a shower; most were afraid that they were going to be taken off and shot. It took a lot of coaxing and reassurance to make the laborers understand that their liberators were Americans and not Russians. H Company's translator, Siegfried helped in this process when he discovered that one of the laborers, a Russian was also fluent in German; he explained the situation to the others.

The Final Battle

At 1200 hours on 11 April, Second Battalion left Witten and moved to a town called Herdecke located on the Ruhr River. By 11 April Allied aircraft were pounding German tanks and infantry concentrations in the Ruhr with ease. The Luftwaffe's fuel was all but gone and the Germans could commit few if any aircraft. British Typhoons and American P-47s flew numerous close support missions. Whenever a unit of the 75th Division was halted due to tanks or infantry, they called in for air support. The 290th Regiment was the lead element in the attack on Herdecke. They shelled Herdecke directly and air-support bombed the last remaining tanks and heavy guns in the area. Victory seemed like it might come at any moment. Thousands of German soldiers were surrendering from the battered under strength German divisions that continued to operate in the Ruhr. Wrecked tanks and armored vehicles continued to be spotted as the men of Second Battalion, 291st Infantry moved towards Herdecke. However, in Second Battalion's sector, the Germans were not yet ready to surrender; the last remaining elements of the 2nd Fallschirmjager Division were determined to make one last ditch attempt at resistance.

Chaiklin's Close Call

As Second Battalion moved towards Herdecke, the men of H Company began to setup their machine gun emplacements in preparation for attacking the town. Chaiklin spotted German soldiers moving around on the outskirts of town. A young artillery forward observer, with limited time on the line, had moved through the position of First Section of First Platoon as they were dug in. The forward observer started shooting at targets down the hill with his Carbine. The shooting attracted the German's attention and mortars were targeted on his position. Chaiklin was in a foxhole and had witnessed the mortars come down very near to the forward observer's position. After five minutes, the shelling had stopped. Despite others warning Chaiklin to remain in his foxhole, he instead took a chance and ventured out to find out what happened to the forward observer. As Chaiklin started down the hill a mortar shell came in at maximum range and hit the hill. The explosion was close enough to Chaiklin, that it singed his eyebrows! It was a steep hill and luckily for Chaiklin all the shrapnel from the shell went into the hill. A short time later, the young forward observer came back, safe and sound.

Attack on the Farm

As elements of the 75th and 95th Divisions converged on the last remaining German troop concentrations in the Ruhr, the Germans made their last stand. Second Battalion, 291st Infantry setup behind a ridge as German artillery rained in on their position. The remnants of the 2nd Fallschirmjager Division had setup on a large farm on the outskirts of Herdecke. 20-mm anti-aircraft guns were depressed to fire on Second Battalion. H Company's Mortar Platoon withdrew to better cover behind the ridgeline and prepared to return fire. The machine gun platoons were pinned down and could not setup. Staff Sergeant Galway, commanding Third Section of the Mortar Platoon had scouted ahead under fire and determined that Germans positioned in a large farmhouse on the farm were directing the 20-mm fire. Galway relayed targeting coordinates to the Mortar Platoon and they opened fire on the farmhouse. A short time later, the concentrated 20-mm fire that had pinned down Second Battalion was silenced. Over a hundred Fallschirmjagers emerged from the farm and surrendered. H Company moved onto the farm and slept in the farmhouses where the Germans had been; they even found some hot food to eat.

The German's Last Stand

On 12 April, the last remaining German troops in the Ruhr Pocket retreated to the banks of the Ruhr River and prepared to make their last stand. The town of Herdecke would not capitulate despite being bombed by aircraft and shelled by artillery from the 75th Division. The SS commanded the town and the fanatical Nazis still thought they had some chance. On the banks of the Ruhr, remnants of one German battalion setup and fired on Second Battalion, 291st Infantry. Machine gunners and mortar men of H Company returned fire and broke up the resistance. The German battalion surrendered. As Second Battalion moved back in the direction of the farm, they were confronted by a weak platoon of old Volkssturmers armed with rifles. They attempted a counter-attack, but it was broke up within minutes and they surrendered. Second Battalion then moved back through the large farm where they had captured the Fallschirmjagers and H Company setup on a hill. They were ordered to prepare to attack the town of Herdecke when word came. The 290th Regiment bombarded Herdecke with mortar fire and Division artillery opened fire on the town. A messenger from the 290th Regiment was dispatched to Herdecke offering the town a chance to surrender. Two days later, on 14 April, the mayor of Herdecke agreed to an unconditional surrender of his town. Elements of the 95th Division arrived onto the farm where Second Battalion, 291st was setup; the Ruhr encirclement was complete and the Battle of the Ruhr was over.

Encounters in the Ruhr

Staff Sergeant Prater ventured around the area as combat concluded. He took some rations off a tank nearby. Prater and three or four men from his Section spotted a little bar in town and they went in. The bartender poured each of them a beer, making no issues of serving Americans. Three little old, white-haired men were sitting on the other side of the room, trying to pay little attention to the GIs. They were very nervous and proclaimed "Nicht Nazi! Nicht Nazi!." After leaving the bar, Prater and his buddies walked down a road, while American tanks drove by. The road led to a little bridge over a stream. On the bridge, they encountered three Russian soldiers from what was probably a scouting party. Prater could not speak Russian and the Russians could not speak English, so both groups settled by saluting each other.

Aftermath of the Ruhr Pocket

The Germans in the Ruhr surrendered quickly and with little trouble. There were some elite troops left, but the vast majority were Volkssturmers and bedraggled soldiers that had lost the will to fight. The Ruhr Encirclement had deprived Hitler of 80% of his fuel supply. With little fuel left, Hitler's once mighty Luftwaffe and his famed Panzer Divisions were worthless. The outcome of the war was all but decided. For the men of Second Battalion, their combat was now over and they earned a period of rest. The 75th Division had fought their way through the Ardennes and confronted the tip of the "Bulge", took part in liberating the Colmar Pocket, and contributed to clearing out the Ruhr Pocket. The men of the 75th Division had earned their third Battle Star for combat in the Ruhr.

Occupation Duty

H Company in Lunnen, Germany

Thompson (1st Platoon) during air-raid- Lunnen, German   1st Platoon Lunnen, Germany

220

H Company chow line- Lunnen, Germany

S/SGT Bob Galway in Feudigen   **S/SGT Dallas Wilkinson (Mortar Platoon)**

Solomon- Civiak- Malarich (Mortar Platoon)   **Mess Sgt Ray Casper with "Liberated" Drinks**

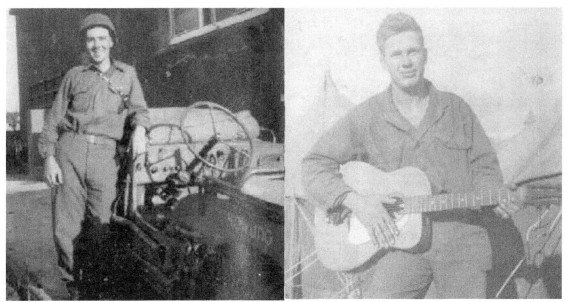

James Solomon- Jeep Driver (Mortar Platoon)   **S/SGT Harry Osborn**

Ira Posnak- guarding entrance to Feudigen   **Hal Simpson- Ira Posnak**

Wrecked 88 gun found near Feudigen   **John Hess and woman freed from DP Camp**

Jim Strong- clearing out Feudigen   **Nazi Mayor of Feudigen (Suicide)**

Feudigen, Germany

Freed from DP Camp, Feudigen

T/SGT Garo- Art Grindstaff "Barber"

Billy Hyatt- George Bozovich (Mortar Platoon)

L-R: Lyons, Cohen, Sotir, Shaffer, with gun- Wallace Kravitz   **Middle: Pete Pontes**

Into Lunnen

On 15 April, after the end of combat operations in the Ruhr pocket, the 291st Regiment moved north from Herdecke to Am Lunnen-Brunnen, just to the northeast of Dorsten where H Company had been setup on a farm two weeks earlier. The men of Second Battalion, 291st Infantry were given hot meals and a chance to take a shower. Trucks moved the men of H Company to an area in town where they took showers and received clean clothing. Third Battalion, 291st Infantry, had captured a large electric plant in town intact two weeks before. The only incident in Lunnen was when a lone German aircraft tried to bomb H Company's position, forcing the men to seek cover in an air raid shelter in town. The men of H Company were organized in the center of town and Captain Goodnight spoke to them about the conclusion of combat in the Ruhr Pocket. They were congratulated for their contribution to the collapse of the German Army in the Ruhr.

Rehabilitation

From 16 to 21 April, the 291st Regiment remained in the vicinity of Am Lunnen-Brunnen as the Regiment was outfitted with replacements. H Company received a new first sergeant, who was a miserable man that was promoted up from buck sergeant and transferred into H Company. He was a horrible choice for first sergeant and likely was only promoted so some other unit could be free of him. Replacement platoon commanders also arrived. Slagle's temporary command of Second Platoon had concluded and he went back to Fourth Squad of First Platoon. The men of Second Battalion were tasked with cleaning equipment and sergeants were tasked with noting what equipment their men needed. After the tough fighting in the Ruhr, supplies had dwindled and now it was a time to receive new supplies. During this time, the men of Second Battalion had the luxury of attending showings of motion pictures that were provided by the Special Service Office. The men would crowd in barns, workshops, and buildings to see the pictures. The only problem was that they had very few pictures to show. John Wayne's "Tall in the Saddle," a cowboy picture was shown many times. Men marched through the streets, overhauled and washed vehicles, and also washed clothing and hung it out to dry. Their combat was over and the men of the 291st Regiment transitioned from a combat team into an occupational force.

The Beginnings of Occupation

On 22 April, the 291st Regiment moved east from Am Lunnen-Brunnen to the vicinity of Bad Driburg, just to the north of Paderborn. The 291st Regiment was to take over a large area of occupation with its companies and platoons spread out in the surrounding areas. Bad Driburg was a resort town with famed mineral springs. The men of H Company took some time to enjoy their surroundings. The civilians in the area were very hospitable to their American occupiers. Despite the war still going on, the civilians were pleasant. There were no incidents of note. The civilians continued with their regular duties and were only restricted with not being able to leave town. One afternoon, Sergeant "Kirk" laid on his back in a field near the edge of town, taking in the beautiful surroundings. Two little girls not more than four or five years old walked over to him and handed him flowers they had just picked. "Kirk" took the girls back home to their mother and was invited in for dinner. Despite a no fraternization policy that was very loosely enforced, "Kirk" became very fond of the family. The father was a soldier that had been killed in the war and the mother seemed very pleased to have a man to cook for. Playing with the little girls in the house after dinner made "Kirk" think about his own daughter that was born just before he departed the United States in October 1944.

Sergeant Lawson's Return

Sergeant Lawson returned from the Aid Station as H Company was setting up in Bad Driburg. He hitched a ride with a jeep driver from Battalion that was delivering a message to Captain Goodnight. Lawson was told he was not in shape to return to his Company, but he would not accept that answer; he wanted to get back to his buddies. Lawson was last seen being carried off on a litter back across the Dortmund-Ems Canal on the morning of 6 April. Lawson was lucky, the bullet had gone clear through his shoulder and he healed quickly. The second bullet that had hit his helmet had given him a concussion. In addition, Lawson had picked up a severe stomach ailment that had made him nauseous. Despite not quite feeling like his former self, Lawson returned to duty. However, after Lawson left Fourth Squad, Slagle had taken over, then "Hay Seed" had taken over for Slagle, and finally the Armenian was promoted to Sergeant after "Hay Seed" was wounded. No one liked the Armenian, but by default he had been promoted.

The Bird Bath

Slagle was laying field phone wire in town for H Company's Command Post, through several backyards. He was still suffering from a sore back from his wound at Colmar in February. As he was laying the wire, a well-dressed German man approached Slagle and told him that he could not lay wire on his property. The man was probably a draft dodger as he was of age to be a soldier. Slagle grabbed the man by the throat and dragged him over to the bird bath in his own backyard and dunked his head in it. Slagle told him to get back in his house or he would shoot him. Slagle continued with his duty of laying the wire and looked up to see the same German looking at him out of a second story window in the house. Slagle stopped what he was doing, picked up his M-1 Garand and aimed it at the man. The German shut the window and closed the drapes. Slagle continued laying the field phone wire.

The Mission

One night while in Bad Driburg, Slagle was awakened by a messenger from Division Headquarters. Slagle and Saul Cohen were both requested by name, as was H Company's translator, Siegfried. They were told to meet a convoy at the edge of town. The messenger saw Lawson and pointed to him, "He's awake, bring him too." Slagle, Siegfried, Cohen, and Lawson walked to the edge of town and met a small convoy of five trucks and three jeeps. The Deputy Division Commander, General Mickle got out of the lead jeep and greeted Slagle. He confirmed that Slagle and Cohen had both been requested due to their intelligence training back at Camp Breckinridge. Mickle told them to board the troop trucks as they were moving east. They did not recognize anyone aboard the trucks and everyone was very puzzled as to what they were doing aboard trucks in the middle of the night. One man whispered, "Maybe they are sending us home!" After a long ride in darkness and through sunrise, the convoy stopped along a small road. The men got out of the trucks to stretch their legs. General Mickle called out to Slagle and requested him to get into his jeep; Lawson followed Slagle. The jeep moved ahead of the convoy along a small dirt road near several bombed out buildings. They saw a large fenced in area off the road and the General told his driver to go there. Slagle and Lawson hopped off the jeep and proceeded ahead to a large gate. There were people all crowded inside of it, along the fences.

"The Most Horrible Sight I Ever Saw in My Life"

Slagle shot the lock off and he and Lawson opened up the gates. The sight that greeted them would haunt them both for the rest of their lives. A group of people looking like they had not eaten in ages approached. They wore clothing looking something like prison clothes with the Star of David on the shirt; they were Jews. A very tall man walked over to Slagle; the man's face was gaunt and his body little more than a bundle of bones. He embraced Slagle and was trying to thank him. Slagle kept a few chocolate bars in his pocket and gave one to the man. He ate a bite of it, embraced Slagle again and died in his arms. It was the worst thing Slagle had ever seen in his life. Soldiers being killed all around him in the Ardennes and at Colmar; all the combat he had been through was nothing when compared to the sights he saw in the concentration camp at Keune. Slagle and Lawson handed out all the food they had in their rations. A short time after Slagle and Lawson entered the camp, the convoy arrived and setup a thin soup chow line to feed the inmates. The sights were horrific and unimaginable. Piles of the dead littered the ground. The stench was unbearable and came from everywhere. People suffering from the extremes of starvation tried to get up and make it to the chow line; many could not get up. Lawson carried soup over to some of the men who could not even sit up and he tried to feed them. As men from the convoy entered the camp to try to help the people, some of the able-bodied Jews crowded around them and cheered.

By late afternoon the people that could eat were fed. Many of the people died from eating too much, too quickly. More Americans arrived and doused the camp with DDT. A Major arrived to take command and he ordered the GIs to sift through all the bodies and look for dog tags. The SS had frequently gone through POW camps looking for Allied soldiers who were Jewish. Many were sent to the concentration camps. At the far end of camp there was a railroad that had been bombed. More bodies were found in the trains. The Major in command ordered the GIs to burn the bodies as quickly as possible. The stench was so horrible that many of the GIs threw up and were so ill they had to be taken out of the camp. Cohen sat with many of the dying and said nothing; he showed no emotion. As the inmates were given showers, given clean clothes, and fed, they moved into buildings near the camp; the former offices of the camp staff. They were to be checked out by medics who arrived and setup an aid station. Cohen had spotted a man who looked like he did not belong in the camp. The man had his head down and would not look at the GIs he had plenty of body fat. Cohen walked over to him and looked him over; the man would not look at Cohen. Siegfried, the translator was called over by Cohen. Siegfried asked the man who he was; he would not say anything, but seemed to understand German just fine. At gunpoint, Cohen ordered the man to raise his arms and remove his prison clothing. Beneath the shirt on his collar was the insignia of the SS; the man was an SS Captain! Siegfried and Lawson ran off to get the Major. A second later, Lawson heard a gunshot; Cohen had shot the German low and he was rolling around in pain. When the Major arrived, he pulled out his pistol and shot the German in the head. Nothing was said of Cohen's actions. A few other Germans were also caught in prison attire; Cohen saw that they did not make it to trial.

Slagle, Lawson, and Cohen remained in Keune through V.E. Day. Every morning they went to work in the camp sifting through bodies looking for dog tags, then burning the bodies. The inmates by then had all been moved out of the camp and were receiving medical attention. They were all Czechs and Poles. Keune was a German town on the border with Czechoslovakia and Poland. The Germans had used the railroad in town to haul Jews from Czechoslovakia and Poland to the various concentration camps in Germany. Eventually, Keune became such a camp itself. Many of the GIs working in the camp were suffering from psychological problems. Even the toughest and most rugged of men could not handle what they saw. A GI woke up one morning, seemingly joyful and walked into a building; he did not come out. Lawson walked in an hour later and found that the man had hanged himself. Another man, while eating breakfast pulled out a pistol and shot himself in the head. Shortly after V.E. Day, Slagle, Lawson, and Cohen were ordered to board trucks for another move.

2LT Robert O. Slagle outside Concentration Camp- Keune, Germany

Areas of Occupation

By 25 April, the 291st Regiment was relieved by elements of the 95th Division at Bad Driburg. The 291st was sent to another area of occupation in the vicinity of Kreuztal, southeast of Dortmund. The 291st Regimental Command Post was setup in Kreuztal and the companies were spread out in the surrounding areas and separated by platoon. H Company was to occupy the province of Bad Laasphe. The Company first arrived in Nieder Laasphe, a small suburb town, where H Company dispersed by platoon for their individual platoon assignments. They remained in Nieder Laasphe for a few days. Chaiklin slept on the second story of a house. In the house he discovered a copy of Mein Kampf. There were no civilians around. Headquarters Platoon remained in Nieder Laasphe. First Platoon was sent to occupy the town of Laasphe, Second Platoon was sent to Puderbach along the Lahn River, and Third Platoon was sent to Feudigen. The three towns of Bad Laasphe, formed a triangle, with Puderback in the north, Feudigen to the west, and Laasphe to the east.

Laasphe

First Platoon moved on foot through hilly countryside to Laasphe, the town they were to occupy. They arrived to the center of town and setup civilian government. In occupation duty there were no more formations, weapons inspections, or close order drills. The men of First Platoon then dispersed to different houses and moved in. Second Section took over several small houses near the center of town. Civilians were kicked out of their homes and were moved across the street to new quarters. It was usual practice to take over the house of a local Nazi official. First Section moved into a big house along a creek at the edge of town. The house belonged to the town's mayor. While sergeants took the beds, the privates were left with couches and chairs. Chaiklin slept on a couch that looked like Freud's. The men had food brought to them in containers for their meals and it was always hot. One afternoon, Chaiklin sat by the creek near the mayor's house that had been occupied by First Section. The mayor's daughter was about 16 and very beautiful. She was sitting by the creek and crying. She spoke pretty good English and was hurt because her house had been taken away from her. Chaiklin found himself in an odd position, trying not very successfully to console the girl.

Puderbach

Second Platoon moved up by the Lahn River to the town of Puderbach. Sergeant Henry and his Squad took over a big white house up on a hill, overlooking the village. Though the inhabitants were friendly, the GIs were warned not to fraternize. Many of the civilians claimed they were "Nicht Nazi!" Second Platoon's first task was to clear out all signs of the Nazis including uniforms, insignias, and weapons. The no fraternization policy was loosely enforced. Bruce Reynolds found himself a girlfriend among the Germans in Puderbach. The girl understood little to no English and Kravitz and the men of his Squad referred to her as a "horse's ass," which she thought was complimentary. By V.E. Day, the war was over and the German civilians were anxious to become friends; it was hard to avoid. There was only one man of military age in town and he was a veteran of the Eastern Front and had been wounded in combat a year earlier. The younger women in town fraternized with him. The man would have nothing to do with the GIs and they ignored him as well. Whenever the GIs saw him, he would turn around and limp away. There were a few children in town that looked typically German with rosy cheeks and blonde hair.

In Puderbach, a cow was in labor and was having difficulty in giving birth. The German farmer needed help. PFC Helmuth Cattau was a farmer from Nebraska and he knew just what to do. He covered his arm with an antibiotic and tried to help deliver the calf. Unfortunately, it was too late and the calf died soon after delivery. Another incident was when Mess Sergeant Lyons messed up somehow and was busted down in rank to a buck private. He was then sent to Henry's Squad. By then, the Squad consisted of Kravitz, "Red" Schaeffer, Leon Cohen, Bruce Reynolds, and "Suds" Sotir. While they lived in Puderbach, once a week a farmer would come by with a horse drawn wagon and a honey basket to clean out the cesspool. He always managed to arrive just as they were getting ready for lunch!

Second Platoon was tasked with 24-hour guard duty on the only road that led into the village. The Germans were not allowed out of town. One evening, while guarding the road, Kravitz spotted a woman riding a bicycle down the road; she was not supposed to be out. Kravitz held up his rifle and said loudly, "Halt, oder Ich scheiss." Perhaps the word should have been "Schiess!" The woman started to laugh. While in Puderbach,

Kravitz received a three day leave pass to Brussels, where he had the opportunity to stay in a hotel, eat decent food, and enjoy an opera at the opera house. Kravitz saw the opera LaBoheme, which he liked very much. For five American dollars, Kravitz bought a bottle of wine for his Squad buddies in Puderbach. The so-called wine turned out to be something much stronger. When Kravitz returned to Puderback he and his buddies opened the bottle and bravely took turns taking swigs. After a couple drinks, it knocked him out. It was so strong, it literally knocked Kravitz out of his seat! He awoke in bed in the morning with a terrible hangover.

Feudingen

H Company's Mortar Platoon moved into the town of Feudingen for occupation duty. The town was located near a valley and they setup for the night across the street from a large mansion. The mansion was intact and Staff Sergeant Prater and his gunner Malarich entered into the house. It was full of furniture and as they moved through the house, they found a closet full of Nazi uniforms. Prater found a 32 caliber Mauser pistol in the home; it was a nice souvenir. Third Section of the Mortar Platoon was tasked with maintaining a roadblock on the edge of town. First and Second Sections moved into a large schoolhouse and were in charge of a displaced persons camp. Russians, Poles, and others from Eastern Europe populated the camp. There were men and women. The men of Third Platoon would hunt deer in the woods surrounding the camp and they would be taken to the DP camp. The people in the camp would cook deer for everyone. They would give the tenderloins to the Mortar Platoon. PFC John Hess, Staff Sergeant Prater's driver came to him one morning and said someone had stolen his jeep. Prater ordered Hess to steal another one! Later on, Hess returned with a jeep, it was better than his old jeep as this one had a wire cutter attached to it. From then on, Hess always removed the carburetor from his jeep so that no one would make off with it.

In Feudingen, Third Section found a house with German girls that liked the American GIs. The no fraternization policy was certainly ignored by most. One night, Page put on a coat and added some brass. He walked up to the house and knocked on the door. One of the girls answered the door and thought she had a colonel standing on her doorstep. She went into the house and told the GIs that a colonel was waiting at the front door! The GIs started jumping out of the back windows of the house! The next day, the men of Third Section were sitting around a swimming pool near the house with the girls. Page was there and was listening to the talk going around. One of the men said to Page, "A damn colonel came to the door last night!" The girl who had answered the door immediately recognized Page. PFC Hewitt pointed at Page and said, "You were the 'colonel,' you son of a bitch!" Third Section drank plenty of cognac while in Feudingen. One morning, Page was accused of being involved with an incident in town during the night. While Page had been drinking, he was sure he did not do what he was accused of. A short time later it was proved that it was not Page, but one of the sergeants who was guilty.

One of the first duties while in Feudingen, was to see about the rumors that there was a German officer in town. While in occupation duty, German soldiers, particularly members of the SS tried anyway they could to escape from town and they were quite creative in their methods. Sometimes they would even wear a dress and try to pass as a woman to get past the watchful eyes of the guards manning the roadblock at the edge of town. Posnak was on guard duty at the roadblock one afternoon when a man in a business suit approached. Posnak asked to see his papers before he could pass through. His papers checked out, but something did not seem right. Posnak and the other guard with him forced the man to take off his coat and they went through his belongings. He turned out to be the SS officer that was rumored to be in town and Posnak had caught him. Posnak was the smallest guy in the Platoon and some of his platoon buddies would tease him about this. However, his buddies changed their attitude after Posnak had captured the SS officer.

The time spent in Feudingen was very much a period of relaxation for the men of Third Platoon, but there were of course some duties that had to be performed. One such duty was that of getting a haircut. This duty fell to one of the jeep drivers, Art Grindstaff. He had worked in a barbershop before getting into the Army and it would seem that he was the ideal man for the job. One afternoon, Grindstaff said to Page, "Let me cut your hair." Page did not want him to, but when Grindstaff told Page that he had worked in a barber shop, Page conceded. Grindstaff butchered Page's hair; it was a terrible haircut! Page said that he thought Grindstaff worked in a barbershop and Grindstaff confirmed that he did, but he was not a barber. Grindstaff shined shoes; he was a shoe shine boy!

236

Platoon Sergeant Garo was to be the next "victim" of Grindstaff's barber skills. Staff Sergeant Ray Casper, the man that had poured the pork grease on the Tiger back in the Battle of the Bulge had survived through the campaigns. He also enjoyed his time in Feudingen; he "liberated" plenty of cognac!

Ira Posnak, the Man with the Camera

PFC Ira Posnak had a camera and he decided to take pictures of the whole Mortar Platoon. Military Photographers did not take pictures of whole platoons. In fact, usually only ranking officers got their pictures taken. However, Posnak took it upon himself to photograph his whole Platoon and in great detail. Squads were photographed together and individuals also posed for pictures. Posnak had begun to take pictures just before the crossing of the Rhine. Posnak's pictures reflect what the terrain looked like that they moved through and the mood of the men from the Mortar Platoon. Pictures were also taken of convoy moves across Germany and even more sentimental pictures were taken of his buddies reading a book, playing cards, or relaxing. Perhaps the most significant picture that Posnak took was of the whole Company assembled just after combat in the Ruhr had concluded. On that afternoon, Captain Goodnight addressed the Company and Posnak captured that very significant moment. Posnak's work as an unofficial photographer captured a rare look into the interactions among platoon buddies.

Into Berlin

After leaving the concentration camp at Keune, Slagle, Lawson, and Cohen were put aboard a troop truck and moved into Berlin. This was in the immediate days following V.E. Day. The Soviets controlled Berlin, but a large contingent of Americans were there as well. Slagle saw Hitler's bunker and they also saluted General Eisenhower as his convoy moved through. The Soviets were like locusts, looting everything imaginable in Berlin. They took food and trinkets of all varieties. They took everything, including the light bulbs and the fixtures. Even toilet seats were taken. Many of the Soviets did not even know what electricity or indoor plumbing was, but they pilfered through it anyway. Slagle moved through the ruins that had been Berlin, amazed by what little was left. The Soviets were extraordinarily polite to the Americans, always saluting and returning salutes. Lawson thought very little of the Soviets and was especially angry when Cohen compared him to the Soviets, playfully mocking Lawson for not having grown up with electricity or indoor plumbing. They spent no more than a day and night in Berlin, only passing through on their way back to the 75th Division. By morning they were back aboard another troop truck bound for Bad Laasphe.

The Beginnings of the Black Market

On the truck ride to Bad Laasphe, Cohen said that he was fed up with the military and thought he had done his part. As a Jew himself, being put through a concentration camp and tasked with cleaning it up was shocking to him. He did not feel that as a combat veteran, he should have had to do that. He talked about how he thought he could make a few bucks by selling products to German and French civilians and even to American rear area units. Cohen was after all, the son of a successful pawnshop owner. Slagle and Lawson both wanted in. When they arrived to Westphalia, they had to wait for another truck to take them to Bad Laasphe. Cohen had some money on him and convinced Slagle and Lawson to give him what they had too. Cohen did just what he was not supposed to do: fraternize with German civilians. He walked into a house and bought a sizeable collection of trinkets from an old woman. He then went into a big manor house in town. The civilians were still living inside. He showed them the money and was given a box full of Nazi armbands and a few German pistols; the rear area unit had not done their job of cleaning out the town. Cohen was a good businessman, even among the enemy.

Cohen showed Slagle and Lawson all the "loot" he got. They went right away to see the Americans in town, a quartermaster unit that had not seen much action. Some of the trucks in town carried supplies including cigarettes and Coca-Cola. Cohen showed the naïve GIs the Nazi arm bands and they wanted to make a trade. Cohen walked back to Slagle with an armful of cigarette packs and a bottle of Coca-Cola for each of them. He told Slagle to walk over with one of the German pistols and trade it for more cigarettes. By the time the troop truck arrived, Slagle, Lawson, and Cohen had three big bags full of cigarettes; almost more than they could carry. Cohen told them that the cigarettes would be worth far more than money in the long run.

Reuniting with First Platoon

Slagle, Lawson, and Cohen arrived into Laasphe on about 10 May. The first GI they saw as they got off the truck was Sergeant Larson. They had a brief reunion before moving on into town. Lawson found Fourth Squad and was dismayed to discover that the Armenian, the coward, had somehow been promoted to Sergeant. The Armenian was very arrogant about his promotion too. That afternoon, Slagle started to cook some stew over a fire when a little German boy walked up and begged for a hand out. The Armenian told the boy to get lost and told them not to feed any Nazis. Slagle gave the boy some food and Lawson told the Armenian, "You had better watch your mouth or you are going to get a knife in your back." The Armenian was probably the least popular man in the Platoon, with Bergheimer having been the only one even less popular. The little boy came by every day and was always given a hand out. Staff Sergeant Slawson was married with children of his own back in the United States; he treated the boy as if he were his son.

Friends

Not much happened while in Laasphe, except for some personal interactions between squad buddies. The day after Slagle, Lawson, and Cohen had arrived to Laasphe, the usual messenger arrived by jeep, but on this day he carried a passenger. "Hay Seed" who had been severely wounded in the battle in Castrop-Rauxel made his return. He had over twenty pieces of shrapnel removed from his side and left arm, but he still had his typical smiling face. Lawson and "Hay Seed" had been best of friends since the summer of 1944 at Camp Breckinridge. In all that time, no one ever bothered to ask what his real name was; "Hay Seed" was enough and he liked the name given to him by his buddies. Lawson spent much of the afternoon reuniting with his buddy. Through all the action they had been through and despite "Hay Seed's" bravery in combat, he still looked like a big, dumb guy. "Hay Seed" was a very simple man with very little intellect, yet he was without question the model soldier and a true hero. Though both Lawson and "Hay Seed" were wounded in the Ruhr, both men somehow knew the other was going to be alright. One afternoon, Slagle, Lawson, and "Hay Seed" went out into the woods to hunt deer. It was really the first pleasure activity the men had ever done together in the many months they knew one another. Slagle walked through some brush and snapped a twig on a tree. A very old German man carrying a musket came out of the woods and threatened to shoot them. The old man was the forest meister and he would not tolerate any disturbance of his forest. Slagle thought he was going to have to shoot the man; it was a challenge to calm the old man down. "Hay Seed" and Lawson spotted deer moving through the forest and a bet was made. Whoever could shoot the deer at a range of about 70 yards with one bullet would be the winner. Without hesitation, "Hay Seed" took a shot; the whole section had deer for dinner that night.

"Something Is Wrong with the Cognac!"

While in Laasphe, one of the men of Second Section had bought a very expensive bottle of Cognac while on a leave pass. One evening, the bottle was passed around. Many of the men did not drink; Slagle, Lawson, and "Hay Seed" being among them. Due to the taunting from their buddies, everyone took a few swigs from the bottle. The cognac was very strong and it resulted in a fight breaking out in the Section. Lawson and the Armenian had a fistfight and Slagle and some of the others tried to break it up. Before long the whole Section was fighting. In the morning, the men were full of bruises and suffering from terrible hangovers. Slagle, Lawson, and several others woke up in a makeshift stockade in one of the buildings. Sergeant Larson arrived to let them out. It was reasoned that something must have been wrong with the cognac as none of the men had ever fought like that before.

The End of Occupation Duty

By 28 May, the 75th Division's occupation duty had been completed. Bad Laasphe was in the British sector and the 75th Division was relieved. H Company's platoons reorganized as a Company in Nieder Laasphe and the Company moved by trucks to a railhead for movement back to France. Not all of the Division would return to France by rail; part of the Division and indeed part of H Company made the trip by truck. The 75th Division was assigned to a large area of camps in Suippes, France where American units were to be processed for returning home. This process was based upon the points system, with 57 points earning a discharge. On the truck ride to the railhead, Slagle and Lawson spent time with their former Sergeant, Bert Larson who had led them through some tough times in the Battle of the Bulge and at Colmar. They had gone from scared boys to become men and combat veterans under the fatherly eye of Sergeant Larson; he kept them alive and taught them much about being soldiers. While in the truck, one of the guys in the Platoon who was a talented artist, began to sketch a few portraits on scrap paper. Slagle and Lawson were two of the men that received sketches. For Lawson, the truck ride was really the end of his circle of buddies. The war was over and they were going home.

Moving On

When they arrived to the railhead, Slagle, Cohen, Lawson, "Hay Seed," and the men of Second Platoon discovered that they would make the journey back to France aboard troop trucks. Their journey took them north to Meunster, an area that had been heavily bombed. In Meunster, a POW Camp had been liberated that contained men of the 75th and 106th Divisions. First Platoon's original Platoon Sergeant, the old Regular Army soldier that was captured back in December near Rochefort, was among the men liberated from that camp. The convoy moved through the battered remains of Meunster, encountering few civilians other than some that rode bicycles back to their former homes that had been reduced to rubble. Slagle had a camera with him and he took pictures of the devastation from the back of the truck. They moved through Cologne and saw the cathedral; one of the only remaining buildings. The convoy then moved back to the south, where they crossed the Rhine at Koblenz on General Hodges' Bridge. They then moved through the heavily battered town of Duren. Very little remained of Duren, but scattered ruins. The convoy then moved further east to Aachen, the site of a major battle back in October 1944. Aachen was also very battered. It was in Aachen where Slagle and Cohen parted ways with their buddies in H Company. A Major met them in Aachen and Slagle and Cohen appeared on a list of names eligible to attend intelligence training studies and to complete Officer's Candidate School. They seized the opportunity. They were first given a week's furlough in Belgium.

Crossing the Rhine on General Hodges Bridge- Koblenz, Germany

Duren and Aachen: the devastation that Slagle saw in that convoy move across Germany

243

Remnants of Meunster   **Cologne Cathedral**

L: Robert O. Slagle- Meunster, Germany

"I Knew then that the War was Truly Over"

During the convoy move across Germany, Slagle and his buddies spent the night on the second story of a building in Meunster. A kitchen was setup on the first level and there was a big pile of trash sitting in front waiting to be collected. It smelled terrible and included all sorts of things besides scraps of food. Slagle, Lawson, and Cohen shared a small room and fell asleep quickly that night. Just before sunrise, Slagle was awoken by German voices. He peered out the window and saw two Germans sifting through the trash. They were POWs that were working in the area and they were not supposed to be out and about at that hour. Lawson and Slagle watched them as one of the POWs, a former officer ordered his subordinate to dig through the trash faster. It was a pathetic sight and was a clear sign that the Germans were very much a defeated people. The German officer caught sight of Slagle and Lawson looking at him; their eyes met and Slagle and Lawson went back into their beds. Cohen stood by the window looking down at the former German soldiers pilfering through the trash; they were in waist deep. Cohen said nothing and he could have easily reported the POWs, but for some reason he did not. Despite how much Cohen hated Germans, he must have felt some semblance of pity for them.

Back to Belgium

After departing from their buddies in H Company, Slagle and Cohen went to Verviers, Belgium and with the large amount of money Cohen had made, they enjoyed themselves in restaurants and nightclubs. By late May, Slagle and Cohen were sent back to Germany to attend Officer's Candidate School at Heidelburg University. They crossed the Rhine for the second time at Koblenz on General Hodges' Bridge. They continued on in the intelligence training that they had begun back at Camp Breckinridge. Rather than living in dorms, Cohen rented a nice apartment not far from the school. He continued his successful side job of black market sales, continuing to make large sums of money. When they completed Officer's Candidate School in June, they were transferred to a unit in Paris. They traveled to Frankfurt, where they boarded a truck to take them into France. They were on limited duty and as their orders had been confused in their rapid departure from the 75th Division, the Army did not quite know where to put them.

Reuniting with H Company

Old buddies: Cook and Wells   Billy G. Wells after the war

Wells' Long Journey Back to H Company

PFC Billy Wells, the messenger for Second Platoon had been wounded on 1 February, during the first morning of combat in the Colmar Pocket. He was sent to a hospital in Nancy, France were he was to undergo surgery. Wells survived and awoke in bed in the hospital. The man in the bed next to him was sure Wells was not going to make it as he was out for three days. The doctors decided that Wells should be sent to England to recuperate. Wells remembered little of the journey that moved him from Nancy, to the docks of Le Harve and the ship that took him back to England. What he did remember was how crowded the ship was, filled with many wounded soldiers. Wells was supposed to have had the dressings on his wound changed daily on board ship, but this did not happen. By the time he arrived to England, his wound was full of infection. He was very lucky that he did not have to have an amputation.

Wells ended up in the 826th Convalescent Center, Stoneleigh Park, in Warwickshire, England. The doctors there cleaned up his hip wound and twice a day, they would insert a rubber tube through the hip wound, pull it apart and squirt saline solution all the way through to flush it out. Then they would pack it full of greased gauze pads. They operated on Wells' arm two times, as the ligaments were too short for him to open his hand; it was shaped something like a claw. After the second operation by the surgeon, Captain Wells (who was of no relation) told him they had done all they could. Wells still could not open his hand all the way and it was up to him to do the rest. He spent hours forcing a soft rubber ball into his hand and squeezing to stretch the ligaments more. He also spent hours rotating a doorknob to regain movement in his hand. When he was more mobile, Wells added dribbling a basketball to his regime. Eventually he had a near normal working hand. Something else happened to Wells while in the hospital in England. Layers of skin on his feet started to peel off. This happened to all of the combat veterans that had trench foot. Being in the warm hospital finally had its effect. Wells' feet were so tender that they could not have a sheet covering them. He slept with either a cage over his feet or the sheet and blanket were folded back so they could stick out. Eventually new skin replaced the old but that area still showed, plus he did not have toenails.

During the stay in the hospital, Wells was taken on a few tours to the surrounding areas. Young English ladies served as the escorts to the patients. The young ladies belonged to an organization that visited the wounded veterans and they helped to temporarily make the GIs forget about their wounds. Wells went to Warwick Castle, St. Mary's Church in Warwick, Ann Hathaway's Cottage, Leamington Spa, Shakespeare's House and Theater on the river Avon, Mary Arden's Cottage and Kenilworth Castle. The cottages had thatch roofs and were very interesting. Wells saw an opera in Shakespeare's

Theater. He enjoyed it primarily because his escort was a pretty girl. On another occasion Wells' escort asked if he would like to go punting on the Avon. It was a nice spring day and Wells' felt adventuresome; he said he would love to go, so off they went to the Avon. It turned out that punting on the Avon was a ride in a long and narrow, flat-bottomed boat with square ends propelled with oars. It was a great ride even though it rained and they had to park under a huge willow tree to keep dry. Wells thought that he would be sent home from England but one of the hospital staff saw him riding a bicycle one-day and said, "I think that you are well enough to return to your Division." Wells did not like it but since the war was over in Europe and he would get to see his buddies, it could not be too bad, and it was not.

Wells was told that the 75th Division was in Germany on occupation duty. He was given written orders to travel by the best means available to their location. Wells' orders noted that he had thirty days to arrive to his destination and it was an opportunity for a sightseeing tour. Wells traveled through England, across the English Channel, through France and Belgium and finally into Germany. He moved through one transient mess and motor pool to another. He made good connections at the motor pools, riding in trucks and jeeps. He visited Colmar where he was wounded and stopped in Liege, Aachen, Koln, Bonn, Frankfurt, and Weisbaden. Unfortunately, by the time Wells finally made it to the 75th Division's occupation area, they had already departed for their next assignment.

Wells had no orders to travel back to France and the Captain in charge of Brambauer told Wells to remain there with his outfit. Wells did not like that and had orders to rejoin his Division, so he found a Chaplain. The Chaplain took Wells to a Colonel and they fixed him up with new written orders to go to Suippes, France, near Rheims. Written orders were needed because if the Military Police stopped you and you did not have them, then you were AWOL. Checking his maps showed Wells that he was headed for territory in France that he had not been through before. He could go through Nancy, where he was in the hospital the first time, then to Metz, Verdun, and Suippes. So, Wells took off again. He was seeing great country but the cities and villages had been destroyed.

Ross' Three-day Leave Pass

While H Company was encamped near the Dortmund-Ems Canal back in early April, Ross was the winner of a three-day leave pass to Paris; it was the first leave Ross had received since arriving to Europe. Ross had been taken by truck back to Belgium and put on a train in the evening. It was an old train with wooden seats and the windows had been shot out during the war. It was a miserable ride and Ross got a sore throat from exposure. When he arrived to Paris the next afternoon, Ross had a fever and was sent directly to the American General Hospital with a severe case of tonsillitis. After a few days, the inflammation went away and his tonsils were removed. After a few more days, Ross felt fine, but because his outfit was so far away in Germany, the Army Regulations kept him in the hospital for ten days. The doctor would check Ross every morning and then he was free to go to downtown Paris until bed check at 2200 hours. Ross was still in Paris on V.E. Day, when the whole city went wild. He went through replacement depots and was attached to another company. Ross eventually returned to H Company after they arrived to Camp New York.

Camp New York: Going Home

Byrd (1ˢᵗ Platoon) moving POWs   **Camp New York- POW enclosure**

The man known as "Hay Seed," June 1945- going home

2LT Robert O. Slagle- Fontainbleau, France   **2LT Robert O. Slagle, November 1945- Paris**

The Camp System

About 29 May, the men of H Company arrived to Camp New York, built on the site of the World War I trenches on the old Marne battlefield. It was one of many redeployment camps in Suippes, France near Rheims. The 75th Division was in charge of camps to process the movement of troops and equipment back to the United States. Camp New York was about 100 miles east of Paris. There was little to do in the camps, but interact with one's buddies and try to get leave passes out of camp. Other than that, everyone was patiently awaiting their turn to go home. To go home, one had to have sufficient points and not everyone did. The cooks were the first to go home, next came the original members of the Company that had earned medals during the war. Bronze Stars and Purple Hearts both contributed a sizeable number of points.

"Hay Seed's" Departure

One of the first men in H Company eligible to go home was "Hay Seed." With his medals, he had more than enough points to go home. When "Hay Seed" found out that he was eligible to go home, he got very upset; he did not want to leave. He was offered a promotion to Staff Sergeant if he would remain in the Army, but Captain Goodnight talked him out of it. Lawson was there as Goodnight presented "Hay Seed" with the Oak Leaf Cluster, his second Bronze Star, earned at Castrop-Rauxel. Goodnight was very much a man of his word and had not forgotten about Lawson. Sergeant Lawson had led a successful patrol across the Maas River in Holland and was actually berated by his then Platoon Leader, Lieutenant Bergheimer. Captain Goodnight told him he would get a medal for his actions on that patrol, but Lawson had long since forgotten about it. Lawson was quite surprised when Goodnight presented him with the Bronze Star. Goodnight shook their hands and invited them to dinner that evening in one of the barracks buildings in Camp New York. That evening, Goodnight hosted a dinner for sergeants and officers from H Company, even some of the original privates in the Company were invited. Goodnight left a lasting impression on all those in attendance with his bravery, fairness, and quiet demeanor. They all treated him like a hero, but Goodnight would have nothing to do with such praise; he was a very modest man. At the end of the meal, each soldier shook Goodnight's hand and saluted him. For Lawson and "Hay Seed," shaking hands with Goodnight was a great honor; they both looked upon him as a hero and as a model leader in every respect. The next morning "Hay Seed" was set to go home. He was supposed to board a troop truck to go to the train station, but Captain Goodnight would have no part of it. Goodnight's driver volunteered to drive "Hay Seed" to the station. His duffel bag was loaded in the back and as he was getting in, Lawson bade him a tearful goodbye and a salute. Many of "Hay Seed's" old buddies came out to say goodbye. As the jeep was pulling away Lawson shouted, "Hey, wait a minute, what is your name and what town are you from?" "Hay Seed" shouted back, "I am a Southern boy from Mississippi!" Lawson never did find out what his best buddy's name really was.

POWs in Camp New York

As the cooks were discharged to go home, there was a need to replace them in the kitchen. At that time Chaiklin's main duties consisted of guarding POWs that would not try to escape. In Camp New York, the POWs did mainly maintenance work, such as collecting garbage, KP, and those with skills were gradually moving into cooking duties. Guarding POWs was onerous. A new lieutenant arrived fresh from the States and he was apparently angry that he missed the war. He insisted that guards carry live rounds in the chamber while they were on guard duty. Anytime a round is in the chamber it is dangerous.

Page from the Mortar Platoon was one of the men assigned to guard the POWs. They slept in pup tents in Camp New York and were escorted out every morning to their duties. The POWs offered absolutely no arguments; they were glad to be working for the Americans and not for the British, French or Russians. Page could have easily taken a nap while the POWs worked, they would not have gone anywhere. If they did try to get out of camp and the French caught them, they would be put to hard labor. As H Company settled into their duties in Camp New York, Staff Sergeant Modrzejewski returned to duty from his wound back in February at Colmar. Modrzejewski went to the officer's quarters and worked there. PFC Larry Silverstein who had been in Third Section of the Mortar Platoon through the war, showed his talent while in Camp New York. Silverstein was a talented artist and he often made sketches of the guys in the Mortar Platoon. One day, Silverstein made a sketch of Page, paying such close attention to detail that he even included the scar on Page's left arm caused by a Zip-O lighter burn.

A Life Lesson

Chaiklin who had arrived as a replacement in February along the Maas in Holland did not have the points to go home. The cooks were going home and there was a call for volunteers to go into the kitchen. Chaiklin, who was always hungry, violated the Army rule of never volunteering for anything and went into the kitchen. It was strictly on the job training. He was taught cooking skills from one of the original cooks, Ross Simms and Ray Ott, the Company Clerk, who eventually became the Mess Sergeant. Ott was a mink farmer from Wisconsin and was close to going home. H Company's new

First Sergeant, Whalen's replacement was a miserable man and a petty tyrant. At one point, Chaiklin traded something in the kitchen for an old Air Force leather jacket to keep himself warm on cold mornings. The First Sergeant threatened to charge Chaiklin with something for wearing it. Captain Goodnight liked Chaiklin and nothing came of the charges.

Goodnight came into the kitchen every morning for coffee at 1000 hours. He began to talk with Chaiklin about everyday things. At one point he asked Chaiklin if he was going to go to college when he got home. Chaiklin said he had thought about it, but he had read that the colleges were full and he did not have money. Goodnight began to tell him how he had gone through college. Even though Goodnight was an All-American college football player with a year in the Pros before being drafted, college had not been easy for him. He was an Indian and undoubtedly experienced the prejudice towards Native-Americans that many people had. Goodnight told Chaiklin how he had worked in an icehouse to support himself through college. He had been an All-American student too as well as an athlete. Goodnight served as an inspiring role model to young Chaiklin.

Into the Kitchen

Chaiklin started off in the kitchen as one of many cooks and gradually it became his kitchen as the original cooks went home. Corporal Simms served as Chaiklin's mentor in the kitchen. Simms was from Ohio and was red-faced, stoutly built, with blonde hair; he was quite a drinker too. Chaiklin had no experience with cooking and Simms taught him a lot. His first lesson was how not to get blown up while starting up an Army Field Range. It was rectangular and looked like a tall refrigerator cut in half. It used gasoline. The Field Range had aluminum griddles and was a top quality product. Simms taught Chaiklin how to make corn fritters, a favorite of the Company. He was taught to mix the batter, throw in some canned corn and deep-fry them. If the batter was made right, they would turn themselves when one side was done. If they did not flip over themselves, then a spoon was used to turn them over. Chaiklin was also taught to make hotcakes using powdered eggs. The hotcakes had to be made just before they were served. If they were left around for long their texture resembled cardboard. Eventually "fresh" eggs were delivered; they were quick dipped in paraffin to seal the shells and they were kept in cold storage. For breakfast it was bacon and eggs. Meat and chicken was delivered frozen and pre-cut. Simms taught Chaiklin to cook chicken, pot roast, and meatloaf. If meats were in short supply, Spam was used in place of it. Chaiklin was taught 50 ways to cook with Spam. There was still rationing at the time and there was not a lot of local produce to cook with as the French farmers were just getting back into production. Potatoes and Brussels Sprouts were among the only vegetables. Beef stew and Spaghetti was two other favorite meals. Simms even taught Chaiklin how to bake a sheet cake.

Corporal Simms was a good teacher, but he also liked to tease his young apprentice. Simms was something of a practical joker. When Chaiklin first got started in the kitchen, Simms told him to pour vinegar into a garbage can full of chickens to tenderize them. Chaiklin poured in a bottle, later to discover that it was pure citric acid! There was a lot of washing chickens to do. Chaiklin was also told to cook a pot full of beans and he filled it up too much and it boiled over; he was not told that beans expand when cooked! These practical jokes at the expense of "Junior," brought great joy to the old timers in the kitchen. Despite the close association between instructor and pupil, Simms was older than Chaiklin and that meant they were not social buddies.

A Cook's Adventures through France

As the cooks began to go home, German POWs took over the menial kitchen duties. Chaiklin worked 24 hours in the kitchen and 48 hours off. His shift began just after breakfast and ended just after breakfast the following day. On his days off, Chaiklin would hitchhike into Suippes and Chalons for a train if a ride was not available. He had a favorite spot in Suippes, where Pedro, an ammo bearer from his Squad would play his guitar. Chaiklin got friendly with the owner of the establishment, who was amused at the crazy Americans that fought each other and smashed up tables and chairs. The owner was making a lot of money for damages. The owner once invited Chaiklin to dinner on the second story, where there was a restaurant. It was the first time Chaiklin had crepes.

At Camp New York, there was a raid on the POW enclosure. They were living in pup tents and it was discovered that the ground was dug out under them. The POWs had saved all the fruit bars from C rations and whatever sugar they could get their hands on, including some stolen from the kitchen. The POWs had 19 stills functioning in camp; the Germans were very ingenious. When Mess Sergeant Ott went home, the next mess sergeant was arrested for feeding the prostitutes that had moved into camp and setup residence in one of the old French trenches.

Assembly Area Command

By 1 July, everything changed abruptly. The camps became an assembly area command, with a new unit patch; Seine et Oise. There was no more training for going to Japan or lectures on atabrine. H Company had come apart as a unit. Many of the men were assigned to new duties and no longer worked together. Some buddies managed to live and work together. Units disbanded and those GIs that still did not have the points to go home, remained and were left with the feeling that they were no longer part of an infantry regiment. Chaiklin remained as his good friend Bert Larson went home to his wife and children in Minnesota. Chaiklin was planning to go on leave to Switzerland that September, but his First Sergeant tried to kill the leave. Captain Goodnight saw to it that Chaiklin got his leave. A few days later, Goodnight received the Silver Star for his actions in the Colmar Pocket and he was offered a promotion to Major, should he choose to remain in the Army. Two days later on 12 September, Goodnight turned down his promotion and was honorably discharged and went home. Chaiklin was eventually moved to the old French barracks buildings in Camp New York and worked in a much larger kitchen. Corporal Simms also came to the new kitchen.

The Privileges of a Cook

One night, Chaiklin went to a dance hall in Suippes; he had a lot to drink that night. The MPs were called and Chaiklin was picked up. It was a cold night and the cool air cleared his head during the ride. One of the MPs was heavy set with a pencil-thin mustache. Chaiklin recognized him as a pool player from the YMCA in his hometown of Bridgeport, Connecticut. He said he knew the MP, but the MP did not know him. Chaiklin then explained how he recognized him. Within a short time, Chaiklin was taken to his kitchen in the middle of the night and he cooked steak and eggs for the MP; all was good. Being a cook offered a certain measure of privileges. Chaiklin was a young man and did not engage in the fairly large-scale practice of selling rations on the Black

Market. Instead, he used his cigarette rations to finance trips to Paris when he could get a pass. Cigarettes cost ten cents a pack and a carton usually went for twenty dollars on the Black Market. Chaiklin was not a cigarette smoker, but did attempt a pipe and a cigar. Chaiklin discovered that a few trades of the right items to the right people got him leave passes. He traded with the medics for some 200 proof medical alcohol. Some grapefruit juice and alcohol went to the First Sergeant in exchange for a three-day leave pass to Paris. A colonel frequently came by Chaiklin's kitchen with his two great danes that liked baked beans. The colonel once said that if the GI would let him, the Germans would, "kiss his ass."

From Camp to Camp

Chaiklin was eventually promoted to Technician Fifth Grade and got a liquor ration. After seven months in Camp New York, Chaiklin was moved to a camp in Mourmellon in January 1946 and remained in the kitchen. Mourmellon was just outside Chalons. Captain Orvale E. Faubus was in command of the unit in Mourmellon. Faubus had worked in the railroad industry and kept a drawer full of Hamilton railroad watches; he later became the segregationist governor of Arkansas. After a few months Chaiklin then moved on to another camp, Herbert Tareyton in Le Harve for another two months. In Herbert Tareyton, he had an unusual experience. A Rabbi came to visit Chaiklin and said he was arranging a Passover Seder for the Jewish community in Le Harve and he had permission to have the kitchen help while he supervised. By then, POWs were doing most of the cooking. One of the POWs, "Curley" was a middle-aged man that said he had worked for a kosher butcher when he was young. "Curley" said that he understood how things had to be. The dinner was cooked and served by the POWs. It was a Passover of contrasts. While in Herbert Tareyton, Chaiklin became ill and was in the hospital for six weeks. He was diagnosed with Mono, but it was likely another ailment caused by drinking unpasturized milk. Many others from H Company had the same ailment. When he got out of the hospital, he collected his belongings and moved to Camp Lucky Strike also near Le Harve.

At Camp Lucky Strike, there was an enlisted and an officer's mess; Chaiklin worked in both of them. He was promoted to T/5 there. One of the things on the menu was Waldorf Salad. The Army version was made with mayonnaise, carrots, and raisins.

259

The G.I.s would not eat it and Chaiklin was visited by supervisors who said he was not following the Army Class-A Menu. The men wanted to eat raisins and raw carrots, not all of it mixed together. If he made the salad, there would be complaints from those who checked the garbage for food wastage. It was a true Catch 22.

One day, Chaiklin watched as Red Cross men loaded a jeep with coffee and nylon stockings and they returned with diamonds. The Black Market was very big in France. Chaiklin remained in the kitchen through June 1946, when he was finally eligible to go home. He was offered a promotion to Staff Sergeant if he would remain in the Army, but Chaiklin took his father's advice and turned down the offer. Chaiklin went home on a big ship and cooked on the voyage. He got seasick one day from the rolling sea and frying pork chops. There was a huge amount of gambling and poker with the card sharks. The voyage was also notable for broadcasting the Lewis-Conn fight live.

Getting Reacquainted with Old Buddies

When Wells returned to H Company in Camp New York, he received a warm welcome from his old buddies, but many of the buddies he remembered were gone. Wells did however find his good buddy, PFC James Cook and also Staff Sergeant Donald Stewart. He also got to know the replacements. Some of the men of H Company lived in buildings, but most lived in reinforced tents with floors. The tents were flammable as Prater and Malarich discovered when their tent caught fire one night. Wells was assigned to a supply room where the men being discharged passed through to turn in excess clothing or get new clothing. It was a nice job, being in a warm building, getting good food, and it was not very busy. Wells and his buddies also got passes to Rheims and Paris often.

One day a notice was posted on the bulletin board noting that they needed someone to work in the dispensary. Wells thought, "Why not?" He always thought he would like to be a doctor. When he got there, he discovered that they expected medics to apply, as the job included giving penicillin shots to the men that had gotten a venereal disease. These men had messed up their chance to go home until they were cured; they did not get any sympathy. Since nobody else showed up for the job, Wells got it. The fact that he was not a medic and had never given injections was discussed. It was decided since these guys had messed up and all Wells had to do was be able to stick a needle in their bare butts, it would be ok. They did show Wells how to fill a syringe and he stuck them in a lot of bare butts for a while. When it came time for some of the men to go home they had a going-away party. When it was his time to go home, Wells arrived to New Jersey, and he was issued orders to report to Camp Atterbury, Indiana; a separation center. Wells received his Honorable Discharge from the Army on 3 May 1946.

Reassignments

In Camp New York, Staff Sergeant Prater was assigned to a Signal Corps to process troops that were to be sent to the South Pacific. Prater's new assignment was to oversee the collection of equipment and manage to get it shipped back to the major supply area around Thionville, in northeastern France. Prater would get the occasional pleasure trip out of Camp New York, when he and a driver took a 6' by 6' truck to Thionville to drop off equipment and then go on to Luxembourg City. He would spend the night and sightsee around the area in the morning. Prater also went back to the Ardennes Forest, to an area just to the south of where he had fought in the Battle of the Bulge.

In August, just after the war in the Pacific had ended, Prater and some of the men in H Company who had been in ASTP studies were offered the chance to stay in France and go to school. Prater and Ross ended up at the University of Paris in a twelve week course of study on "Language and Civilization" at the Sorbonne. They lived at the Cite University, on the outskirts of Paris, in the Swiss House. A short metro ride took them to school each day. They spent a few hours each morning learning the French language, then took their course at the Sorbonne. On several afternoons each week, they were taken on sightseeing trips outside Paris to visit museums, cathedrals, factories, and other points of interest. After several months, Prater's number came up for transfer back to the United States. He was offered a place in Officer's Candidate School, but Prater wanted to go home. The voyage home was uneventful and Prater was honorably discharged at Jefferson Barracks in St. Louis. Prater immediately went home to Springfield, Missouri and enrolled in Drury College again in January 1946. Ross departed Europe on 5

February 1946 and arrived to New York on the 16th. Ross was honorably discharged at Fort MacArthur, California on 24 February.

The "Little Red Schoolhouse"

One day, shortly after arriving to Camp New York, a jeep pulled up to the front of the tent where Kravitz and the men of his Squad were standing. An officer jumped out and called out, "Can anyone type?" Without any hesitation, Kravitz's hand went up. Kravitz was ordered to pack his duffel bag and found himself in a jeep heading for Rheims. Kravitz left H Company that day and was reassigned to work as a clerk in the "Little Red Schoolhouse," which had been General Eisenhower's Headquarters. This was the building where the Germans signed their unconditional surrender treaty that ended the war in Europe. Kravitz was no longer in the 75th Division; for the next six months he lived in Caserne Colbert, a French Army barracks, where he shared a room with three other GIs who also worked as clerks in various offices in the "Little Red Schoolhouse." More than a hundred men and women worked as clerks there and they held ranks ranging from colonels down to privates. Kravitz missed his buddies in H Company and he managed to visit them on his days off and some of them came into Rheims to visit him.

While working in Rheims, Kravitz had information about units that were being redeployed. When Kravitz saw that the unit in which his hometown friend Earl was a part of, come up for redeployment, Kravitz arranged to go out to the camp and find him. Kravitz found his friend sitting on a cot in a dusty tent and he nearly fell off of his seat when Kravitz walked in; they had a great reunion. In November 1945, Kravitz had a week's furlough to Switzerland. Three cartons of cigarettes were worth quite a lot. Kravitz came back to Rheims with three Swiss wristwatches. When he returned to the "Little Red Schoolhouse," Kravitz discovered that he had been promoted to Technician Fifth Grade. In late December, Corporal Kravitz had enough points to be discharged. He asked the colonel in command for an expedited discharge so that he could register for the spring semester at the American International College in his hometown of Springfield, Massachusetts. By Christmas, Kravitz had received his shipping orders. Kravitz crossed the Atlantic on a converted ocean liner through very stormy weather. He spent a good part of the voyage in his bunk, seasick. In January, Kravitz returned to New York then to

Fort Dix, New Jersey and back to where his service first began almost three years earlier; Fort Devens, Massachusetts. Kravitz received his honorable discharge at the end of January 1946 and enrolled in a special college class for returning veterans in February.

A View from Paris

During the summer of 1945, while in Paris, Slagle and Cohen lived together in a nice apartment. They were still in the Army, but Cohen managed to pay for enough leave passes to keep them out of regular duty. Cohen continued his black market dealings and became a very wealthy man. As Cohen and Slagle moved through downtown Paris one evening, a Moroccan moneychanger pulled a knife on Slagle. He kicked the man below the belt, threw his knife for distance and Slagle and Cohen quickly ran off. On many evenings they went to the USO Shows and any band concerts they could find. There was plenty of nightlife in Paris and they never ran out of things to do. The food was excellent and both men started to gain some weight from the heavy French cuisine.

Living a Dream

In June, while in Paris, Slagle and Cohen attended a band concert from the Glenn Miller Orchestra. It was Slagle's favorite band and he loved the music and knew most of the songs by heart. Slagle really missed playing the alto sax and clarinet and remembered his days playing on the Steel Pier in New Jersey before he got into the Army. During the show, Slagle got a chance to meet some of the musicians that had been with the band for several years. When he told them he was a musician and played the sax, one of the musicians said they needed a sax player and he should audition. The next day, Slagle joined the band. The Glenn Miller Orchestra playing in Paris was one of two bands to hold the name of the late Glenn Miller. This was an offshoot band that was going to travel across Europe and perform for the troops. After months of war, Slagle was living his dream of playing in the Glenn Miller Orchestra. While playing in Paris, the Glenn Miller Orchestra opened for Bob Hope, who Slagle had the opportunity to meet. They spent a few weeks in Paris, then went on tour to Salzburg, Austria where they spent the remainder of June and part of July. Slagle enjoyed the culture and the life of a bandsman. On V.J. Day, the Glenn Miller Orchestra was performing in Marburg, Germany. They toured all around Germany through August. The Band then returned to Paris where Slagle continued on into the end of August 1945. Cohen often came to see his buddy play the sax.

During their time in Paris in August, Cohen sent a letter to Lawson in Camp New York along with some money. Sergeant Lawson paid his First Sergeant for a week's furlough to Paris. Lawson, a simple country boy, looked forward to seeing Paris. He lived in the apartment with Slagle and Cohen for the week. They took Lawson to the USO Shows and to many different restaurants and nightclubs. Slagle and Cohen, who had completed Officer's Candidate School, frequented a popular officer's club on the first landing of the Eiffel Tower. One night they went and took Lawson as well. They got him in with no trouble. While in the club a drunk colonel tried to pick a fight with Slagle for allowing Lawson into the club. The colonel missed with a punch and Slagle hit him hard in the gut, knocking the colonel out cold. A round of cheers went up from the patrons in the club.

Lawson enjoyed Paris, but was starting to feel ill. At first they thought it was due to staying out too late and eating too much rich food, but Lawson felt progressively worse. When he returned to Camp New York, he spent time in the Aid Station; his head was spinning. The doctors could not find anything wrong with him and discharged him and requested that he be given limited duty. Lawson took a weekend trip to Paris again to visit his buddies, but still felt bad. Slagle and Cohen were shocked by how bad Lawson looked. A week later, Lawson asked his First Sergeant if it would be possible to go home on medical discharge. The request went ignored. A few days later, Cohen sent Lawson about one thousand dollars in a letter; he told him to bribe the First Sergeant and take the rest home with him. Lawson paid off the First Sergeant and went home in early August. Lawson had done more than his fair share while in the Army. As he was awaiting his discharge papers in an office in Le Harve, Lawson caught a glimpse of a familiar face; Second Lieutenant Bergheimer, his former Platoon Leader. Lawson took a close look at Bergheimer; he did not see the smart mouthed bully he remembered, he saw a bedraggled, beaten down man. Bergheimer recognized Lawson, lowered his eyes and said nothing. It was obvious that Bergheimer was recovering from his wound and had been assigned to office duty. By the time he boarded the ship, Lawson was so ill, he thought he would die before he could make it home.

264

Getting Discharged

By early September, Slagle and Cohen were ready to go home and they had the points. However, due to the fact that they had completed Officer's Candidate School and were awaiting their official promotions to lieutenants, the Army would not discharge them. They were supposed to sign a six-year term of duty with the Army, but both men refused. About that time, as their careers were stalled, they discovered that they were eligible to take a class at the Sorbonne in Paris. Slagle and Cohen lived a few blocks away from the campus in another nice apartment, with Cohen footing the bill. They took a class on Cinema Arts and Slagle worked on a documentary film project about France's sewer system. They took many class trips all around France, visiting all the big tourist locations. Fontainbleau was another popular destination and at a lake in the area they had a chance to go fishing.

Homesick

In early December 1945, Slagle passed by a storefront in Paris where a musician was playing Christmas songs. Slagle wanted to go home; he was homesick. He parted ways with his good buddy Cohen and took home his earnings of over a thousand dollars. Cohen decided to stay in Paris; he was making a lot of money and was really enjoying himself. After completing his course at the Sorbonne in late November, Slagle reverted back to Army duties; this time working in a Colonel's office. During his time as an office clerk, Slagle met two other men who also were patiently waiting for their discharges. Ralph Miller was from Chicago and was about ten years older than Slagle. Thomas Parenti had been a Sergeant in L Company, 291st Infantry since Camp Breckinridge; he was a decorated veteran who had qualified for OCS. Parenti was from Philadelphia and he and Slagle quickly became good friends. Slagle, Miller, and Parenti were determined to get home by Christmas. On 5 December, Slagle, Miller, and Parenti finally received their honorable discharges from the Army. They traveled from Paris to Le Harve and tried to find a means to get home. They decided to sign on with the Merchant Marines as deck hands and got aboard a ship bound for New York. They left the Port of Le Harve on 13 December.

The Voyage Home

Slagle, Miller, and Parenti enjoyed the voyage for the first day or so, but then the situation greatly changed; they went through a major storm while at sea. The storm made even the most seasoned sea dogs ill. The storm struck fear in the whole crew and they were not sure if they were going to make it. Miller became horribly ill and could not do any work. Slagle and Parenti faired little better. After a seven-day journey, whereby they survived the storm, they made it to New York. As they moved through customs, Slagle and his buddies were stopped and customs wanted to hold their duffel bags for inspection. Likely, the customs officials would have confiscated their "loot" for themselves. Slagle told them to go to Hell and pushed his way through the line. A fight erupted between discharged Servicemen from the ship and the customs officials. Slagle escaped through the confusion and went on his way. He stayed the night in New York and went home to Hadden Heights, New Jersey the next day. Slagle got home on 22 December and celebrated Christmas with his family. When his parents moved to New Hampshire in January 1946, Slagle used the G.I. Bill and the money he made with Cohen to pay for a college education. He went to Clark University in Worchester, Massachusetts and studied Economics and Geography. On weekends, he looked for work as a musician. He met his future wife one Friday night, when he happened to stop in a dance hall in Worchester, looking for work.

"There Were All Kinds in H Company"

Thus, is the story of the men of H Company, 291st Regiment, 75th Infantry Division through the Battle of the Bulge, the Colmar Pocket, and the Ruhr Encirclement. The men of H Company were average men, like those found in all other battalions and regiments within the 75th Division. The men were from all walks of life, some from the city and some from the country. Some came from very humble beginnings, while others came from comfortable lives. Some were very well educated, while others were barely literate. Some were typical Americans, while others were from immigrant families. Some were Protestants and some were Catholics, and some were Jews. The men of H Company were very much a melting pot of many different types of men, but together they did their part. Despite the many differences between them, the men formed strong bonds and even some life-long friendships emerged. GIs on the front line form a special bond that only exists between men that have gone through the same ordeals together. They identify each other as buddies. After nearly 70 years, many of these men still fondly remember their buddies that they served with in H Company.

The Men of H Company After the War

Owen L. Goodnight Jr.

Owen Goodnight returned home to Texas in late September 1945. He married and had two daughters. He also returned to play Pro Football for the Chicago Bears and Baltimore Colts. In 1950 he retired from the Pros and began his coaching career at Pasadena, Texas. He later moved on to San Marcos, Texas where he became head football coach and athletic director at San Marcos High School for 16 years. His teams won the District of Central Texas Championship three times and also the State Championship once. Coach Goodnight was named Central Texas Coach of the Year for three consecutive years. He was later inducted into the Texas State Coaches Hall of Fame. He held more wins than any other coach in the state of Texas. Goodnight suffered a fatal heart-attack just as he was being introduced at the Spring Sports Banquet in 1967. It was to have been his final honor as athletic director and coach as he was to become the Vice Principal of San Marcos High School. In 2007, Goodnight was honored with a school that bears his name in his hometown of San Marcos, Texas: Owen Goodnight Junior High School. Captain Goodnight is remembered by the men of H Company as a truly rare man. Humble, soft spoken, brave, and heroic are just a few words that many of the men who served with him use to describe their captain. Goodnight is fondly remembered by his men.

Robert O. Slagle

Officer's Club: GHQ Tokyo- middle Slagle   Slagle- Seoul, South Korea 1952

Robert O. Slagle before retirement- 1984

Granddad and Grandson: Robert O. Slagle- James Slagle McClintock 1983

Slagle always said that his experience in the war was the start of his career in intelligence; he learned the basics from General Mickle. Slagle returned home, studied Economics at Clark University in Worchester, Massachusetts, and met his future wife, Dolores at a dance in 1946. He married in 1947, got his B.A. in Economics from Suffolk University in 1949, and received his Masters in Military Geography from Boston University in 1950. When he found out that he had his first child on the way, he decided to enlist in the Army Reserves. He was commissioned as a Second Lieutenant and sent to the Army Intelligence School at Fort Riley, Kansas. Slagle taught intelligence courses there based on his own war time experiences. He was an expert in photo interpretation. Shortly after his son Glenn's birth in 1951, Slagle was told that he would be taking part in the Korean War. He was sent to Kimpo AFB, South Korea. He served as an Intelligence Officer attached to an Air Force unit. He was working on target acquisition to USAF bombers over North Korea. While at Kimpo, he was strafed by a North Korean Bed Check Charlie, took an unsanctioned flight in the back seat of a RT-33 jet at low level over North Korea (where he earned his second Bronze Star), and survived a mortar attack on his barracks at Kimpo. He was later assigned to GHQ Headquarters, Tokyo and served on the Defense Geographic Survey of Japan in 1952. He probably saw more of Japan than most Japanese had seen, while driving a jeep through the back country of Japan with a Nisei interpreter.

Slagle returned home in April 1952 and continued his service in Army Intelligence. In 1955, he returned to civilian life (though continuing on in Intelligence) and he brought his family along to Wiesbaden, Germany, where he served as Senior Advisor to the Commanding General USAFE. In 1956, this commander was General Ben Davis, the former commander of the Tuskegee Airmen during WW II. Slagle formed a close friendship with Davis, at a time when prejudice was still very prevalent. At a dance in the Officer's Club one night, General Davis asked Slagle's permission for a dance with his wife, which was a memorable moment in her life. While stationed in Germany, Slagle traveled all through Europe, to the places he fought in during the war. He returned to Paris, Villers St. Gertrude in Belgium, to the Ardennes, the Rhine, and to his ancestral home in Castrop-Rauxel. He even became fluent in the German language.

Slagle returned home in 1960, bought a house in the Washington DC suburbs on the GI Bill, raised his children, and continued on as a civilian in Intelligence and National Security. In his career, he would become a Team Leader, Director, and Division Chief. He wrote numerous articles, project studies, and estimates on a wide-range of topics pertaining to the Soviet Union and its capabilities. In 1971 he predicted that the Soviet Union would collapse by 1990, due to failures in collective farming. He was proven correct, when it happened in 1992. He concluded his career as a specialist in long-range economic and military projections and strategy. He retired in 1984, raised his only grandson from birth and enjoyed his Golden Years. He loved his music and often spent evenings playing the saxophone and recording his voice to the music of Glenn Miller and Frank Sinatra. Slagle passed away in 1996 at the age of 71.

S. Phillip Lawson

Lawson left Le Harve in late August 1945. He was severely ill on the voyage back to New York. He was to be discharged at Fort Dix, New Jersey, but was sent first to a hospital in New York City. He spent two weeks there until he was well enough to go home to Georgia. Lawson took a several day long train ride to Savannah, Georgia and then hitched rides back to his family farm. He was still ill and suffering from what seemed to be a permanent stomach ailment and severe headaches. Lawson had a hard time returning to civilian life. He had nightmares and constantly had thoughts of his buddies that were killed in combat. He put his uniform and all of his war-related items into an old chest and put it into his attic, never to think of it again. When his father died in 1946, Lawson took over the family farm and in 1948, he married the daughter of a neighboring farm owner. They had 8 children and 25 grandchildren. Lawson still does farm work, even at the age of 89. Every so often he walks outside at night with his rifle slung over his shoulder and checks around "looking for Germans."

Lawson said that he only agreed to talk to me because he knew my grandfather. He says that my weekly conversations with him over the span of a year helped him to get over the events he went through 70 years ago. He told me a lot of stories about my grandfather that I never knew. Over the summer of 2010, he went up into his attic and pulled down his trunk where his uniform was kept for 65 years. For the first time in his life, he started to tell his family about his war experiences. His youngest grandson picked up his Bronze Star and asked how he got it. Lawson says the thing he is most proud of is his first great-grandson, S. Phillip Lawson II, born in July 2010, while I was interviewing him for this book. Lawson never would tell me what the "S" stood for in his first name. Lawson continues to live on his family farm, an hour from Savannah, Georgia. He still thinks of his buddies from the war and particularly about those that never made it home. He often wonders what became of his best buddy, "Hay Seed."

On 4 April 2012, Lawson came on a World War II tour group to Washington DC, where I met up with him in person at the World War II Memorial. You could easily pick him out of the crowd, since he wore overalls and was chewing on a piece of a corn cob; a true farmer. We had a nice visit and I brought some of my grandfather's old pictures from the war with me. It brought both a smile and a tear to his eye to see pictures of his old buddies. He laughed incessantly when he pointed out "Hay Seed" in one of the pictures.

Saul Cohen

Saul Cohen remained in Paris until the summer of 1946. He returned home with a small fortune and bought his father's pawn shop in the Bronx. He opened up several other stores and eventually moved to New York City, where he became a successful businessman. In July 1955, a sports car pulled up on Lawson's farm in Georgia. Cohen had tracked him down to pay his old buddy a visit. Lawson invited Cohen to stay as long as he wanted, but Cohen said he would just stay overnight. Lawson gave him the full tour of his farm. Cohen pointed out every little thing wrong with the farm and very rudely told Lawson to spend money in repairs. Lawson had no money to spare, he was going through some tough times and could not even afford shoes for his children; Lawson thought he would probably lose his farm. The next morning, Cohen had breakfast with Lawson and his family and was in a rush to leave. When Lawson's wife went into the guest room to tidy up, she found a large envelope full of money, thousands of dollars, and a note from Cohen that read "I hope this will keep your farm going. Buy your kids some shoes!" Lawson wanted to find Cohen and return his money, but he was long gone. Several years later, Cohen called him and wanted to see how Lawson was doing. Cohen's money had saved Lawson's farm. Lawson has always been grateful to his buddy, Cohen. Saul Cohen passed away after a heart-attack in 1967. He was married and divorced five times.

Billy Wells

Billy Wells receiving medal at French Embassy

When Billy Wells returned home, he thought he would like to become a draftsman. However, upon returning home, he discovered that his father had bought a grocery store and expected his son to be his partner. He worked there for about three weeks and decided it was not for him. Wells then began to study to be a draftsman, but after a month decided that was not for him either. He reunited with his high school

275

sweetheart and her family said they could use him on their farm. They married shortly thereafter. After a few years the World War II era prices began to drop and there was not enough land for them to farm. Wells and his father then bought a dragline and went into the excavating business; Wells had found his calling. Wells and his father bid on jobs and started a business, but his father became ill and they went bankrupt. Wells discovered that he had reinstatement rights at the Naval ammunition depot that he had worked for before he was drafted. He went back to work there and thus began his 40 year career with the Federal Government. Billy Wells retired in 1984 and now resides in his home state of Indiana.

"Willard"

"Willard" was the Sergeant who commanded Third Squad of First Platoon, who was severely wounded at Colmar when a mortar landed on top of him. He had lost both his legs above the knee, his left arm, and two fingers on his right hand. Half of his face was blown away. No one thought he would live, but he did. He was evacuated to a hospital in Nancy, France in critical condition. He went through surgery many times, just to keep him alive for a few more days. He was eventually sent to a hospital in Scotland, where he remained until October 1947. When he recovered enough to sit up in bed, a nurse wrote a letter for him to his girlfriend in Philadelphia. He told her of his condition and not to wait for him to come home. He did not want to live and assumed his life was over; he was a cripple. His girlfriend would not give up on him; she wrote him several letters every week and one of "Willard's" nurses would write a letter back to his girlfriend. "Willard" returned home in November 1947 and thought about going somewhere else, other than home. He was very upset and thought everyone would mock him for his condition. When he returned home to Philadelphia, his arrived to a big celebration in his honor among his family and friends; he was treated like a returning hero. His girlfriend waited for him and they married a week later. They had two sons and four grandchildren. "Willard" became an amateur poet, a children's author, and an accomplished oil painter, using his one hand with three fingers. He spent much of his life visiting hospitals and speaking to disabled veterans and also children with physical disabilities. I interviewed "Willard" in October 2009. "Willard" passed away in his hospital bed two days after I last talked with him. "Willard" was a very humble man and wanted to be remembered for what he did with his life, not what happened to him in the war.

"Kirk"

"Kirk" returned home to his wife and daughter in the suburbs of Philadelphia in December 1945. They had three more children and nine grandchildren. "Kirk" was not sure what he wanted to do with his life, so he got into the restaurant business with a friend shortly after he got home. He owned and operated a Greek diner for over 50 years. His three sons each started their own restaurants when they grew up. I talked to "Kirk" many times in early 2009. He never said much about his war experiences to his family and preferred that his full name not be put into print. He said "Kirk" was the name that his buddies would know him as. He had a lot of stories to share and many very sad memories. He lost a lot of friends in the war and he was forever changed after he took part in liberating a labor camp in the Ruhr. Many of the laborers were Greek. He had fond memories of many of his platoon buddies. Lawson remembered him well. "Kirk's" daughter took over his successful diner when he passed away in September 2009.

Wallace Kravitz

Wallace Kravitz dressed for Granddaughter's wedding, Dec. 2014

Wallace Kravitz was discharged in January 1946 and then enrolled back into American International College in his hometown of Springfield, Massachusetts. He was an accounting major with a minor in education. It was too late to enroll in the spring semester, so he got into a night class on accounting that was for returning veterans. He lived with his parents while he went through college, graduating with honors in June 1948. He traveled with a group of veterans back to Europe and spent three weeks each in England, France, and Holland. Kravitz returned home to pursue his studies at Syracuse University, where he received his Masters in business education in June 1949. He taught business subjects at Courtland High School in New York for five years then moved on to Long Island to teach in other schools. He went on to become department chairman of Mineola High School in New York. Kravitz also wrote several books on accounting.

His wartime romance did not last long after he got home. He eventually met his wife, Mollie through a blind date setup by his sister in law. They married in August 1954 and were married for 48 years, until his wife passed away. Kravitz has two children and four grandchildren. For his 85th birthday, his son and family took him to San Diego and while there he saw a man wearing a 75th Division cap. The man was Ed Coltrin, who had saved Captain Haddock's life during the Battle of Grand Halleux. After so many years, Kravitz reunited with the veterans of the 75th Division and later the surviving veterans of H Company. Wallace Kravitz resides in Scottsdale, Arizona, to be close to his son and family.

Henry H. Smith

Henry H. Smith   **Henry H. Smith: Horseshoe Champion**

     Henry H. Smith was discharged on 17 February 1946 at Fort Dix, New Jersey. He went straight to Owensboro, Kentucky where he reunited with Anna Laura Conley. She was the girl whom he had just three dates with back in the summer of 1944 while he was at Camp Breckinridge. Smith had carried a picture of her in his shirt pocket, against his heart for the duration of the war. Henry and Anna were married just three days later on 20 February. They went to stay with Smith's family in Covington, Virginia for about a month, then moved to Hillsboro, New Hampshire where they worked in a woolen mill. His wife was very homesick, so they decided to move back to Owensboro after just a few months. Smith's brother-in-law was a shoe repairman and his parents bought a shop in Henderson, Kentucky. Smith moved to Henderson and learned the trade. The family bought five shops and Smith and his wife eventually ran one in Owensboro. In 1953, Smith got another job, working the nightshift at a plastic factory. He became a foreman and worked there for six years. In 1959, he decided to go back to the shoe repair shop and continued on there until 1971, when he and his wife decided to move back to Covington, Virginia and open a shop there.

Smith began to have health problems in 1973 and sold his shop and went to work for the buyer. On Thanksgiving night, Smith had a massive heart-attack and was clean out of his body. They broke his ribs and brought him back, but they did not think he would live. Smith spent 29 days in the hospital and was told he could not work again. Since then, Smith has been in the hospital 45 times and has had open-heart surgery and a pacemaker. His wife has also been in poor health.

Smith had two sons, and one was named after his H Company buddy, Marcel Lambert that was killed at Poteau in the Battle of the Bulge. Smith has six grandchildren and two great-grandchildren. Smith and his wife eventually moved to Greenspring Retirement home in Springfield, Virginia. Henry and Anna Smith then moved to Farmville, Virginia nearby to one of their sons. Anna passed away on 2 June 2013 after 67 years of marriage to Henry.

On 31 May 2015 I visited Henry H. Smith at his home and filmed an interview with him on his experiences during the war. I asked a number of questions about that terrible day: "Bloody Monday," 15 January 1945 in Grand-Halleux, Belgium. Present and listening intently to Smith's commentary were his two sons Bill and Andre, both of whom knew very little about what their father had gone through in the war. In all my years of research and correspondence for this book, I found that afternoon to be one of the most treasured and rewarding moments I have ever experienced.

Bill G. Prater

Bill G. Prater with his medals- Christmas 2014

In January 1946, Bill G. Prater used the G.I. Bill and returned to his studies in Drury College. The next semester, he transferred to Washington University in St. Louis.

In the Fall of 1947, Prater was accepted into the Washington University Medical School and completed his "Doctor of Medicine" degree in 1951. He met his wife, Marie during his residency at Washington University McMillan Eye Hospital; they married in 1956 and had three children. Also in 1956, Prater performed the first corneal transplant in Springfield. Prater became a consultant for the Missouri Crippled Children's Clinic, the Division of Welfare, Bureau for the Blind, and the Missouri Sanitarium in Mt. Vernon. He was also the civilian consultant for Fort Leonard Wood Army Hospital. He operated at both Cox and St. Johns's Hospitals, served on the Executive Committees of both, was Chief of Staff at Cox and served a term as President of the Greene County Medical Society.

Prater retired in 1994 at age 70. He has enjoyed retirement and along with his wife, they have had many travels around the world. They own a condo in Aspin, Colorado where they spend vacations with the family. Bill and Marie Prater have six grandchildren. Prater returned back to Belgium and France and visited Grand Halleux. In 1998, he became a member of the Compagnie des Mousquetaires de Armagnac due to his involvement in France during World War II. Dr. Bill G. Prater and his wife reside in Springfield, Missouri.

Jim Strong

Jim Strong was a Corporal by the time the war was over. He returned home and studied at the University of Michigan. He entered the family Insurance business. Strong organized many trips to return back to Europe to visit the battlefields where he fought and to visit his buddies that are buried at Henri-Chappel cemetery. Strong kept a list of names and addresses of his buddies from the Mortar Platoon and others from H Company. He organized a reunion in 1979 at his home in Long Island, New York. It was a wonderful occasion where many old friends had the chance to see each other again after so many years. Strong also wrote many articles about his experiences in the war and wrote an account of the Mortar Platoon's actions at Grand Halleux. Jim Strong passed away in 1998.

Floyd R. Ross

H Company Reunion 2004: L-R Leonard Verilli- Billy Wells- Floyd Ross- Elton Page

Floyd Ross returned home to California, went to college, and entered the insurance business. He went to work with Continental Insurance Company. In 1969, his best buddy from the war, Jim Strong called him and invited Ross to come for a visit. Strong owned an insurance and real estate business in Long Island, New York. Strong offered Ross a job in his company and Ross accepted the offer. They worked together from October 1970 until Ross' retirement in 1987. Ross resides in Ontario, California. Because of his dedication to his H Company buddies, he learned to use a computer to keep in touch and to write the H Company "Howler" Newsletter. It is because of Ross' strong determination to keep in contact with his buddies, that much of the information for this book could be compiled.

Elton T. Page

Elton "E.T." Page at 2004 Reunion

Elton "E.T." Page did not have enough points to go home in the summer of 1945. He was offered a 30-day furlough home if he would reenlist for six years and stay with the Army. Page took the furlough and went home to see his family in North Carolina. After his furlough, Page was sent to Fort Benning, Georgia to prepare to return to Germany for occupation duties. He became an M.P. and was stationed in a little town near Heidelberg, Germany. He did not like M.P. duty and was given three days to find a new assignment. Page was transferred to another station near a trade school in Heidelberg. He ended up running a gas station for military vehicles in the area. Page spend three years in Germany and while there, he met his wife and took her back to the US when his tour of duty in Germany concluded.

In 1950 Page was sent to Japan as a replacement and served in the Korean War. He took part in the Pusan Landings on 16 September 1950. Page spent 13 months in Korea and returned back to the US. He retired as a Sergeant First-Class with 20 years in the Army. After the Army, Page got into vacuum cleaner sales and did very well. Page attends the 75th Division Reunion each year and is well regarded for his humor. Elton T. Page resides in Winston-Salem, North Carolina.

Ira Posnak

Ira Posnak received his honorable discharge in March 1946. When he returned home to New York, he became a draftsman and spent a year working for the RCA Institute. He married in 1949. He bought and lived on a chicken farm from 1950-1954. They returned to Brooklyn, where Posnak worked for several construction companies. Several years later he started night school and attended Polytech Institute in New York, where he earned a degree in civil engineering. He completed his degree, while working a fulltime job to support his wife and two daughters. Posnak was an avid reader of non-fiction, he loved fishing, and he had an extensive collection of American stamps that he began collecting as a child. Ira Posnak passed away on 31 October 2009. His Combat Diary was a critical source of information in the organization of this book.

Harris Chaiklin

Buggenum Holland, where he first joined H Co.   **Dr. Harris Chaiklin**

Harris Chaiklin took Captain Goodnight's advice and used the G.I. Bill to go to school. To this day, Chaiklin holds Goodnight in high regard. He remains awestruck that Goodnight, a man that seemed to reside on Mount Olympus, took the time to be so encouraging. When he returned home, Chaiklin went to the University of Connecticut and completed his Undergraduate in Sociology in 1950 and his Masters in 1952. He received his Masters of Science in Social Work in 1953 from the University of Wisconsin. In 1951, Chaiklin received his Doctorate in Medical Sociology from Yale

University. He also served in the Reserves from 1946 to 1954, where he became a First Lieutenant. From 1953 to 1986 Dr. Chaiklin was an active practitioner of social work as a caseworker with the Jewish Board of Guardians in New York City, with Jewish Family Service in New Haven, Connecticut, and with Jewish Family and Children's Service in Baltimore, Maryland. He also has worked private practice and with the John F. Kennedy Institute Family Center. In addition to being a social worker, Dr. Chaiklin has been a university professor since 1959. He taught social work at University of Connecticut, Smith College of Social Work, and the University of Maryland School of Social Work. He also was a visiting professor at Haifa University in Israel and at Morgan State University. Dr. Chaiklin has written a book, as well as articles and book chapters, in addition to editing and book reviews during his career. Dr. Chaiklin is married with four children and many grandchildren. He travels frequently and continues to be actively involved with the cause of social work. Dr. Chaiklin resides in Baltimore, Maryland.

My Personal Contact with Dr. Chaiklin

Dr. Chaiklin was very influential in my decision to write this book. Though he was not present for much of the chronology of H Company, his daily contact with me has helped me to understand more about the war than history books or official documents could ever provide me with. He helped me to understand that H Company was made up of many different types of men from many different backgrounds. A comment he made early on etched itself into my mind as I wrote this book "There were all kinds in H Company." Chaiklin showed me that while movies and television may project an image of the typical American GI as brave and fearless, the realistic image is one of an average guy that went off to fight a war and hoped to return home to reunite with his family.

I visited Harris and Martha Chaiklin on 26 April 2015. Through our years of correspondence, we had never met in person until that day. It was a rare opportunity to meet a man that so fundamentally encouraged and aided me in my research. I do not believe that I would have ever written this book if it were not for his commitment to see H Company's story put into print. I will forever be grateful to Dr. Harris Chaiklin for his kindness and willingness to share his history and memories of the war and for editing my tome.

Others from H Company

Richard Haddock, H Company's first captain, spent several years in VA hospitals after he lost both legs at Grand Halleux. He was honorably discharged and returned home to Long Island, New York. Some of the men in H Company continued to visit their former captain.

Hoffman Wong, who was also severely wounded at Grand Halleux, remained in a VA hospital until 1947. He returned home to California and owned and operated a car repair shop. Floyd Ross met him by chance in 2003.

Bert Larson received his honorable discharge and returned home to Minnesota in August 1945. He owned and operated a costume jewelry business. Harris Chaiklin once visited him during a teaching trip in the 1950s. In 1977, Larson attended the H Company Reunion in Long Island. About a week later, Bert Larson passed away. He is fondly remembered by the young men who served in his squad.

Mike Murza was honorably discharged in December 1945. He returned home to south Philadelphia and played in many Big Bands in the area. As the Big Band era dwindled, he used his savings to open up a music store, where he taught youngsters and amateur musicians alike. Murza married in 1948 and had two children and one grandson. Murza became a popular local musician and teacher. Mike Murza passed away after a heart-attack in 1978. His grandson now operates his music store, which still focuses on the music of the Big Band era.

Richard Modrzejewski recovered from his injuries at Colmar and stayed in the Army. He became a career soldier, serving in the Korean War and he retired as a Major.

Leslie Hicks received his honorable discharge and came home in May 1945. He went to trade school and became a machinist. He spent most of his career teaching his trade at night school. He lives in Colrain, Massachusetts and in Florida during the winter.

Bergheimer recovered from his wounds. He remained in the Army and stayed in Europe after the war. In 1947 he was promoted to First Lieutenant and served as

Executive Officer to an Intelligence unit in Austria. However, his reputation caught up with him, when in 1948 he was caught stealing money from his subordinates. He was court-martialed and spent two years in military prison.

Finding "Hay Seed"

"Hay Seed" was never heard from again. After much research through original records, it was thought that "Hay Seed's" real name might have been Harold Nelson from Hattiesburg, Mississippi. This name appears on a listing of replacements that arrived to H Company in July 1944 while at Camp Breckinridge. This fit in exactly with Lawson's recollection of when "Hay Seed" arrived. Researching old census records produced a Harold Nelson who lived in the suburbs of the same town since at least 1950. With the aid of Phillip Lawson and his family, we were finally able to track down "Hay Seed."

In November 2014, Lawson's son visited the farm that was once owned by "Hay Seed." He found "Hay Seed's" son, Barry who still lived in the area. Barry told us that his father, Harold Nelson had married in 1946. Harold may not have been his birth name. Barry thought it was funny that we knew his dad's nickname; "Hay Seed." He was thrilled to finally learn how he got that name. "Hay Seed" was a bricklayer and well digger for his whole life. He never learned to read and could not even write his own name. Barry remembered his father as being a very kind man, but knew very little of his war service. "Hay Seed" died in 1987. He was cleaning the gutters on his house and fell off a ladder. A piece of shrapnel in his body had moved in the fall and it pierced his lung. He was 62 years old. His wife passed away a year later. After his father died, Barry went through his father's dresser drawer and in it, had found his medals from the war: 8 Bronze Stars and 6 Purple Hearts.

Christmas 2014 was very special for Phillip Lawson; he invited "Hay Seed's" son and whole family to spend a week at his farm.

Eugene Druillard

Captain Druillard from G Company survived the war and was shortly thereafter promoted to Major. He was a graduate of West Point and was a career soldier. After the war, he married, had two daughters, and became an instructor at the US Army Infantry School. He used his own wartime experiences to educate another generation. His recollections of the battle in Castrop-Rauxel, Germany became a case study in the Infantry School. Druillard retired as a Lieutenant Colonel, having spent a number of years in the reserves. He was a public school educator in Northern Virginia, where Glenn Slagle (Robert O. Slagle's son) met him while in high school.

Druillard and Slagle reunited and formed a friendship that lasted for the rest of their lives. Druillard was heavily involved with preserving the 75th Division's history and in particular, that of the 2nd Battalion, 291st Infantry, and G Company. He was an active member of 5 veterans organizations. He wrote many articles, organized many veterans trips back to Europe, and sought out all of the men who once were under his command in G Company. There was an annual G Company reunion that continued on through 2010. Druillard's highly detailed account of his experiences at Grand-Halleux is the prominent source of information for that battle. Druillard wanted the 75th Division to be remembered for what it did during the war. Eugene Druillard passed away on Christmas Day 1997.

Buckner S. Conn

"Bucky" Conn, as his friends called him, returned home to Jeffersonville, Indiana and became a livestock producer and a career letter-carrier for the US Postal Service. "Bucky" maintained a great friendship with his former Captain, Eugene Druillard. Druillard entrusted "Bucky" with a copy of his wartime diary and many other written accounts. All of these sources were used to write this book. "Bucky" wrote a newsletter called "The Guidon" that was a G Company Newsletter continuing on through 2010. There were many highly detailed wartime accounts preserved in the newsletters. He organized the annual G Company Reunion and made great efforts to preserve the history of the 75th Division. His bond of friendship with his wartime buddies was admirable. "Bucky" wrote a poem on his experiences during the Battle of Grand-Halleux that captured that event, perhaps better than any after-action report could. It should be noted that I first contacted "Bucky" by letter only a few days after his wife passed away. I did not know of this until sometime later. Despite his grieving process, he made every effort to contact me and to send me all of the resources he had on the 75th Division. We maintained a friendship for several years, whereby he read my drafts for this book and helped to add more details concerning G Company's history within this book. "Bucky" passed away on 21 June 2014.

Epilogue

My grandfather, Robert O. Slagle was a member of H Company. My grandparents raised me and I spent most of my youth with my grandfather. One of my earliest memories at the age or three or four was going into his den in the basement and being amazed by all the books and papers that surrounded the whole room. I saw a big book with the 75th Division patch on it and I remember asking what it was. From an early age, I was fascinated with history and it was not long before my grandfather began to tell me small stories about his days in the Army during World War II. He would never say much and if I asked questions he would change the subject. As I got older, he would tell me more; I always pressed him for more. He once told me he was going to write a book on his war experiences, but he never had the time to do it. He battled cancer and was very ill during the last two years of his life. I spent a lot of time with him then and he started to talk a lot more about his war memories. Talking of them seemed to give him some comfort. My grandfather passed away in November 1996 and I continued my interest in history and in particular, his history. My Uncle Glenn (Robert's son) remembered many of my grandfather's stories from the war and I wrote all of them down.

Many years later I thought that I would attempt to locate information on his unit. I knew he was in H Company, 291st Infantry, 75th Division. I decided to go through his den and see if I could find any information. I first went through that big book I had first seen as a young boy, the "Pictorial History of the 75th Division." In it, I found names he wrote down and a few notes. As I went through college and into graduate school I wrote many research papers, mostly on military history subjects. It gave me an idea: to write a book based on my grandfather's stories. I decided to take the initiative and go through everything in his den. Hidden away in an old record box, I found a collection of pictures from World War II. He had never shown them to the family. I once asked if he ever had any pictures from the war and he told me he did not. My grandfather lost a lot of friends in the war and it was a painful subject for him. Besides the pictures, I found a battered up piece of paper with names and hometowns; it was a list of the men he knew in the war that had survived. Some were from H Company, others were from other companies in the

291st Regiment, but most were men he knew from the Division Band or from playing in the Glenn Miller Offshoot Band after the war. With the aid of the Internet, I looked up many of these names; most were long since deceased, but I did find a few still living.

I began to correspond with some of these veterans. I sent each of them a letter identifying my grandfather and myself. I expected to hear nothing considering I was looking for information 60 years and more after the war. However, I did hear from them. Several of them specifically asked that their names never be put into print in anything I would write. Many of them had never uttered so much as a word about their experiences to their family. Phillip Lawson proved to be a valuable source of information. He called me one day after receiving my letter and shouted at me and told me to never bother him again. Two weeks later he called me back and told me to shut up, get a pencil and paper and start taking notes. Our first few calls lasted two hours or more and I ended up with far more information than I ever thought I would get. He did not recognize the name Slagle, but after I sent him a picture of my grandfather, he immediately recognized him: they were in the same squad. Lawson had tried to forget about the war, it was painful for him to remember, but he now tells me that recounting his experiences has given him some relief and made him feel better. I also talked with two other veterans who wished to be known only by their nicknames; "Willard" who was a sergeant and "Kirk" who began his service as a private and eventually was promoted to sergeant. Both of them knew my grandfather and had many stories of their own war experiences to share.

By 2009, I thought I had made contact with everyone I would find from H Company, but then, I found Harris Chaiklin. He was a replacement in H Company and was in the same platoon and squad as my grandfather. I have maintained an almost daily e-mail exchange with him since January 2010. His lucid memory of very specific events has made much of the second half of this book possible. Chaiklin put me into contact with Wallace Kravitz whom I have also maintained a frequent e-mail exchange with. He too, provided me with details about his war remembrances. Then, I learned that Floyd Ross wrote a newsletter for veterans and friends of H Company called the "Howler." I sent out letters to all those on the "Howler's" mailing list and received many responses back. I first received a call from Bill Prater who had saved many papers on H Company, a picture album of his platoon in the war, a Combat Diary of the 291st Regiment, and had his own remembrances to share. We have continued our correspondence since June 2010. I then heard from Henry Smith, another member of H Company with memories of events I had not heard before. We have continued to exchange letters and e-mails. I also heard from Billy Wells and we have maintained an almost daily e-mail exchange since June 2010. He had a lot of memories of his own and was able to help me with specific details of Camp Breckinridge and the Battle of the Bulge. He also had copies of some of H Company's Morning Reports.

Later, I heard from Floyd Ross who had taken classes to learn how to use a computer so that he could write a newsletter to help to stay in contact with his buddies from the war. He sent me a big parcel of pictures and copies of his "Howler" newsletters where I learned more about the men of H Company. We also had many phone conversations and letter correspondences where he recounted some specifics about men in the company that were lacking in my notes. Mr. Ross was very helpful in answering even the smallest of questions I had about H Company; his memory was quite incredible. I corresponded also with Elton T. Page who shared his experiences. He had many stories about himself and his platoon buddies after the war in Germany. I also had a phone conversation with Max Engle, who was an original member of H Company, back from the days when the 75th Division was first activated at Fort Leonard Wood. I made contact with Leslie "Joe" Hicks who was able to provide me with specific details of several battles. The final member of H Company that I made contact with was George Ramirez, who vividly remembered how my grandfather took command of his platoon during the battle in Castrop-Rauxel, Germany. Ramirez gave me some closure on how my grandfather went from PFC to Second Lieutenant.

I corresponded with Ray Brejcha, the last known living veteran of the 75th Division Band, who provided me with information that was very helpful in understanding my grandfather's association with the Band. Incidentally, Mr. Brejcha was one of the men that my grandfather had mentioned to me by name. I also corresponded with "Bucky" S. Conn, a veteran of G Company who sent me some information about the Battle of Grand Halleux and wrote a poem about his experiences. Mr. Conn writes a newsletter called "The Guidon" for the veterans of G Company. Overall, I interviewed 18 veterans of H Company and Second Battalion, 291st Infantry. One of my personal connections to the men of Second Battalion relates to G Company's Captain Druillard. He lived two streets away from where I grew up and he and my grandfather were friends. They had lunch together often and I frequently went along. I remember Mr. Druillard well as he often drew me pictures of soldiers or tanks and once made me a sketch of the 75th Division patch. Finally, I made contact with Rhona and Risa, the daughters of Ira Posnak. They sent me some pictures that their father took during the war and a combat diary that he wrote. Posnak's diary proved to be an essential part of my research for this book. He noted the towns that H Company moved through during the war and other events in their daily lives. It helped to put H Company's story together, chronologically.

The conversations and correspondence I have had with all of these veterans have made this book possible. I have learned so very much from the remaining veterans of H Company and gained a great respect for each of them and what they went through. This book is a compilation of *their* war put into chronological order and written as a narrative. It is not just a military history, but rather an account of what life was like for the men of H Company. I tracked down many of the 75th Division and 291st Infantry records and also written accounts from many of the veterans. A list of these is included at the end of the book. Originally I had planned to write a book on my grandfather's war experiences. The book has instead evolved into a history of H Company and indirectly a history of Second Battalion, 291st Infantry. I did not write this book for military historians or for military officers; I wrote it for the enlisted men. It is my hope that it will be shared with children and grandchildren; perhaps members of another generation that will serve in the Army. I hope that the reader will gain an appreciation of just what these men went through from training camp through the largest battle that American soldiers ever fought in, The Battle of the Bulge, and through to the end of the war. I have made every effort to explore all areas in this book, to provide the reader with a nearly complete view of what life was like for them. There are positive and negative views of people and events in this book from the veterans I have interviewed; I have censored nothing other than language. I have also attempted to show different viewpoints from within the same company, from members of the two machine gun platoons, the mortar platoon, and from a messenger. I have also emphasized my grandfather's movements between H Company, the 75th Division Band, and his association with the Deputy Division Commander.

The Interviews

I used the same methodology to interview each veteran. I first sent them a letter with my address, phone number, and e-mail. I identified myself, my grandfather, and that I was looking for information to help in writing my book on H Company. Most responded to me. I later discovered that those who did not were unable to, primarily due to health concerns. Each veteran had their own preferences for contacting me. I asked each to recount any memories they had of the war and I took extensive notes. After collecting and organizing my notes and reviewing the official documents I was able to locate, thus somewhat understanding the "big picture" as it were of H Company, I then began to ask specific questions. Some of the veterans remembered very little, others remembered a great wealth of details. Acting somewhat as a "messenger" between the veterans, I continued to pass along details I collected to the others, which often struck up memories of particular events. Overall, I have collected some fifteen notebooks full of notes from my interviews. In addition, I was given pictures, written accounts, and many other documents from those I interviewed. All of these items were very helpful in writing this book. Each veteran still living had read and provided a critique of this work before publication. It was a great honor to have had the opportunity to correspond with each of these veterans. It was a lifelong dream fulfilled to have had the opportunity as an adult, to get to know more about my grandfather and the men he served with nearly 70 years ago.

James Slagle McClintock

<u>Appendix:</u>

I.   The title of this book, "Unlikely Heroes" was suggested by Dr. Harris Chaiklin. He was not present during the Battle of the Bulge, but 2nd Battalion, 291st Infantry's battle along the Ouerthe River was a primary event in the stopping of the German "bulge." This, combined with the young age of the men, along with a lack of winter clothing and weapons, and the fact that they were "green" at this time gives credit to the title.

II.   A complete list of all men of H Company killed during the war does not exist. What is depicted in this book are recollections from the surviving veterans and the few casualty lists that were preserved. The names of the many replacements killed in 1st Platoon at Colmar do not survive. They had been on the line for only a few days; some even less. Due to the large number of casualties and losses of both officers and senior NCOs, the paperwork either never survived the war or was inaccurately recorded by the men that took up the duties of record keeping.

III.   **The following pictures were taken at Camp Breckinridge, KY in June 1944**

L-R: Front row #2 Hoffman Wong, #4 LT Contell, #5 Leonard Verilli
    2nd row #2 Ira Posnak, #5 John Malarich, #6 Harold Castanaga, #7 Robert Byrnes
    3rd row #2 Bruce Reynolds, #2 Schafer, #5 Wallace Kravitz
    Back row #7 Carl Bruton

L-R: **Front row #3 Post, #5 Boyce turner, #6 David Goodman, #8 Lyons, #9 James Flud**
    2nd row #7 Glen Johnson
    3rd row #4 Bustin, #5 Floyd Ross, #6 Jim Strong, #8 Bob Galway
    Back row # 2 John Robertson, #4 Art Grindstaff, #5 Gordon Vining, #6 Robert O. Slagle,
      #7 Henry Lee

L-R: Front row #2 Frank Cook, #3 Bill Counselman
   2nd row #8 Billy wells
   3rd row #2 Bernard Raymond, #7 Leslie Hicks
   Back row #2 Colin chisholm, #5 Bert Larson

IV.   The Men of H Company (rank and platoon assignments are noted if known)

Amil, Raymond (SGT)
Axom, Norman (2nd Platoon)

Baker, Julian (SGT- 2nd Platoon)
Balch, Dan (S/SGT)
Barker, Henry (PFC)
Bee, Cassel (PFC)
Bennington, Carrol (PFC)
Bergheimer, Albert (2LT, 1st Platoon)
Bessner, John (SGT, Headquarters Platoon- KIA)
Blankenship, Oliver (PFC, 2nd Platoon)
Bonecutter, Melvin (PVT- PFC)
Bonnet, Jack (PFC)
Bozovich, George (PFC, Mortar Platoon)
Brannon, William (SGT, 2nd Platoon)
Bruton, Carl (PFC, Mortar Platoon)
Bryant, Norman (PFC)
Bustin, Frank (T-4, T-5)
Byrd, Lynn (PVT, 1st Platoon)
Byrnes, Robert (T/SGT, 2nd Platoon)
Cage, Robert (PFC, 2nd Platoon)
Carpenter, Clair (PFC- SGT)
Carroll, Clarence (S/SGT, 2nd Platoon- KIA)
Casper, Raymond (T-4, T-5, S/SGT)
Castanaga, Harold (SGT, 2nd Platoon)
Cattau, Helmuth (PFC, 2nd Platoon)
Chaiklin, Harris (PFC, 1st Platoon)
Chisholm, Colin (SGT, 2nd Platoon)
Civiak, Joseph (PFC, Mortar Platoon)
Clark, Shepman (PVT)
Cliff, Gerald (T/SGT)
Cochrane, Vince (Mortar Platoon)
Cohen, Leon (PFC, 2nd Platoon)
Cohen, Saul (PFC, 1st Platoon)
Contel, Richard (1LT)
Cook, James Jr (PFC, 2nd Platoon)
Cook, Frank (PFC- CPL, Mortar Platoon)
Counselman, William (PVT, Mortar Platoon)
Cpravalo, Joseph (PVT)
Craig, William (1LT, 2nd Platoon-KIA)
Craig, John (1LT, 2nd Platoon- KIA)
Dempsey, Eugene (PFC, Medic- 2nd Platoon)

Donnely, Thomas (CPL- SGT)
Diakoff, Eugene
Dunham, Harold (PFC)
Faber, Edward (PVT- PFC)
Finke, Eugene (PFC, 1st Platoon- KIA)
Flud, James (S/SGT, Mortar Platoon)
Gaffney, James (PVT)
Galbreth, Albert (PFC, 1st Platoon)
Galway, Robert (CPL- S/SGT, Mortar Platoon)
Gardner, Raymond (PFC- Headquarters Platoon- KIA)
Garo, Stanley (T/SGT, Mortar Platoon)
Goodman, David (Mortar Platoon)
Goodnight, Owen L. Jr (1LT- CAPT)
Granat, Zigmund (PVT)
Green, Alvin
Grindstaff, Arthur (Mortar Platoon)
Haddock, Richard (CAPT)
Hain, Albert (PFC, Headquarters Platoon- KIA)
Halloran, Edward
Hartranft, Charles (PFC, Mortar Platoon- KIA)
Hayes (PFC, Medic- Mortar Platoon)
Heim, Ralph (PVT)
Henry, John (PFC- SGT, 2nd Platoon)
Hess, John (Mortar Platoon)
Hewitt, George (PFC, Mortar Platoon)
Hicks, Leslie (S/SGT, Mortar Platoon)
Hopkins, Wilford
Houck, Luciene (PVT)
Huff, Kenneth (PFC)
Hunnett, Joseph (PVT)
Hyatt, Billy (PFC, Mortar Platoon)
Jeckovich, John (PFC, 2nd Platoon)
Johnson, Glen (CPL, Mortar Platoon- KIA)
Johnson, Walter (PVT)
Jones, Richard (SGT, Headquarters Platoon)
Kilgore, Tom (CPL, Mortar Platoon)
Killington, Charles (PVT- PFC)
Kravitz, Wallace (PFC, 2nd Platoon)
Lacey, William (PFC, 2nd Platoon)

Lambert, Marcel (PFC, 2nd Platoon- KIA)
Lane, Thomas (PFC)
Lape, Donald (PFC- KIA)
Larson, Bert (PFC- SGT, 1st Platoon)
Lawson, S. Phillip (PFC- SGT, 1st Platoon)
Lee, Henry (S/SGT, Mortar Platoon- KIA)
Lemmon, Harry (PFC)
Linseaum, Doek (PVT)
Lyons (S/SGT)
Malarich, John (CPL, Mortar Platoon)
Mason, Luther (PVT)
Maxwell, Robert (1LT)
McBeth, Edward
McCarron, William (PFC)
McDonnell, Bernard (PVT- KIA)
Modrzejewski, Richard (S/SGT, Mortar Platoon)
Moon, Thomas (PFC, 1st Platoon)
Morrison, Michael
Murphy, William
Murza, Mike (PFC, 1st Platoon)
Nelson, Harold (PFC- SGT)
Nionakis, John
Osborn, Harry (S/SGT, Mortar Platoon)
Ott, Raymond (S/SGT)
Page, Elton T. (PFC, Mortar Platoon)
Parker, Herbert (PVT)
Passiatore, John (PVT)
Pearman, Leon (PVT)
Pearson, Michael ((PVT)
Pearson, Tom (Mortar Platoon)
Pettigrass, Peter (Headquarters Platoon)
Pontes, Peter (PFC, 1st Platoon)
Posnak, Ira (PFC, Mortar Platoon)
Post (Mortar Platoon)
Prater, Bill G. (CPL- S/SGT, Mortar Platoon)
Ramirez, George (T-5 – T/SGT, 2nd Platoon)
Raschka, Everett (PVT- PFC)
Raymond, Bernard (PFC, Mortar platoon)
Reader, William (CPL, Mortar Platoon)

Resse, Charles (CPL)
Reeves, John (T-5)
Reynolds, Bruce (PFC, 2nd Platoon)
Richkas, Tony
Rimes, Logan (PFC)
Robertson, John (PVT)
Romono, Louis (PFC, Medic-1st Platoon)
Ross, Floyd R. (PFC, Mortar Platoon)
Rubart, Charles (T/SGT)
Sarakwash, Michael (PFC, 2nd Platoon)
Scaduto, John (PFC, Mortar Platoon)
Scaggs, Howard
Schafer, Howard (PFC, 2nd Platoon)
Schesko, Kenneth (PVT)
Scheuler, Dilbert (PFC)
Schimank, Lorenz (PVT)
Schlaefflin, Walter (PVT)
Schroeder, Roy
Scott, Robert
Shelansky, Henry
Siegfried, Luther (PFC, 1st Platoon)
Siggelakis, James (PFC, 2nd Platoon)
Silberstein, Larry (PFC, Mortar Platoon)
Simpson, Hal (PFC, Mortar Platoon)
Simms, Ross (S/SGT)
Slagle, Robert O. (PFC- 2LT, 1st Platoon)
Slawson, Stan (S/SGT, 1st Platoon)
Smith, Burley (2LT, Mortar Platoon)
Smith, Charles (S/SGT)
Smith, Henry H. (PFC, 2nd Platoon)
Smith, Leonard (PVT)
Smith, Leslie (Mortar Platoon)
Soloman, James (PFC, Mortar Platoon)
Sotir, Sautter (PVT, 2nd Platoon)
Spade, Arnie (SGT, Headquarters Platoon)
Spatt, Robert (PFC)
Speck, William (PFC)
Sposta, Andrew (2nd Platoon)
Staton, Rocker (1LT, Mortar Platoon)

Steward, Donald (S/SGT, 2nd Platoon)
Stewart, Johnny P. (SGT, 1st Platoon- KIA)
Strong, Jim (PFC- CPL, Mortar Platoon)
Sullivan, Martin (PVT- KIA)
Tabor (CPL)
Taylor, Henry (CPL)
Thomas, Carol (PFC)
Thompson, Tommy (PFC, 1st Platoon)
Thorpe, Richard (Headquarters Platoon)
Thrower, Harold (PFC)
Turner, Boyce (Mortar Platoon)
Underwood, Carl (2nd Platoon)
Vaicunnas, John (PVT)
Vining, Gordon (S/SGT)
Vinsentin, Louis (PVT- PFC)
Visich, Edward (SGT)
Verrilli, Leonard (Mortar Platoon)
Wallis, Leroy (2LT, Mortar Platoon- KIA)
Walter, Johnson (PVT)
Weatherhead, William (PVT)
Welch, John (PFC, 2nd Platoon- KIA)
West, Charles (PFC, Mortar Platoon)
Whalen, Michael (1SGT)
Wilkinson, Dallas (S/SGT, Mortar Platoon)
Wilson, William (S/SGT, 2nd Platoon)
Williams, Lyle (PFC)
Withham, Richard (S/SGT)
Wong, Hoffman (SGT, Headquarters Platoon)
Ziegler, Martin (2LT- KIA)

IV.   On Sunday, 28 June 1981 the Grand Halleux Memorial Plaque was presented and dedicated at Grand Halleux, Belgium. The names of all men killed from the 291st Regiment during the Battle of the Bulge were placed on the plaque.

The Plaque reads:

GRAND HALLEUX BELGIUM
JANUARY, 1945
IN MEMORIAM
TO THOSE GALLANT AMERICAN SOLDIERS
AND STALWART BELGIAN CITIZENS
WHO GAVE THEIR LIVES IN
THE BATTLE OF THE BULGE
Grant Unto Them, O Lord, Eternal Rest
291st Infantry Regiment, 75th Division
UNITED STATES ARMY

V.   A memorial to 2nd Battalion, 291st Infantry exists on two bronze plaques at the Zachary Taylor National Cemetery in Louisville, Kentucky. The plaques contain the names of all known casualties from 2nd Battalion during the war.

VI.   On 24 July 1992, The 75th Division Memorial was dedicated at Freedoms Foundation in Valley Forge, Pennsylvania.

VII.   Buckner "Bucky" S. Conn wrote a poem to commemorate his experiences and that of G Company during the Battle of Grand Halleux:

COUNTERATTACK!
On 3rd January '45, counterattack was begun.
Objective: To get those Krauts on the run.
Enemy resistance against the 82nd was strong.
To suffer many casualties didn't take long.

So the 75th, in reserve, had a short stay.
Soon we were ordered to get into the fray.
At the Salm River (82nd closed up there)
We were to relieve them—no time to spare.

Then our long so-called "Death March" began,
Challenging the stamina of each infantryman.
We lugged weapons and gear, mile after mile,
Staggering onward, sometimes single file.

We marched into town at dusk on a Sunday,
Unaware next day would be "Bloody Monday."
Tired, cold and hungry—numb to our fears,
Groggy as tho' we had not slept in years.

Effected the relief; situation seemed calm,
Night of the 14th we arrived on the Salm.
In recon patrol venturing into the dark,
Bullet through helmet, on man's scalp a mark.

At dawn we advanced thru deep fallen snow,
Ordered to strike German hard crushing blow.
O'er five hundred yards of wide open field
Against dug-in enemy not wanting to yield.

Kraut bullets and shrapnel flew all around,
Causing us to hit the hard-frozen ground.
Our troops in dark olive drab were clad;
No camouflage snow-suits were to be had.

Conspicuous targets from the order to go;
Black on white against frigid snow.
Of our young comrades-in-arms, many got hit

And those who survived had become frostbit.

Our tanks ineffective; the field was mined
And not much artillery support did we find.
Our infantry must bear brunt of the battle,
Odds against them—slaughtered like cattle.

Next day our Company was one weak Platoon
For survivors, war could not end too soon.
Our weapons kept ready, we struggled ahead,
Knowing that many of our comrades were dead.

Events elsewhere? We were not in the know,
As we advanced thru the woods up to Poteau.
That crossroads the Germans had to defend
To save their troops—they lost in the end.

France-Holland-Germany? Still not in sight.
Belgian Ardennes? By far our worst fight.
A village (Grand-Halleux) we do recall yet
And our buddies lost there we never forget!

Sources:

Picture Credits
I.   All pictures of Robert O. Slagle, courtesy of the Slagle family
II.   Camp Breckinridge barracks, courtesy of Henry H. Smith

III.　Billy Wells and buddies, courtesy of Billy Wells

IV.　H Company on march to the Ouerthe, courtesy of S. Phillip Lawson

V.　All photos of the Mortar Platoon originally photographed by Ira Posnak, photos preserved and courtesy of the Posnak Family and Bill G. Prater

VI.　Dortmund-Ems Canal, 1st Platoon at Lunnen, pictures by Bert Larson, courtesy of Harris Chaiklin

VII.　H Company group pictures from Camp Breckinridge, courtesy of Floyd R. Ross

VIII.　All additional photos, courtesy of the men pictured in them

Interviews

Brejcha, Ray (e-mail correspondence and Phone calls 2010-2012)

Chaiklin, Harris (e-mail correspondence 2010-2014)

Cohen, Seth *Son of Saul Cohen (*Phone calls 2011-2012)

Conn, Buckner S. (Letter exchanges 2010-2012)

Engle, Max (Letter exchanges and phone calls 2010)

Hicks, Leslie Joe (Phone calls 2010)

"Kirk" (Phone calls 2009)

Kravitz, Wallace (e-mail correspondence 2010-2011)

Lawson, S. Phillip (Phone calls 2009-2014)

Murza, Richard *Grandson of Mike Murza* (Phone Call 2010)

Page, Elton T. (Phone calls 2010-2012)

Prater, Bill G. (Letter exchanges and phone calls 2010-2012)

Ramirez, George (Phone calls 2013-2014)

Ross, Floyd R. (Letter exchanges and phone calls 2010-2012)

Slagle, Glenn B. *Son of Robert O. Slagle* (Oral recollections 1996- 2014)

Slagle, Robert O. (Oral History 1992-1996)

Slawson, Sarah *Wife of Stan Slawson* (Letter exchange and phone calls 2009- 2013)

Smith, Henry H. (Letter exchanges and e-mail correspondence 2010-2014)

Wells, Billy (e-mail exchanges 2010-2011)

"Willard" (Phone calls 2009)

Collected Primary Sources and Personal Written Accounts from Veterans:

Brejcha, Raymond J *Raymond J.Brejcha World War II chronology* (2007)

Conn, Buckner S. *Counterattack!* (A poem and history of Grand Halleux)

Conn, Buckner S. *The "Death March"* (Article from the Guidon Newsletter) 1982

Conn, Buckner S. *The Guidon* (G Company, 291st Infantry's Newsletter) 1970s-2010

Conn, Buckner S. *The Situation in the Ardennes- 24 December 1944*
    (Article from the Guidon Newsletter) Dec. 1985

Conn, Buckner S. *Unforgettable Grand halleux* (Article from Guidon Newsletter) 1982

Charles, Harold *75th Infantry Division* (After Action Report, Dec. 1945)

Drain, Jesse *After-Action Report: Ardennes January 1945* (Battle of the Bulge)

Drain, Jesse *After-Action Report: Colmar Pocket February 1945*

Drake, Sam *F-291* (Article from Guidon Newsletter) 1982

Druillard, Eugene *Personal Account of a Company Commander* (1947)

Druillard, Eugene *G-291 At Grand Halleux* (1982)

Druillard, Eugene *The Battle of the Bulge* (General History of 75th Division) 1992

Druillard, Eugene *My Experiences in World War II* (unpublished manuscript) 1993

Haddock, Richard *Morning Reports* (26 Dec 1944- 14 Jan 1945)

Jenkins, Douglas *G-291* (Article from Guidon Newsletter) 1982

Justice, Bob *E-291* (Article from Guidon Newsletter) 1982

Kravitz, Wallace *The Army Career of Wallace Kravitz* (2010)

Lundeen, Carroll *The Morning Report- E-291 –16 January 1945* (1945)

Mickle, Gerald S. *A Brief History of the 75th Infantry Division- 1944*
    (Bulgebuster Newsletter) Oct. 1964

Petersen, Glen N. *Wounded in Action* (Article from Guidon Newsletter) Dec. 1985

Prater, Bill G. *World War II Memoires* (1999)

Ross, Floyd *H Company Roster* (reconstructed July 2010)

Ross, Floyd *Howler: H Company, 291st Infantry Newsletter* (2003-2011)

Ross, Floyd *A Short Military History of Floyd R. Ross* (2010)

Sarkwash, Mike *The Crossing of the Rhine, Friday, 23 March 1945* (1945)

Slagle, Robert O. *My Life Since 1943* (1995)

Slawson, Stan *1st Platoon Section Leader's Diary, 20 Dec 1944- 7 May 1945*

Smith, Henry H. *Notes and drawings on Battle of Grand Halleux and Poteau Crossroads*
    (2010)

Stewart, Fred *Casualty Note to Ray Brejcha* (March 1945)

Strong, Jim *H-291* (Article from Guidon Newsletter)

Strong, Jim *History- His Story, H Company, Grenades/Guns & Guts* (Guidon)

Thompson, John *"Roles of two 1st army Corps revealed"* Chicago Tribune (1945)

US Army *A German in H Company* (The Mule, 75th Division Newspaper) unknown date, 1944

US Army *291st Regimental After-Action Report* (in booklet form) Dec 1945

US Army *291st Infantry Combat Diary* (1945)

US Army *Map of Battle of Grand Halleux* (291st Infantry's actions)

US Army *The 75th Infantry Division in Combat* (1945)

US Army *After Action Report Ardennes Offensive, 2nd Battalion, 291st Regiment* (1945)

US Army *After Action Report Colmar Campaign, 2nd Battalion, 291st Regiment* (1945)

US Army *After Action Report Ruhr Pocket , 2nd Battalion, 291st Regiment* (1945)

Whalen, Michael *First Sergeant's Hand-Written Morning Reports 26 Dec 1944- 4 April 1945* (Some are degraded and unreadable)

Henry H. Smith and James Slagle McClintock 2015

Harris Chaiklin and James Slagle McClintock 2015

Made in the USA
Middletown, DE
24 January 2021